Understanding European Union Institutions

What are the institutions of the European Union?

How do they work and what to they contribute to the functioning and development of the European Union?

Understanding the institutions of the European Union is vital to understanding how it functions. This book provides an introduction to the main institutions, and explains their different roles in the policy making and evolution of the European Union.

Features and benefits of *Understanding European Union institutions*:

- It introduces and explains the function of all the main institutions, dividing them into those that have a policy-making role, those that oversee and regulate, and those that operate in an advisory capacity.
- It provides students with an overview of the history of the European Union and the development of its institutions, and considers their continuing importance to the success of the European Union.
- It is clearly written by experienced and knowledgeable experts in, and teachers of, the subject.
- It is presented in an accessible way, providing boxed key facts, summaries, guides to further reading, sample questions and contact information.

Alex Warleigh is Reader in European Governance and Deputy Director of the Institute of Governance, Public Policy and Social Research, Queen's University Belfast.

EUROPEAN UNION
Please visit our *European Politics Arena* at www.politicsarena.com/euro

Understanding European Union Institutions

Edited by Alex Warleigh

London and New York

First published 2002 by Routledge
11 New Fetter Lane, London EC4P 4EE

Simultaneously published in the USA and
Canada
by Routledge
29 West 35th Street, New York, NY 10001

*Routledge is an imprint of the Taylor & Francis
Group*

© 2002 Alex Warleigh, selection and editorial
matter; the contributors, individual chapters

Typeset in Century Old Style by Keystroke,
Jacaranda Lodge, Wolverhampton
Printed and bound in Great Britain by
TJ International Ltd, Padstow, Cornwall

British Library Cataloguing in Publication Data
A catalogue record for this book is available
from the British Library

*Library of Congress Cataloging in Publication
Data*
Understanding European Union institutions /
edited by Alex Warleigh.
     p. cm.
     Includes index.
     1. European Union.   I. Warleigh, Alex.

JN30 .U5 2001
341.242′2—dc21   2001019940

ISBN 0–415–24213–4 (hbk)
ISBN 0–415–24214–2 (pbk)

For Jason Adams, Chris Augerson, Michael Carmody, Clive Davis, Christopher Lack, Ciarán O'Ceallaigh and Carl Stychin
(in alphabetical order, so you boys play nicely now)

And for Emma Harrison, Jo Seery, Josie Kelly, Andrea Ellner, Viki Lloyd, Louise Hilditch and Rachel Monaghan
(in no particular order, since you girls share so instinctively)

Contents

CONTENTS

CONTENTS

Illustrations

Figures

Tables

Contributors

Charlotte Burns, Ph.D. candidate, University of Sheffield.

Michelle Cini, Jean Monnet Senior Lecturer in European Community Studies, University of Bristol.

Philip Giddings, Senior Lecturer in Politics, University of Reading.

Roy Gregory, Emeritus Professor of Politics, University of Reading.

Anthea Harris, Sessional Lecturer in International Relations, University of Reading.

David Howarth, Lecturer in Politics, Queen Mary College, University of London.

Jo Hunt, Lecturer in Law, Cardiff University.

Brigid Laffan, Jean Monnet Professor of European Politics, University College Dublin.

Philippa Sherrington, Lecturer in European Integration, University of Warwick.

Alex Warleigh, Reader in European Governance and Deputy Director of the Institute for Governance, Public Policy and Social Research, Queens University Belfast.

Acknowledgements

I would like to thank all the contributors to this volume for their expertise and dedication, especially Philippa Sherrington.

For comments on early drafts of some of the chapters, I am grateful to Ben Rosamond and Thomas Christiansen.

Part I

HOW DOES THE EU WORK?

Chapter 1

Introduction

Institutions, institutionalism and decision making in the EU

Alex Warleigh

Why study the institutions of the EU?

In order to understand how any political system works, it is necessary to understand its institutions and how they interact. Institutions act as forums in which actors cooperate, argue, deliberate and make the decisions which eventually constitute public policy. Institutions can also shape the values and belief systems of those who work within them. As a result, they influence not just what actors do, but often also how they view the world in which they live as well as the people and ideas with which they must engage in order to realise their goals.[1] This is no less true for the European Union (EU; the Union) than for its member states. Indeed, given the fact that EU institutions are to some degree independent of the Union's member states and often try to represent – or construct – a 'European' interest, their activities have long been of considerable importance to scholars of European integration (Haas 1964, 1968). In a basic but vital sense, the Union's institutions are a necessary part of EU studies because they supply most of the actors who are engaged in the policy-making process. Moreover, institutions are key variables in understanding how the EU works because the integration process itself is shaped by their patterns of contestation and cooperation; that is, by the way they interact. The aim of this book is thus to show how the Union institutions both shape integration in Europe and reflect its problems, pressures and possibilities for reform.

Institutions can be defined in both limited (or formal) and broad (informal) ways (Hall and Taylor 1996; Peters 1999). Formal definitions concentrate on physical or legal structures, such as the European Parliament or the Treaty on European Union. Informal definitions add to this an understanding of more abstract factors such as ideas, values and behaviours. In this latter view, institutions both shape and reflect the thinking and behaviour of those who work and live within them. Indeed, ideas, values and practices (routine behaviours) can become institutions themselves: collective understandings of values or legitimacy frequently become an entrenched point of reference in debates about policy development, often shaping perceptions of what should or can be done about a policy problem just as much as the material resources and power that can be brought to bear upon it. For example, concerns about the concept of national sovereignty – the ability of a state to make its own decisions without imposed deference to the wishes of another state – often shape responses to proposals for institutional change in the EU both at popular and elite levels. In this book, the focus is on more formal definitions since the aim is to provide a clear and thorough understanding of how each of the official bodies which shape EU legislation operates; that is, their respective powers, purpose and role in the EU system. However, this should not be taken to mean that informal institutions are unimportant. As Charlotte Burns in particular makes clear in her chapter on the European Parliament (Chapter 4), it is often through using informal means that EU actors have been able to wield their greatest influence. Moreover, decision making in the Union centres not just on the various institutions (and the actors within them), but also on the networks they create in order to assemble the necessary resources and overcome obstacles placed in their way by actors whose concerns oppose their own (see below). However, in order to establish how each institution 'matters' in EU decision making it is necessary first to focus on the rules which govern them and the functions they are prescribed by Treaty in the integration process.[2]

It must, however, be recognised at the outset that there are certain factors which oblige the student of the EU to acknowledge limits to the use of institutions as an analytical tool if they are understood too crudely. Individuals can matter just as much as institutions; in the absence of a leader (or 'entrepreneur') able to take the initiative and broker deals with other actors in the policy-making process, institutions can lose much of their influence. This has famously been the case with the Commission, for example, whose influence under the leadership of Jacques Delors has not been matched since (see Cini, Chapter 3, this volume). Institutions can thus be of variable influence over time. Inside EU institutions, individuals are free to take up different positions on any issue, and sub-institutional factors may mean that it is important to know which *part* of an institution an actor works in. For instance, committees of the European Parliament often take different views about the same issue, and even within these committees there is usually a majority view rather than a unanimous one. It can thus be misleading to think only of 'institutional' positions on a given issue, and indeed cross- and intra-institutional alliance building between actors sharing similar concerns is usually the key to making the EU system work (see below).

Moreover, despite the fact that the EU's institutions were created to be partially independent from the national governments, this independence must not be exaggerated. As Murray Forsyth (1981) points out, governments seeking to develop a collective system of problem resolution are obliged to allow the institutions thereby created a certain freedom in order to meet their objectives and avoid making the system stagnate thanks to constant interference from one national capital or another. This does not equate to giving such institutions *carte blanche* to develop the system as they see fit. Instead, as noted by scholars such as Laura Cram (1997), the EU institutions other than those which represent the national governments (the EU Council (or 'Council of Ministers') and the European Council) have been able to shape the process of integration in a sporadic way through the creation and pursuit of suitable opportunities. The institutions of the EU have become entrenched in a new and complex arrangement which 'fuses' them together with the national systems of the member states in an unusual symbiosis (Wessels 1997). In order to understand the role of Union institutions it is thus necessary to remember the considerable importance of member state governments for two major reasons. First, as pointed out by Andrew Moravcsik (1999), member governments collectively retain the ability to alter the powers of each EU institution to suit their own ends, a process often driven primarily by domestic (i.e. national) politics. Second, EU policy is implemented not by the Union institutions but by the governmental organs and agencies responsible for each policy area within each member state. Union institutions are thus competent in only part of the policy-making process.[3]

Nonetheless, as the process of European integration has progressed, the 'architecture' of the EU – its institutional arrangements – has often been re-evaluated and reconstructed, with the addition of new institutions and significant changes in the powers and functions of the foundational parts of the system. A key theme of the present book, this evolution continues today, as the often tortuous process of refining the Treaties which form the legal basis of European integration is set to continue until at least 2004, the date of the next scheduled Intergovernmental Conference. Although frustrating for federalists, this continuous if uneven process of evolution is what lends the study of the EU institutions much of its interest. If they are 'fused' with national governments, by the same token they do not simply replicate the institutions of the nation state, and thus serve as a kind of laboratory for those concerned with how politics can be adapted in an era in which globalisation is lessening the independence of nation states. Although begun in response to specific historical circumstances (the end of the Second World War, which brought EU states economic ruin, the loss of great power status and, eventually, the Cold War rivalry between the then superpowers, the US and the USSR), the EU is one example – albeit by far the most advanced and sophisticated – of the phenomenon of regional integration, which is currently enjoying something of a revival globally, thanks to the existence of such trading blocs as NAFTA, Mercosur and ASEAN. As such, the institutions of the EU can provide object lessons for practitioners and scholars in other areas of the globe, even at the conceptual level (Rosamond 2000). As a cautionary element in this particular story, it should however be noted that the institutional architecture of the Union is one of the major contributors to the crisis of the so-called 'democratic deficit' (Bellamy and Warleigh 1998). Thus there are also important normative reasons to acquire a solid understanding of the workings and problems of the Union institutions: the remedy for the image and legitimacy problem that has stained European integration for much of the past decade at least.

In sum, and despite the importance of the corollaries mentioned above, understanding the EU's institutions is necessary for anyone concerned with or about European integration. By revealing the degree of power and nature of the tasks that member governments are prepared to delegate to the Union at any one time, the EU institutions serve as an indicator of the direction and condition of the integration process. Study of the institutions themselves, and how both they and actors from within them interact, helps us to understand the functioning of the EU system and its production of public policy, often in ways unanticipated by the member governments. Frank admission of some of the institutions' shortcomings based on a knowledge of their history and functions can inform blueprints for reform both of each institution and of the Union system itself, particularly with regard to issues of democracy, participation and legitimacy (Bellamy and Warleigh 1998). To reiterate what has become part of the 'New Conventional Wisdom' in EU studies (Church 2000), institutions 'matter' very much in European integration. In the following section of this chapter, I explore how this significance has been expressed in terms of EU, or 'integration', theory.

'New institutionalism' and EU theory

Institutions have been returned to the centre of analysis in all fields of political science as part of a shift away from behaviouralism and its privileging of individual choice by actors in a context considered to be more or less free of important constraining factors (March and Olsen 1984, 1989). Scholars realised that attention needed to be paid to the ways in which the organisational factors in political life (e.g. structures, laws, values) provide a kind of order in what would otherwise be a fairly anarchical scramble for influence between isolated actors. People do not always act according to a rational calculation of cost versus benefit. They may not have all the necessary information to make such a calculation, and thus have to make as educated a guess as possible about the most beneficial course of action. They may even make choices which are not 'rational', but which make sense in the context of a wider moral or symbolic framework. For example, it was highly irrational of Rosa Parks to refuse to give up her seat on the bus to a white person and risk imprisonment by the US authorities. Nonetheless, as an act of principle in the fight for racial equality, it was a bold gesture of great symbolic importance.

Faced with an information gap, people need to have a means of interpreting the problem at hand, and making sense of the range of options open to them. For new institutionalist scholars, this form of reference is offered by institutions, which provide symbols, rituals and rules in order that actors can 'frame' – i.e. interpret and decide between – the choices they have. According to March and Olsen (1989: 16), institutions must be seen as 'fundamental features of politics . . . [which] contribute to stability and change in political life'. In other words, institutions help organise political activity and can also help provide the means of change when actors desire it. Institutions are, in a sense, the arena in which politics happens. They provide continuity, so that the political system does not have to be rebuilt with the departure of key actors. They provide a sort of resource bank comprising the experiences of people who have previously engaged with them. They are thus not neutral or necessarily benevolent; the influence of institutions can be very conservative, which is why struggles for change can be difficult. Analytically speaking, however, it is important to acknowledge that institutions can matter just as much as individual choice in shaping what an actor does, because they can govern not just what one is able to do but also what one conceives to be possible or legitimate. Institutions can limit political activity as well as shape it. Institutions, in short, are about power (March and Olsen 1989: 164): they create and mould identities, define what is considered successful or legitimate, and give authority to certain actors and not others. Table 1.1 explains the three main variants of the way the role of institutions in political life has recently been conceptualised, 'new institutionalism'.

Historical institutionalism is perhaps the most comprehensive of the three approaches.[4] Its understanding of institutions embraces both formal and informal factors, allowing it to account for the influence of structures, practices and values/beliefs on what actors do. It argues that institutions are important in so far as they are incorporated into the organisational system of the polity. In fact, in this way they become the primary shapers of what actors do; when faced with a choice of options, actors will decide between them by reference to the means available and accepted views of what constitutes legitimate behaviour. Through a process of accumulation, individual choices build up and reinforce conventions and structures, thereby shaping in turn the range and nature of choices available when subsequent decisions are made. This is the concept of 'path dependency'. For example, choices about the funding of public welfare and education are heavily influenced by previous decisions about the level of taxation. Moreover, by isolating any policy area, it is possible to see how current options and decisions are affected by (the need to respond to) previous choices, such as the issue of UK higher education policy, in which the recent obligation on students to pay part of their tuition fees is a response to the underfunding of previous expansion in the university sector. Path dependency should not be taken to mean that actors have no real freedom of manoeuvre in the face of

Table 1.1 The three new institutionalisms

Variant	Definition of 'institution'	Main tenets	Strengths	Weaknesses
Historical	Formal and informal behaviours and beliefs which are embedded in the polity's organisational structure	Institutions are the main determiners of action. Past behaviours govern present and future context and action ('path dependency')	Shows how institutions and individuals are linked, formally and informally. Allows the analysis of contestation between actors. Shows how action shapes future choices and has unintended consequences	Imprecision about how exactly institutions shape behaviour. Can underestimate actors' power of choice. Can focus too narrowly on structural factors
Rational choice	Tool for solving policy problems created by key actors and preserved if it provides more benefits than costs	Institutions allow actors to meet their self-determined aims when unilateral action is impossible	Focus on actors and the instrumental use of institutions. Explains how and why institutions survive	Excessive reliance on the concept of predetermined actor choices. Narrow view of what shapes behaviour
Sociological	The means by which actors interpret both their action and that of others	Institutions make political action possible by providing the means by which the need for, and best course of, action is interpreted	Emphasises the role of institutions as legitimisers and framers of behaviour and identity	Underestimates the role of contestation in politics

Source: Based on Hall and Taylor 1996

overwhelming accumulated pressures, however. Indeed, it is quite possible for actors consciously to abandon the 'path' either they or their predecessors have constructed. Historical institutionalists can sometimes over-emphasise the role of structures and underplay the scope for action of actors, and they are often a little imprecise about how exactly institutions shape behaviour informally (although by showing how resource dependencies constrain actors they offer a more complete account of institutions' formal influence). However, this approach to the role of institutions in political life usefully demonstrates how individuals and institutions interact, and also helps us to understand how the legacy of past actions contributes to shaping the present context.

Rational choice institutionalism offers a very different, and arguably more limited perspective. In this view, institutions are only formal and used instrumentally – that is, purely as a tool – by actors who are in complete control of them. For rational choice scholars, it is at best highly unlikely that institutions have a significant influence over the strategic choices actors make. Instead, actors either build new institutions or use those that already exist in order to realise their objectives (which they have already determined themselves without reference to any external factor). There may of course be limits to the goals actors can realise by using institutions, but they will do so if they thereby gain more than they would from unilateral action. Similarly, institutions survive if actors consider they produce more gains than costs. There is thus no significant sense in which ideas, values or cultural context shape actors' decisions. Rational choice approaches are parsimonious (clear, specific and well constructed), and offer persuasive explanations of how and why institutions persist over time. They also avoid over-emphasis of the role of structures, because they concentrate almost entirely on the role of the actor. However, they are rather narrow in their view of what shapes behaviour for the very same reason. Rational choice institutionalism cannot satisfactorily explain how actors' values and choices are shaped by their fellows or the context in which they find themselves; instead, it wants to argue that such influence is at best tangential, an argument which often appears out of kilter with reality. Moreover, the relationship between actor and structure can be much more bi-directional than rational choice institutionalism allows: the repeated use of institutions, even instrumentally, can often shape actors' conceptions of what is appropriate or feasible action. By a process of interpersonal communication, such new or refined understandings can even extend to other actors. Furthermore, there can be unsought (if not necessarily unwanted) consequences of instrumental use of institutions: new institutions can thereby be created. For example, German regional government lobbying of the EU institutions both helped to alter the institutional architecture of the Union and ensured that regional politicians elsewhere were aware of the possibility of working at the EU level, even if this did not produce the kind of 'Europe of the Regions' many activists had wanted (see Warleigh on the Committee of the Regions, Chapter 10, this volume). Thus rational choice institutionalism is of limited analytical value.

Sociological institutionalism presents the third approach. In this view, institutions are conceived as a Gestalt of symbols, rituals, beliefs and worldviews which allows actors to understand – or interpret – the context in which they find themselves. Institutions thus serve as a frame of reference which allows actors to inject meaning into an otherwise unintelligible world. They allow actors to judge what is the best, or most appropriate, form of action to take, and also enable them to understand the actions of others. In this view, institutions thus serve as crucial mediators both between the individual and the world at large, and between different individuals. They are what allow us to make sense of what we, and others, do. This approach offers the fullest narrative of how institutions can shape both behaviour and identity. However, it fails to account for the more formal element of institutions sufficiently. It also tends to underestimate the extent to which actors are capable of instrumental use of institutions (and each other). It also underestimates the role of contestation in political life: although institutions do shape and reinforce identity and values, thereby helping to understand situations, these values and identities are the subject of greater struggle and more divergent understandings than sociological institutionalism allows. There is no automatic agreement about how to interpret a given phenomenon; institutions are not ready-made, universally valid templates to use in interpreting the world. Moreover, institutions are not value-free or independent from external influence; they can be used and created by powerful actors seeking to realise their objectives, at the expense of others if need be. Thus, with the sociological approach, it is necessary to remember that even if institutions serve as a means of interpreting the world, that interpretation is unlikely to be neutral or unshaped by the (prior) actions of others.

The three variants of the 'new institutionalism' are thus highly divergent, though they all give centrality to the role of institutions in shaping political action. There are links between them; even in the brief account given above, it is clear that each approach complements the others by focusing on different functions institutions can play in a political system (Peters 1999). The greatest, and highly significant, differences are between rational choice and sociological institutionalisms. Nonetheless, taken together and by using their respective strengths, the three approaches can help us understand the ways in which institutions 'matter'. As a result, they are essential parts of the political science conceptual toolkit which have been used in recent attempts to study the European Union, to which I now turn.

Although efforts to study and highlight the role played by institutions in the process of European unification and decision making were not neglected by early scholars of what is now the EU, the understandings this work generated were highly coloured by the theoretical frameworks which scholars adopted. The two major schools of thought in what Michael O'Neill (2000) has called the 'foundational' period of integration, neofunctionalism and intergovernmentalism, proposed understandings of the role of Union institutions which both opposed each other and were part of deterministic general theories of what the integration could, or should, achieve (Warleigh 1998). Neofunctionalists expected Union institutions to be autonomous, purposive actors both capable of and seeking to deepen the integration process. Intergovernmentalists held precisely the opposite view, and debate between the two schools of thought was regularly focused on this issue.[5] Both traditional approaches to theorising the EU were overtaken by unexpected events in the integration process, and undermined by conceptual flaws. Although revision of both, and attempts to make new theories derived from the best parts of each, were attempted, they did not prove successful (Warleigh 1998), with the sole exception of liberal intergovernmentalism (Moravcsik 1991, 1993). Instead, attention has been centred on the development of less ambitious theories based on an empirical understanding of how the EU system functions on a day-to-day basis (Peterson 1995; Garrett and Tsebelis 1996). Such a conceptual shift is not without cost. It may lead scholars concentrating on isolated parts of the Union policy-making process to fail to see the 'big picture', and thereby retreat unnecessarily from the attempt to devise broad understandings of the EU process (Warleigh 2000b). Worse still, it may itself become ossified as a new orthodoxy (Hix 1998: 41), and thereby repeat the unhelpful rigidity of the earlier approaches to EU study. However, new institutionalism (NI) has ensured that institutions have retained their importance in the 'post-foundational' (O'Neill 2000) theoretical study of the EU. New institutionalist approaches have successfully been deployed to fill part of the gap created by the shift away from neofunctionalism and intergovernmentalism as catch-all theories of integration.

Indeed, Pollack (1996) has argued that NI is the best way to harness the various useful insights generated by orthodox EU theory, since it allows scholars to accept both the continuing primacy of national governments in EU decision making (see below) and the role played by actors such as the Commission and Parliament. In this view, EU institutions are the arena in which member governments enter into argument about policy choices and thereby shape the policy outputs of the EU system. Pollack considers that member states and the EU institutions are best conceived in a *principal–agent* relationship, in which the former use the latter as a means of securing their (collective) goals – a good example of the rational choice approach discussed above. Institutions such as the Commission may play important roles, but for Pollack they are ultimately controllable by the member governments, which have the power to agree Treaty changes and whose agreement is necessary for any legislation to be produced. This is by no means the only NI view of EU politics. Indeed, Wayne Sandholtz (1996) has used the approach to demonstrate that EU institutions can be independent of member state constraint, and even control them (as is the case in competition policy and, more controversially, in pronouncements of the Court of Justice). NI can also be used to explain how the EU institutions change over time, and how the Union makes its decisions through the use of networks (see below) in which actors derive much of their power and resources from their institutional provenance (Peterson 1995).

The concepts of path dependency and unintended consequences which are so central to historical institutionalism can explain the uneven development of the EU in ways which traditional theories cannot match (Pierson 1996), a factor made more important by the approach's insistence that meaningful study of the Union requires a long time-frame rather than analysis of isolated events, no matter how important. It is easy to view single events as emblematic of the whole process of integration, particularly those of great importance such as the signing of new treaties. However, taking such a step can blind scholars to the day-to-day, regular practice of politics, in which actors other than national governments may well be more influential (Peterson 1995; Warleigh 2000b). NI is well suited to this kind of analysis, since it explains how, once established, policies and structures can generate new sets of interests which increase their value and lead to their expansion without the teleological implications of the spill-over mechanism central to neofunctionalism (Pierson 1996).[6] Moreover, taking part in the process of integration can cause a shift in the way national governments behave as well as their own (internal) structures (Sandholtz 1996): thus NI helps scholars focus on the interaction between the EU and national levels of governance, and gives centrality to the 'relationships of mutual dependence that tie together the various actors' (Dehousse and Majone 1994: 93).

A further benefit of NI is its insistence that we take into account not just 'vertical' (i.e. between (sub-)national and EU levels) but also 'horizontal' (i.e. between the EU institutions themselves) linkages (Wincott 1995); our attention is thereby directed to all the essential levels of action, without necessarily privileging one over the others. Indeed, we are obliged by NI scholars to focus on and acknowledge the great variation in the functioning of the EU both across policy areas and over time (Bulmer 1994). In turn, this is likely to produce a more accurate, and less deterministic, understanding of how the EU works, especially since although NI does not consider the EU institutions or the actors within them to be neutral players, it is 'entirely agnostic on the end-goal of the integration process' (Bulmer 1998: 370). Consequently, NI can accommodate divergent accounts of EU policy making, and avoids one of the major problems of 'foundational' EU theory: its erection of pre-determined end-points of the integration process, which reality has so far failed to match in either maximalist (neofunctionalist) or minimalist (intergovernmental) manner. In addition, NI can help us appreciate the ways in which actors decide between different policy options according to perceptions of interest which are shaped by both their own involvement with the integration process and the interventions of other actors so engaged, i.e. 'learning' and 'socialisation' into new sets of norms and values which they may otherwise not have encountered (Checkel 1999).

Thus NI is of great help in allowing us to understand the operation of the EU system. It is not a uniform approach, and the differences between its three variants ensure that it has not produced a universally agreed account of how the EU works. Nonetheless, it helps define what is important in EU study, thereby framing hypotheses and selecting suitable avenues of enquiry. NI may also help build bridges to the study of other political systems, which could in turn create useful insights for scholars of the EU (Dowding 2000). It has also generated a more nuanced understanding of how the various actors in Union politics come together to make public policy decisions. It remains to detail this understanding, a task which is addressed in the following section.

Decision making in the EU: complexity, coalitions and the lobbying imperative

The EU is an evolving political system, whose rules and decision-making practices have changed considerably over the course of its history. The first incarnation of the Union, the European Coal and Steel Community, set the basic institutional pattern for the Union of today: a Court of Justice, a High Authority (the predecessor of the Commission), a Council of Ministers (to represent member governments), and an Assembly (the predecessor of the Parliament). However, the way in which the Union makes decisions has altered quite significantly over the past fifty years, as has the power balance between the main institutions. The 'single institutional system' mentioned in the Treaty is anything but static, and different parts of it have been accentuated in different ways at different periods in the history of integration. To generalise, the powers of the EU as a whole have grown significantly, and the Union is competent to act in many more policy areas than was initially the case; however, the corollary of this expansion has been the retention of much power by the member states, and the Commission has not become the 'European government' sought by several of the founders of European integration. Instead, legislative power has become more equally shared between the Council and Parliament. That said, the central actors in EU decision making remain the member governments. The latter are responsible for the 'history-making' (Peterson 1995) decisions, such as new treaties. They are also the most powerful actors in day-to-day decision making, in so far as their agreement is necessary for any legislation to exist. Since the Treaty on European Union of 1992, the EU has been divided into three 'pillars' – respectively the European Community, the Common Foreign and Security Policy, and Police and Judicial Cooperation in Criminal Matters (formerly and still better known as Justice and Home Affairs). In pillars two and three, the member governments have allowed the other EU institutions only a minimal role, since the issues covered are considered to be highly sensitive. In the first pillar, the institutions enjoy the whole range of powers described below and in the various chapters of this book.[7]

However, this does not mean that member governments are in complete control of the process. As they have so far been willing to create only a limited, albeit deep, form of joint governance system, they are obliged to rely on informal politics (especially coalitions between concerned actors both within and outside the Union institutions) to fill the gaps in the evolving, and presumably still incomplete, political system. This can allow unexpected influence to be wielded by actors without much formal power (Warleigh 2000a). As discussed above, unintended consequences can result from even 'rational choices', meaning that the process of integration may throw up circumstances unanticipated by member governments. No single government can control EU decision making; instead, the national ministers must forge compromises to which they can all agree, so the power of the member governments is a collective one. Moreover, the other institutions of the EU are capable of exploiting and creating opportunities to extend their own influence.

This is particularly evident in the day-to-day functioning of the system, i.e. the routine making of policy. The three basic branches of government – legislature, executive and judiciary – are discernible in the EU, although the demarcation lines between them are not as clear as in most national systems (Hix 1999). This is because both the initial design of the EU structure, and the way it has since developed, relied upon complex interdependencies between the institutions rather than a strict and clear separation of powers as in the constitution of the USA. In addition, the Union is (presumably) still evolving. The founders of the EU were unable to create a new federal state since the necessary support was lacking at both elite and popular levels. Instead, they set in train a process which binds the member states and the EU institutions ever more closely together, while leaving the difficult constitutional problems such as the separation of powers and relationship between the different tiers of government to be decided gradually or simply emerge organically. The exception to this pattern is the Court of Justice, whose monopoly of the judicial function is clear, albeit in a sometimes difficult partnership with national courts and legal systems (Shaw 1996). The legislature of the EU is the Council, in tandem with the European Parliament (EP). As Charlotte Burns points out in her chapter, the role of the EP as part of the legislature has grown enormously since the early days of integration, and where the co-decision procedure applies the balance of power between the two institutions is roughly equal. The executive function is carried out by the Commission, which is also responsible for ensuring that the various responsible national agencies and branches of government properly implement and enforce EU legislation. The Commission is in addition tasked with making proposals for legislation, which gives it the power to set the EU's legislative agenda.

There is no single process of policy making in the EU. Apart from the variation between the three pillars, policy areas work in different ways, with the main variables being the degree of power allowed to the EP and the decision rule in the Council: unanimity or qualified majority (QMV). An exception is the area of monetary policy, in which the European Central Bank has almost entirely autonomous power within the tasks given it by the Treaty (see Howarth, Chapter 5, this volume). The balance between unanimity and qualified majority voting in the Council has been controversial since the beginning of the integration process, and provoked a major crisis in the 1960s. Although unanimity applies in far fewer cases today, as the Nice Treaty reveals, the 'defence' of the veto power in areas which national governments consider essential for the preservation of their sovereignty remains dogged. QMV is allowed when progress in a given policy area is deemed both sufficiently necessary to the success of the integration process and unlikely to occur if unanimous support for every legislative proposal within that policy area is required, an excellent example being proposals relating to the creation of the single European market. However, even when the Treaty allows QMV, it is usual for the Council to try to reach a consensus rather than vote, in order to preserve as much national power as possible, and voting is very much the last resort (Hix 1999: 73–4). Moreover, thanks to the process of 'comitology' (whereby 'national experts' issue essentially binding 'advice' to the Commission about policy implementation and fine print of legislation), member governments have been able to claw back some of the power ostensibly shared with other institutions (Hix 1999: 41–4).

In some policy areas, such as environmental issues, the EP has long been a key player (Collins *et al.* 1998). In others, such as agriculture, the EP may be relatively peripheral even if the policy area itself is highly 'Europeanised'. In still other areas of policy, both the degree of Europeanisation and the role of the EP may be low (e.g. defence policy). To make matters still more complex, this pattern changes over time. Environment policy, for example, was not an official competence of the EU until the Single European Act of 1986. At the time of writing, the Union's competences in foreign and defence policies appear to be undergoing a distinct upgrading. A further complicating factor is the 'enhanced cooperation' procedure introduced in the Amsterdam Treaty and simplified at Nice. This procedure allows a majority of member governments to proceed with integration unencumbered by a reluctant minority, with the chief proviso that initial laggards are able to join subsequently. Already, member governments 'opt out' of integration in certain policy areas (for example, only twelve of the fifteen member states are participating in the single currency), so the range of actors involved in EU decision making is set to alter according to a new variable: the will (or ability) of member governments to participate in a given policy. Consequently, there is no generalisable and constant process of decision making in the EU.

Helen Wallace (2000) has in fact identified five 'policy modes' present in Union decision making. According to this analysis, the Union has several operating methods, all of which are currently in evidence. The first is what might be termed the 'traditional' method, applicable to the pillar one issues as described above. The second is the 'regulatory' model, which again features most strongly in pillar one but sees the EU act not as the decider of detailed legislation but rather as the setter of a general framework with which national policies must be in keeping. Importantly, this mode of policy making increases the room for difference between national policies and reduces the need to concentrate resources at the EU level. It has thus become increasingly popular with member governments (Majone 1996). The third mode is 'multi-level governance', on which an abundant literature exists.[8] In this variant of decision making, actors from local and regional government, as well as national and EU levels, play a role in deciding and implementing Union policy. This mode is most evident in structural and cohesion policies (pillar one). A fourth mode is policy coordination. This is a technocratic mode centred on the exchange of information and best practice between the member governments (mainly pillars two and three).

Finally, there is 'intensive transgovernmentalism' – cooperation largely outside the traditional institutional framework (e.g. pillars two and three).

The main legislative procedures, described in detail by Charlotte Burns in her chapter, are nonetheless worth introducing briefly here: consultation, assent and co-decision. Under the *consultation procedure*, the EP is asked for its opinion on a proposal by the Commission, but this does not have to be taken into account by the Council (although the latter does have to wait for that opinion to be issued before it can proceed to legislate). This was the original legislative procedure of the Union, and it is still in place although its scope has been significantly reduced. The *assent procedure* was introduced by the Single European Act. This gives the EP the power to veto proposals if it is not satisfied with the Council's decision, but not the power to amend the proposal; it is thus a rather blunt weapon, and one limited to a small number of policy areas (although this includes the approval of enlargement treaties). *Co-decision*, it has been estimated, will soon apply to approximately 70 per cent of EU legislation (Maurer 1999: 43). It gives the EP the power both to amend and to veto legislation should it see fit, and locks it into an intricate and complex relationship with the Council. Thus as a guide to the general pattern of EU decision making, a simplified diagram of the co-decision procedure is included below (Figure 1.1).[9] Other bodies, such as the Economic and Social Committee and Committee of the Regions, are consulted either if the Treaty requires this, or if the Commission, Parliament or Council so decide. These bodies are purely advisory, but they can sometimes be influential in terms of shaping policy outputs (see Warleigh, Chapters 9 and 10, this volume). Implementation of policies is left to the member governments, as mentioned above, although in clear cases of non-compliance the Commission is able to prosecute recalcitrant national authorities at the Court of Justice, which can impose significant fines (see Hunt, Chapter 6, this volume).

Official institutions at either national or EU level, of course, are not the only sources of actors involved in the policy-making process. Interest groups from both industry and civil society have mobilised in great numbers in an attempt to influence legislation which affects their concerns.[10] These actors can be a useful source of information and expertise for EU decision makers, particularly given the limited resources and budget of the Union. Their favourable views on legislation offer the EU a certain legitimacy which it would otherwise lack (Lord 1998: 75–7), since this indicates that those primarily affected by EU activity have sanctioned it. This is particularly useful for the Commission, whose role in the policy-making process has been under often critical re-examination in recent years (see Cini, Chapter 3, this volume). Such actors do not have formal power to decide EU policy. However, as a source of ideas and as brokers of agreements between actors with similar concerns in different institutions, such actors can be highly influential (Warleigh 2000a). Furthermore, when they are part of an official round of consultation about a proposal, such actors can shape its very core (Richardson 1996). In order to make the highly complex and varied EU system operate successfully, actors have to make alliances (or coalitions) both within and outside their own institutions. Because the various functions of government are shared rather than separated between the main institutions, the latter are highly dependent upon each other. To make sure a policy proposal which one supports survives all the way through the legislative process from initial discussions and drafting in the Commission through decisions by

COMMISSION

Issues a proposal, usually after consultation with actors from the other institutions and interest groups. Forwards this proposal to:

| EUROPEAN PARLIAMENT
(AND OFTEN ALSO ECONOMIC AND SOCIAL COMMITTEE, COMMITTEE OF THE REGIONS) |
| --- |

Which decide their (initial) positions, and forward them to the

COMMISSION

Which collates the contributions of the other institutions, decides which amendments it will accept, and forwards them to the

COUNCIL OF MINISTERS

Which produces a Common Position, that is in turn sent to the

EUROPEAN PARLIAMENT

Which either approves the text (then in turn adopted by the Council) or proposes amendments, which, after the Commission has given its opinion, are forwarded to the

COUNCIL OF MINISTERS

Which either accepts the amendments (by QMV if the Commission is in support; by unanimity if the Commission opposes), or, together with the European Parliament, enters into a

CONCILIATION COMMITTEE

Which either agrees legislation, or fails to produce a joint text, in which case the common position is confirmed as legislation by the Council unless the European Parliament uses its veto.

Figure 1.1 The co-decision procedure (simplified)
Note: At all points in this process, coalitions between actors within and outside the institutions are usually in existence, and intensive lobbying is carried out.

Parliament and Council requires constant vigilance. The acquisition of allies in the other responsible Union institutions (not to mention national and even, on occasion, sub-national governments) is thus essential in order to ensure that success at one stage of the process is not undone by failure – or being marginalised by more powerful interests – at another.

This process of alliance construction is not easy. It requires great skill and resources to broker an agreement which is capable of gaining all the necessary majorities between actors within (and outside) the various institutions. In some cases, coalitions are more or less permanent and contribute over time to definite change in the style or content of a policy area (Sabatier 1998). In most cases, coalitions are situation-specific, ending along with the passage of the relevant proposal through the last stage of the legislation process, although some of the actors involved may well cooperate again (Warleigh 2000a). Importantly, the need to construct these 'policy coalitions' (Warleigh 2000a) is felt by even the most powerful actors in the process, the national governments. Within the Council, depending on the decision rule, national governments need to generate either a qualified majority in favour of their position, a blocking minority if they oppose a proposal, or (in the case of unanimity) an agreement from all their partners not to use their veto. When co-decision or assent procedures apply, these actors need to ensure the support of the EP. The Commission needs to ensure that the Parliament will back its proposals, and therefore has to take at least some of the latter's concerns into account when drafting or redrafting them. Internally, actors from any Directorate General (DG) have to construct bargains with those in other DGs in order to ensure that their work becomes an official Commission proposal. The EP requires the Commission to accept its amendments and forward them to Council; it also depends on the latter to accept its amendments, for even where it has the veto power it is usually more beneficial to agree even a sub-optimal policy deal than to have no legislation at all.[11] Internally, actors in each EP committee must ensure that they can secure a majority in favour of their position both within the committee and in the EP as a whole. Inter-institutionally, actors with the same (or at least complementary) goals often cooperate in order to overcome blockages imposed elsewhere in the decision-making process by actors from their own institutions. For example, actors from DG Environment in the Commission often count on the support of the EP (in particular its environment committee) to reinforce proposals weakened by other DGs inside the Commission. The result of this coalition construction is that every actor in the decision-making process, whether or not from an EU institution, adds lobbying to his job description.

Thus decision making in the EU focuses on the Union institutions in several ways. First, as formal actors with specific Treaty-prescribed functions in the business of producing public policy, which, for the strictly political institutions, are shared rather than clearly separated. Second, and consequently, as participants in a process of inter-institutional bargaining and compromise forging, in which each institution must take into consideration the interests of the others. This means that decision making is as much informal as formal: outside the formal processes, actors will seek to ensure that support for their position is a broad as possible. Third, by way of extension, the Union institutions serve both as sources and as focal points of advocacy and of policy coalitions, engaging with a broad set of official and societal actors in an attempt to secure their policy goals.

How to use this book

Apart from the introduction, each chapter in this book is devoted to a particular institution of the EU. The chapters can be read individually, or together in order to generate a holistic understanding of the Union's institutional actors. The format of the chapters is identical in order to facilitate comparison between the roles, evolution and activities of the institutions.

Each chapter begins with a check-box of key facts by way of an introduction. It then proceeds to detail the formal powers, functions and operating procedures of the institution in question. The second section, again preceded by a box of key facts, is devoted to an analysis of the institution's evolution over the course of the integration process to date. The third section, commencing with a further key information box, is devoted to an analysis of the role played in the Union decision-making system by the institution in question. The final section cautiously speculates about the likely future of the institution, drawing on historical and current trends. Each chapter concludes with several devices designed to facilitate learning. First, there is a bullet-point summary of the main points raised and arguments sustained. Second, there are three test questions to be used in order to check that the reader has drawn from the chapter an understanding of the most salient issues. Third, there are recommendations for selected further reading, as well as a full list of references made in the chapter. The selected further reading section indicates those texts that are considered to be particularly useful sources of information by the chapter's author, either because they are suitable as a general guide or because they deal particularly well with a key issue. In each case, the author clarifies why the particular text has been recommended. Finally, each chapter includes information to be used by those interested in making contact with the institution in question.

The book is divided into four parts. Part I includes only the introduction, which serves to relate the aims of the book and sets out the conceptual underpinnings of institutional studies of the EU. Part II deals with the 'policy-making' institutions: the European Council and Council of Ministers; the Commission; the European Parliament; and the European Central Bank. The latter is included in this section because although it does not contribute directly to the general process of policy making, it is responsible for the monetary policy of member states taking part in the Euro (single currency). Part III covers the oversight institutions – those whose duties centre on making sure the EU system functions properly. It includes chapters on the Court of Justice and Court of First Instance; the Court of Auditors; and the Ombudsman, respectively responsible for the legal, financial and administrative oversight functions. Part IV is devoted to the official advisory bodies, the Economic and Social Committee and the Committee of the Regions. Although these two committees are without legislative power, and thus fall outside Part II, they can certainly be influential, and an understanding of their role – in all its limitations – is essential to an understanding of the EU's policy-making system.

The book is not written to put forward any particular theoretical perspective, except to reflect and contribute to the recent shift towards detailed study of EU institutions as part of the increased scholarly and public interest in European integration. Consequently, the chapters do not produce a single normative conclusion. Instead, they reflect the various experiences of the EU institutions, themselves locked into a process of contested evolution. It is hoped that by adopting such a stance, the book will help readers to understand the various pressures on and within the integration process, and thereby increase their awareness of why and how the EU has evolved in its complex, idiosyncratic manner.

Notes

1   See below for a further, more conceptual exploration of the role played by institutions in policy making ('new institutionalism').

2   The Treaty Establishing the European Community, as amended by the Amsterdam Treaty, recognises in Article 7 only five institutions: the European Parliament, the Commission, the Council, the Court of Justice and the Court of Auditors. The other bodies discussed in this book are officially 'bodies' of the EU, but their Treaty-defined nature makes them institutions in the 'formal' academic sense as well as its 'informal' variant. For the sake of convenience, the contributors to this book refer to all EU bodies as 'institutions' but acknowledge the defining force of the Treaty provisions. One high-profile body of the Union is absent from this book, namely the European Investment Bank (EIB). Not to be confused with the European Central Bank responsible for the single currency, this body is an independent public finance organisation owned by the member states as shareholders, and exists to part-fund programmes of economic development across the European continent. Although it plays a vital role in financing the EU, and enlargement to Central and Eastern Europe in particular, the EIB plays no role in the policy making of the EU as such. Neither does it have a role in overseeing the functioning of the system, or in advising the decision-making institutions. Consequently it is outside the scope of this study.

3   A possible and partial exception is cohesion policy, in which the 'partnership' principle officially makes actors at local/regional, national and EU level responsible for policy design and delivery within the Treaty framework established by member governments (Hooghe 1996).

4   The following paragraphs draw on Hall and Taylor (1996).

5   For a thorough and perceptive discussion of the various integration theories, see Rosamond (2000).

6   *Spill-over* was the term given by neofunctionalists to the almost automatic process of deepening and widening of integration that they considered to be at play in the EU.

7   Since the decision-making processes of pillars two and three are almost entirely intergovernmental, they are not described at length in this chapter. It is interesting to note, however, that the pillar structure is itself evolving. The Amsterdam Treaty removed many policy issues from pillar three and transferred them to pillar one. The powers of the Commission in these pillars were also increased to a small degree by the same Treaty. However, matters of pillars two and three remain firmly outside the competence of the Court and Parliament.

8   See Rosamond (2000) for an overview, and Marks *et al.* (1996) for the key primary text.

9   For the sake of clarity, Figure 1.1 does not capture the full complexities of the evolving co-decision procedure. For a fuller impression see Maurer (1999).

10 For excellent overviews, see the collected essays in Greenwood and Aspinwall (1998) and Wallace and Young (1997).

11 It is interesting to note that in the period to 1999, the conciliation committee failed to produce an agreed EP–Council text only twice, since both institutions usually stand to lose more from a legislative vacuum than a compromise (Maurer 1999).

References

Bellamy, R. and Warleigh, A. (1998): 'From an Ethics of Integration to an Ethics of Participation: Citizenship and the Future of the European Union' (*Millennium* 27:3, 447–70).

Bulmer, S. (1994): 'Institutions and Policy Change in the European Communities: The Case of Merger Control' (*Public Administration* 72:3, 423–44).

Bulmer, S. (1998): 'New Institutionalism and the Governance of the Single European Market' (*Journal of European Public Policy* 5:3, 365–86).

Checkel, J. (1999): 'Social Construction and Integration' (*Journal of European Public Policy* 6:4, 545–60).

Church, C. (2000): 'Afterword' (*Current Politics and Economics of Europe* 9:2, 231–5).

Collins, K., Burns, C. and Warleigh, A. (1998): 'Policy Entrepreneurs – The Role of European Parliament Committees in the Making of EU Policy' (*Statute Law Review* 19:1, 1–11).

Cram, L. (1997): *Policy Making in the EU – Conceptual Lenses and the Integration Process* (London: Routledge).

Dehousse, R. and Majone, G. (1994): 'The Institutional Dynamics of European Integration – From the Single Act to the Masstricht Treaty', in S. Martin (ed.) *The Construction of Europe – Essays in Honour of Emile Noël* (London: Kluwer).

Dowding, K. (2000): 'Institutionalist Research on the European Union: A Critical Review' (*European Union Politics* 1:1, 125–44).

Forsyth, M. (1981): *Unions of States – The Theory and Practice of Confederation* (Leicester: Leicester University Press).

Garrett, G. and Tsebelis, G. (1996): 'An Institutional Critique of Intergovernmentalism' (*International Organization* 50:2, 269–99).

Greenwood, J. and Aspinwall, M. (eds) (1998): *Collective Action in the European Union* (London: Routledge).

Haas, E. (1964): *Beyond the Nation State* (Stanford, Calif.: Stanford University Press).

Haas, E. (1968): *The Uniting of Europe* (Stanford: Stanford University Press).

Hall, P. and Taylor, R. (1996): 'Political Science and the Three New Institutionalisms' (*Political Studies* 45, 936–57).

Hix, S. (1998): 'The Study of the European Union II: The "New Governance" Agenda and Its Rival' (*Journal of European Public Policy* 5:1, 38–65).

Hix, S. (1999): *The Political System of the European Union* (London: Macmillan).

Hooghe, L. (ed.) (1996): *Cohesion Policy and European Integration* (Oxford: Clarendon Press).

Lord, C. (1998): *Democracy in the European Union* (Sheffield: Sheffield Academic Press).

Majone, G. (1996): *Regulating Europe* (London: Routledge).

March, J. and Olsen, J. (1984): 'The New Institutionalism: Organisational Factors in Political Life' (*American Political Science Review* 78, 734–49).

March, J. and Olsen, J. (1989): *Rediscovering Institutions – The Organizational Basis of Politics* (New York: Free Press).

Marks, G., Hooghe, L. and Blank, K. (1996): 'European Integration from the 1980s: State-centric v Multi-level Governance' (*Journal of Common Market Studies* 34:3, 341–78).

Maurer, A. (1999): *(Co-) Governing After Maastricht: The European Parliament's Institutional Performance 1994–1998* (Luxembourg: European Parliament Directorate General for Research, ref. POLI 104.EN).

Moravcsik, A. (1991): 'Negotiating the Single European Act: National Interests and Conventional Statecraft in the European Community' (*International Organization* 45:1, 19–56).

Moravcsik, A. (1993): 'Preferences and Power in the European Community: A Liberal Intergovernmentalist Approach' (*Journal of Common Market Studies* 31:4, 473–524).

Moravcsik, A. (1999): *The Choice for Europe – Social Purpose and State Power from Messina to Maastricht* (London: UCL Press).

O'Neill, M. (2000): 'Theorising the European Union: Towards a Post-foundational Discourse' (*Current Politics and Economics of Europe* 9:2, 121–45).

Peters, B.G. (1999): *Institutional Theory in Political Science – The 'New Institutionalism'* (London: Sage).

Peterson, J. (1995): 'Decision Making in the EU: Towards a Framework for Analysis' (*Journal of European Public Policy* 2:1, 69–93).

Pierson, P. (1996): 'The Path to European Integration – A Historical Institutionalist Analysis' (*Comparative Political Studies* 29:2, 123–63).

Pollack, M. (1996): 'The New Institutionalism and EC Governance: The Promise and Limits of Institutional Governance' (*Governance* 9:4, 429–58).

Richardson, J. (1996): 'Policy-making in the EU: Interests, Ideas and Garbage Cans of Primeval Soup', in J. Richardson (ed.) *European Union Power and Policy Making* (London: Routledge).

Rosamond, B. (2000): *Theories of European Integration* (London: Macmillan).

Sabatier, P. (1998): 'The Advocacy Coalition Framework: Revisions and Relevance for Europe' (*Journal of European Public Policy* 5:1, 98–130).

Sandholtz, W. (1996): 'Membership Matters: Limits of the Functional Approach to European Institutions' (*Journal of Common Market Studies* 34:3, 403–29).

Shaw, J. (1996): *Law of the European Union* (2nd edn) (London: Macmillan).

Wallace, H. (2000): 'The Institutional Setting: Five Variations on a Theme', in H. Wallace and W. Wallace (eds) *Policy Making in the European Union* (4th edn) (Oxford: Oxford University Press).

Wallace, H. and Young, A. (eds) (1997): *Participation and Policy-making in the European Union* (Oxford: Clarendon Press).

Warleigh, A. (1998): 'Better the Devil You Know? Synthetic and Confederal Understandings of European Unification' (*West European Politics* 21:3, 1–18).

Warleigh, A. (2000a): 'The Hustle: Citizenship Practice, NGOs and "Policy Coalitions" in the European Union – The Cases of Auto Oil, Drinking Water and Unit Pricing' (*Journal of European Public Policy* 7:2, 229–43).

Warleigh, A. (2000b): 'History Repeating? Framework Theory and Europe's Multi-level Confederation' (*Journal of European Integration* 22, 173–200).

Wessels, W. (1997): 'An Ever Closer Fusion? A Dynamic Macropolitical View on Integration Processes' (*Journal of Common Market Studies* 35:2, 267–99).

Wincott, D. (1995): 'Institutional Interaction and European Integration – Towards an Everyday Critique of Liberal Intergovernmentalism' (*Journal of Common Market Studies* 33:4, 597–609).

Part II

THE POLICY-MAKING INSTITUTIONS

Chapter 2

The Council of Ministers and the European Council

Philippa Sherrington

Key facts

The Council of Ministers is the collective noun for the member state representatives who meet to take the final decision on all EU legislative proposals. As one of the original institutions, the Council of Ministers was given this authority, and its intergovernmental character was jealously guarded by the member states who wished to protect their national interests within the supranational framework of the EU. Over time, it has assumed a distinct and sometimes puzzling identity because, while it legislates, it also engages in bargaining, agenda setting and agenda management. It also acts as the external representative of the EU. Decisions can be taken by either a simple majority, a qualified majority or unanimity. Although Treaty amendments have increased the provision for qualified majority voting, member states prefer to seek a consensus. The European Council is an extension of the Council of Ministers and is the forum for heads of state or government to meet and discuss policy direction, negotiate and approve Treaty amendments, and sometimes resolve disputes between member states over EU policy matters. Unlike the Council, there are no provisions for majority voting – it conducts its business purely through intergovernmental negotiations, although in future, if the Nice Treaty is ratified, it will decide the Commission President by qualified majority. Despite being formally recognised as an institution only by the Single European Act, the European Council is seen as a necessary forum for problem solving in the EU.

The Council: organisation and responsibilities

The Council of Ministers of the EU was established by Article 145 of the Treaty of Rome and is one of the four original institutions.[1] Its creation was perhaps not as inventive as the Commission or the European Parliament in that it represents the traditional interaction between member states. However, to define the Council simply as an intergovernmental institution is misleading. While it does possess such characteristics, it has developed a more distinct identity than other intergovernmental organisations. The Council has many idiosyncrasies, with a heady mix of supranational and intergovernmental characteristics. It is the supreme decision-making authority in the EU. The Council's principal role is to take the final decision on all legislative proposals that become EU law either in consultation with other EU institutions, or by sharing its legislative power with the European Parliament (EP) under the co-decision procedure (or cooperation procedure prior to the Amsterdam and draft Nice Treaties). In all matters, it is required to consult with the Economic and Social Committee, and with the Committee of the Regions if appropriate. Depending upon the decision-making procedure set out in the Treaties, the Council takes decisions by simple majority, qualified majority, or unanimity. Within the first pillar, there has been an incremental growth in the number of areas governed by the qualified majority provision. For Council decisions based on a Commission proposal, a qualified majority of sixty-two out of eighty-seven votes has to be found. For other decisions the same sixty-two votes have to be cast by at least ten member states. The number of votes per member state is allocated on a rough principle of population size. As can be seen in Table 2.1 (p. 33), the larger member states all have an equal number of votes, after which there is a descending scale. This was agreed not on precise statistical proportions to population size, but as an approximate reflection, with the underlying notion that all states are really equal supposedly still in play (a point that has caused many difficulties in preparing for the future enlargement of the EU).

Formally, the Council cannot act alone and relies upon the Commission to put forward proposals for its consideration. However, the argument can be made that member states will push for certain Commission proposals to be made, or request that the Commission embarks on drafting legislation in a particular policy area through the use of Article 152, so in some respects this can be seen as indirect action on the part of the Council. In addition, the Council will make political statements, opinions and recommendations outside of the formal legislative process, but which carry the weight of member state agreement. The Council also performs an agenda-setting role by taking broader decisions on future EU policy developments, discussing general economic policies of member states, and ratifying international agreements on behalf of the EU. It provides the Commission with the mandate to act on behalf of the member states in areas such as the implementing decisions for the Common Agricultural Policy (CAP), association agreements with third countries, and carrying out accession negotiations. With the EP, the Council is responsible for the approval of the annual Community budget. The Council's distinct character arises out of the fact that in acting as a legislator, the Council also negotiates. It is the forum in which EU member states engage in a bargaining process in order to reach legislative and policy decisions that are acceptable to all.

The Council is composed of a representative from each member state. The Council is a generic term for many councils, differentiated by their policy concerns. These technical or sectoral councils deal with the wide-ranging policy remit of the EU, from fish to telecommunications, and there are approximately twenty different formations. Thus Council membership corresponds to the policy area under discussion and national ministerial portfolios – ministers responsible for transport will meet within the Transport Council, environmental ministers within the Environment Council and so on. Arguably, the most important of the technical councils is the General Affairs Council, composed of the foreign ministers of the member states. Not only does the status of these ministers place such authority upon the General Affairs Council, but so does its policy remit. Foreign ministers deal with a broader range of issues than their colleagues in other councils. External political and economic affairs dominate the agenda, but often the General Affairs Council gives formal approval to a wide range of other proposals simply because it meets the most frequently. More importantly, foreign ministers are perceived to have greater political authority, and they are frequently asked to resolve issues upon which other technical councils have failed to reach agreement. Other councils make up the ministerial pyramid effect according to the relative involvement of the EU in a policy area, and the frequency of meetings. The Council meets on average ninety times per year. The General Affairs Council convenes the most frequently, usually once a month, with Agriculture and the Economic and Finance Council (EcoFin) close behind. It has also been argued that these two councils have a heightened status and greater permanence comparable with that of the General Affairs Council (Hayes-Renshaw and Wallace 1997). Other councils assemble according to their workload in that particular year, or such as the Education Council convene only biannually due to the limited involvement of the EU in education policy (Sherrington 2000). Ministers also meet informally to discuss EU policy issues. An informal meeting can range from lunch-time conversation during a formal session to planned gatherings or weekend breaks: in all of these, the actual substance of the discussions is not recorded. The Council sometimes holds joint council meetings when there are such distinct policy overlaps that an integrated discussion is deemed useful. The most common has been joint Environment and Energy Councils. Brussels is the home to the majority of Council sessions, except during April, May and October when meetings are held in Luxembourg, or special sessions convened by the presidency and held somewhere in that member state.

Sitting at the top of the Council's pyramid structure is the European Council, the name given to the summit meetings of heads of state or government. These meetings are usually held at the end of each presidency, although informal or emergency meetings have been convened on occasion to deal with urgent matters, or to try and achieve some initial discussion on problematic issues prior to the set-piece European Council meeting. The French Presidency's motives were exactly this when it convened an informal European Council in Biarritz in October 2000, hoping to obtain some sense of the key stumbling-blocks on institutional reform prior to the Nice European Council. The boundary between the work of the Council and that of the European Council is that the former is more concerned with day-to-day decisions, i.e. what could be termed 'routine' policy making. Decisions made at the Council level might not be seen by some as simply a matter of routine where agreement on a Regulation or Directive requires a radical adjustment to domestic law. Nevertheless, the Council is primarily involved with keeping the EU's legislative machinery ticking over. By contrast, the European Council has traditionally focused upon the direction of European integration by negotiating Treaty revisions and holding general policy discussions. In this sense overall responsibility of EU policy making lies with the European Council (Aggestam 1997: 88). However, there have been occasions – and these have increased in recent years – whereby the Council has requested that an agenda item be referred 'up' to the European Council because the ministers concerned could not agree and wish to defer to the authority of their prime ministers or heads of state. This is similar to the earlier example of the work of the General Affairs Council. It is here that the distinction between the European Council as a separate institution, or as part of the Council becomes blurred, as in such instances the European Council is engaging in Community decision making but within a more intergovernmental forum.

The work of the Council and the European Council is supported by the Committee of Permanent Representatives, specialist committees, working groups, and the Council's General Secretariat. The Committee of Permanent Representatives is known by its French acronym 'Coreper', and comprises ambassadors and senior civil servants based in Brussels. It is split into two parts, reflecting both seniority and policy concerns of these national representatives. Coreper is responsible for preparing Council meetings and carries out much of the preliminary negotiations on a policy proposal. In some cases, Coreper is able to reach agreement by itself, and then simply requests formal approval from the specific Council by placing the item as an A point on the Council agenda. B points normally indicate that there are still outstanding issues that ministers are more appropriately equipped to resolve. Given the vast amount of preparatory work that is needed to cope with the ever-increasing EU policy agenda, Coreper is itself supported by specialist committees and hundreds of working groups. For example, the Political Committee supports the work of the General Affairs Council, and there is a Specialist Committee on Agriculture. Working groups are usually convened on an ad-hoc basis. In both cases, the task of these committees is to research the detail of the proposal with the aim of drafting a text that will satisfy all member states. The General Secretariat of the Council provides the entire Council with the necessary administrative support and guidance. It is subdivided into policy responsibilities, and consequently members of the Secretariat are often seen as experts in their field, able to provide continuity of information and in-depth knowledge of a particular policy area. It is required to work in an impartial manner, and has often been crucial in times of difficult negotiations.

Each member state takes a turn in presiding over the Council, and is responsible for setting and managing the EU agenda, chairing the discussions in all levels of Council meetings, and acting as the Council's external representative. The job of Council Presidency is rotated between member states every six months (January to June, July to December). Until 1993, this was structured according to the alphabetical list of member states in their own language, i.e. Deutschland (not Germany), Espana (not Spain). From 1993, it was agreed that the Presidency should be rotated alternately because of the differing workloads of the two semester terms. For example, the second semester is somewhat shorter as there are very few meetings in the traditional holiday month of August, and this period often inherits proposals from the first semester. The alternating rotation ensures that a member state does not consecutively preside over the same semester. With the accession of Austria, Finland and Sweden in 1995, the Presidency rotation was changed again. This time, modifications were made so that the troika system includes at least one larger member state in each rotation. In 2000, Portugal and then France presided over the Council. For 2001, it is the turn of Sweden and Belgium, and in 2002, Spain and Denmark. The *troika* is the term given to an arrangement whereby member states cooperate in their work as Presidency of the Council. Prior to the Treaty of Amsterdam, this comprised the current, preceding and forthcoming presidencies. As a result of Treaty changes, and the appointment of a High Representative for the Common Foreign and Security Policy (CFSP) (Javiar Solana), the troika is now made up of the actual Presidency, the High Representative and the Commission. The forthcoming Presidency may join the troika if the matter under discussion will spill over into its term of office.

What is evident is that as with any institution, the Council comprises and is supported by a complex web of internal structures and mechanisms that have evolved since 1958. Yet the persistence of member state authority over the nature of this evolution, whether espoused formally through Treaty revisions or informally through political agreements, reflects the very essence of the Council's dominant power and functions within EU policy making, and its national and supranational characteristics.

Evolution of the Council

The Council as an EU institution remains the final decision maker even though Treaty revisions have resulted in an increased legislative role for the EP. The underlying assumption, as espoused by Monnet and his followers and legally reflected in the Treaty of Rome, was that as the Community evolved, the grip of member states acting as the Council would decrease. The Treaty of Rome, while providing the Council with the legitimacy to take the final decision on all legislative proposals, also built in the scope for qualified majority voting to be incrementally introduced into the legislative process as the Community developed and the areas of policy competence deepened. It was believed that this would alter the nature of the Council, and for the federal idealists perhaps eventually result in the erosion of Council control to that of an upper house in a two-chamber system. The initial area where qualified majority voting was to be phased in was agriculture – a primary concern for the Original Six given issues of food supply in the aftermath of the Second World War, and especially for France due to the political strength of agriculture and the farming lobby. However, partly due to the power of agriculture within French domestic policy, and partly due to de Gaulle's ideological and political positioning within the European framework,

Date	Event
1957	Treaty of Rome establishes the Council of Ministers as the primary decision-making institution.
1966	Following the empty chair crisis of 1965, member states agree to the Luxembourg Compromise and the right to veto if there is a threat to the national interest.
1972	Paris Summit formalises the meetings of heads of state and government.
1986	Single European Act extends provision of qualified majority voting by introducing the cooperation procedure requiring the Council to work in partnership with the EP in areas covered by this procedure. The European Council is formally recognised.
1992	Maastricht Treaty introduces co-decision procedure which extends qualified majority voting and Council–EP dialogue.
1994	Ioannina Compromise asserted that further consensus should be sought under qualified majority voting if there existed a blocking minority of between twenty-three and twenty-six votes.
1997	Treaty of Amsterdam simplifies and extends the co-decision procedure and introduces a High Representative for CFSP.
2000	Nice European Council alters the weighting of votes, and extends qualified majority voting in preparation for enlargement. Larger states are seen as the winners.

the move to qualified majority was muted by the Luxembourg Compromise of 1966. France demonstrated its reluctance by walking out of the Community in the summer of 1965, which became known as the 'Crisis of the Empty Chair'. The only palatable solution for de Gaulle was an agreement that asserted the right of veto if 'very important interests of one or more of the member states are at stake'. While this agreement to disagree had no legality, it framed the mentality of future Council decision making. On a more organisational level, this was further reflected by the formalisation of the European Council in 1974, and its treaty recognition by the Single European Act (SEA). It is somewhat ironic that in order to mark the end of the Gaullist period, President Pompidou of France convened a meeting at the Hague in 1969 of heads of state and government. In aiming to assert his European credentials, Pompidou, together with his five colleagues, implicitly agreed that some sort of further stamp of political authority was required upon the direction of the Community, which gave birth to the European Council.

Commentators throughout the 1970s often cited the Luxembourg Compromise as one reason for the so-called stagnation of the Community, that the right of veto was somehow slowing down the decision-making process. Although research has now shown contrary evidence to this (Sloot and Verschuren 1990), it has shaped the manner in which the Council prefers to conduct its business – by consensus. The repercussions of the Luxembourg Compromise were also reflected in scholarly discussions about the nature of European integration at this time. The neo-functionalist idea of spillover could, and can, be seen in the growth of EU policy competence, yet the political spillover is not as neofunctionalists constructed it. While there is no doubt that member states are engaged in a continual process of community building, there is not the degree of transfer of loyalties implicit in neofunctionalist ideas.[2] The Single European Act re-enforced qualified majority voting into the legislative process, and somewhat reinvigorated the neofunctionalist debate. The primacy of completion of the internal market was reflected in member states' agreement that a cooperation procedure be introduced. This gave the EP a second reading on legislative proposals concerned with the internal market, as well as aspects of regional development, social policy and research. It also required the Council to take its decision by qualified majority vote. What the cooperation procedure did was to alter the relationship between the Council and the EP by restricting the Council's room for manoeuvre and encouraging a greater level of dialogue between the two institutions. However, these shifts were only in those policy areas covered by the procedure and the Council still retained the final decision. More importantly, the requirement for qualified majority voting was negated by the consensus-seeking approach that member states prefer.

As a consequence of the relative success of the cooperation procedure, but also due to the changing context of European integration in the late 1980s and early 1990s, member states agreed to a further change in decision making through the introduction of the co-decision procedure, set out in the Treaty on European Union. What needs to be stressed here is that member states have been highly adept at pushing forward the notion of collective and supranational decision making in a way that still manages to protect their interests. The experience of cooperating with the EP was not unduly negative, and, coupled with the understanding about consensus rules, it was agreed that further amendments to the legislative processes would be enabling for the deepening policy agenda, as reflected by the commitment to Economic and Monetary Union (EMU). The co-decision procedure introduced three readings for the EP on proposals concerned with the internal market, environmental strategy, consumer protection, health and education (see Burns, Chapter 4, this volume). The EP was given the right to reject the Council's common position and thus throw out the proposal. However, a conciliation committee, based on that used for Council–EP budgetary procedures, was put in place to avoid the rejection of proposals. By contrast to the cooperation procedure, co-decision gives the EP precisely that, and has further altered the Council–EP dialogue. The Treaty of Amsterdam extended the scope of co-decision from fifteen to thirty-eight articles, and simplified the procedure to try and ensure that proposals are not lost. It also reduced the application of the cooperation procedure to purely EMU matters. What this reflected was a clear indication that member states acting as the Council have been willing to address issues of the legitimacy of EU decision making by enhancing the role of the EP precisely because the experience of co-decision has not resulted in a decline in their own political control. However, the Ioannina Compromise can be seen as a mechanism for ensuring this retention of authority. Within the context of further enlargement of the EU, concerns grew that the accession of Austria, Finland, Sweden (and still at that time Norway) would alter the balance of decision making within the Council. Spain and the UK were particularly anxious about this, and what resulted was a decision which, like the Luxembourg Compromise, does not amend the treaties but is a tacit agreement. It states that if between twenty-three and twenty-six votes of the member states are opposed to a decision under qualified majority, the Council will aim to seek further consensus through negotiations.

This concern over relative power within the Council increased with the prospects for a dramatic enlargement with the future accession of countries of Central and Eastern Europe. The distribution of votes was supposed to be resolved at the Amsterdam European Council, but given the sensitivity this evoked, and perhaps a sense of non-urgency in 1997, the decision of re-weighting of votes was not taken. This Amsterdam 'leftover' was addressed at the Nice European Council in December 2000, and reflected the imperative of enlargement.

The priority for member states had to be one of reforming the voting system as simply as possible (Raunio and Wiberg 1998). However, the larger member states had carefully and strategically linked this with the size of the Commission in their deliberations at the Helsinki European Council in December 1999, arguing that they had to be compensated for the loss of a Commissioner and the only palatable solution was to increase their voting power in the Council. At the informal European Council meeting in Biarritz in October 2000, this large versus small member state cleavage was even more discernible. A re-weighting of votes was agreed at the Nice meeting, and the number of Commissioners will be limited to one per member state from 2005 until the EU reaches a total membership of twenty-seven countries. However, as can be seen from the voting figures given in Table 2.1, what emerged is a strengthening of the power balance within the Council in favour of the larger member states. From 2005, it will take only three of the larger member states to block Council agreement.

Naturally this has been criticised as a display of lack of confidence and trust in an enlarged EU by existing member states, and it sends out rather negative messages concerning the future cohesion and institutional efficacy of the Council, and EU policy

Table 2.1 Weighting of votes in the Council

Member state	Current	+ 2005
France	10	29
Germany	10	29
Italy	10	29
United Kingdom	10	29
Spain	8	27
Belgium	5	12
Greece	5	12
Netherlands	5	13
Portugal	5	12
Austria	4	10
Sweden	4	10
Denmark	3	7
Finland	3	7
Ireland	3	7
Luxembourg	2	4
Total	87 (62)	237
(threshold)		(169)
Poland		27
Romania		14
Czech Republic		12
Hungary		12
Bulgaria		10
Lithuania		7
Slovakia		7
Cyprus		4
Estonia		4
Latvia		4
Slovenia		4
Malta		3
Total		345
(threshold)		(258)

making in general. While qualified majority voting has been shown to be the method of last resort (Sherrington 2000), and despite incremental increases in its coverage (the Nice conclusions extend the qualified majority provision to a further twenty-nine, but still limited, areas), there is no doubting its growing significance in an enlarged Council.

Maintaining its authority: the Council as EU policy maker

Of all the EU institutions, the Council is the most important in that it holds the final decision-making power. It relies on the other institutions involved in the

The Council's contribution to EU policy making

The Council is the legislature of the EU, and member states have ensured their hold over the final decision phase of EU policy making, despite Treaty amendments which have increased the role of the EP to that of co-legislator in certain areas. By establishing the rules of the game to be those of consensus building, the extension of qualified majority provision has not weakened its position, although it has resulted in a more cooperative relationship with the EP. Its internal structure has also enabled it to cope with the ever-increasing policy agenda. The Presidency often acts as a necessary broker in times of protracted negotiation, and Coreper and the working groups prepare and filter proposals to ease congestion at ministerial level. The Council works with the Commission in the preparation of legal acts and often invites the Commission to assist in brokering an agreement, but through the European Council and Treaty articles it has ensured that it too can influence the policy agenda. At times, and in different policy sectors, the Council is a robust legislative machine. On other occasions it reflects the difficulties of being a supranational institution representing national concerns.

policy-making process to perform its function, and consequently complex inter-institutional relationships exist. Yet, through its hierarchical status, and internal ability to run a relatively efficient machine, the Council retains its authority. The Commission, as initiator, provides the Council with the policy substance upon which decisions can be taken. The Commission thus regarded the formalisation and treaty recognition of the European Council as somewhat threatening to its position as policy initiator, a concern which has grown as the involvement of the European Council has increased (see Cini, Chapter 3, this volume). The Council also relies upon the Commission within the negotiating process, and it requests the Commission's presence at the table. Frequently, member states will call upon the Commission to provide amendments to secure the life of a proposal. Relations are conducted at all levels, both in formal and informal settings. However, and contrary to the blueprints for the EU's structure, the Council has retained its authority in this respect. As discussed, the Council–EP dialogue has shifted significantly in recent years due to the provision for cooperation and co-decision. Shackleton (2000) feels that co-decision has gone some way to further legitimising the EP, and is optimistic about co-decision eventually becoming the norm for decision making. There is no doubt that co-decision has resulted in a cultural shift in Council–EP perceptions of each other, and the use of informal negotiating practices has been built upon through experience, and is now regarded as crucial for co-decision (Earnshaw and Judge 1997).

New institutionalism can be a useful analytical tool for helping to understand EU policy making, and in this case how the Council's operating procedures and styles of negotiation shape decision outcomes (Rosamond 2000). The way in which the Council has established a consensus-building approach to its role as legislator is clearly crucial both to an understanding of its position within the EU's policy-making system and to its character as an EU institution. In principle, member states accept the logic of increasing the coverage of qualified majority voting, but this falters when they have to agree which areas are to be changed to qualified majority. Under qualified majority, a member state can be outvoted, which can undermine its account-ability to its domestic audience. Unanimity, it may be argued, means that each member state remains accountable to its national parliament. Member states engage in decision making under what is now generally referred to as the 'shadow of the vote'. It is the thought that a vote could be taken which enables consensus seeking. In addition to the formal negotiations, informal mechanisms for seeking out agreement have been of particular significance in terms of establishing policy styles within the Council. Different sectoral councils have established their own identities by their preferred negotiating approaches, which fact is reflected by the respective policy outcomes. Thus understanding the contribution that the Council makes to EU policy making also requires comprehension of the informal practices that occur within its various components and incarnations.

The importance of the Presidency has grown concurrently with EU member-ship. The term of office is an opportunity for each member state to take ownership and management of EU affairs. This provides positive outcomes in terms of burden sharing, and of raising public awareness in the particular member state holding office, and for problem solving. The Presidency often acts as a broker in negotiations, aiming to seek out a consensus. It will often enter into bilateral negotiations with a member state, known as 'confessionals', to identify the stumbling-blocks and hopefully resolve the issue. To some extent, this has secured the authority of the Council in terms of producing policy outcomes, as it is a crucial mechanism for achieving agreement. The Presidency also opens up the possibility for all member states to exert influence by placing items on the agenda that are of particular national concern, or by pushing the negotiations on a proposal in the desired direction. This implicit function of the Presidency is clearly dependent upon numerous internal and external conditions which may have been inherited or come to light at that time, and some of which may be uncontrollable. Nevertheless, and whatever the balance of successes and failures, the Presidency has emerged as an accepted means both for this form of agenda management and for control of EU policy making. The effective contribution of the Council to EU policy making is reinforced by the role of Coreper, the working groups and the General Secretariat. Working behind the scenes, their input and problem-solving abilities early in the decision-making process have resulted in a more efficient Council than might otherwise be the case. The fact that agreement can be reached, so that it simply requires ministerial approval, has been of immense significance as the demands upon the Council's time have increased (Hayes-Renshaw and Wallace 1997; Lewis 1998; Sherrington 2000).

The Council's involvement in EU policy making has been a favourite target for reform due to the fact that it meets *in camera* and the related opaqueness of its operation. With the increased calls for more direct accountability of the EU in general, the Council has responded by increasing transparency and openness. Eurobarometer surveys consistently demonstrate poor public awareness of and trust in the Council (European Commission 2000), and member states first responded to this at the 1992 Edinburgh European Council. Since then, Council decisions have meant the publication of meeting schedules for each Presidency, for Coreper and the Special Committee on Agriculture. Open debates are held, usually the first General Affairs

Council of each Presidency, and Council press releases now specify which member states voted against or abstained under qualified majority procedures. However, these open debates are essentially pre-rehearsed, and little in the way of real negotiation takes place. Public access to Council documents is governed by a 1999 decision which states that this shall not prejudice the protection of the public interest, individual privacy, commercial secrecy, the EU's financial interests, or the confidentiality of information supplied by individuals or member states. These terms clearly cover a variety of reasons for denying access, which have been used in approximately one-third of written requests to the Council. Furthermore, the 'Solana decision' of July 2000 introduced new categories of 'top secret', 'secret' and 'confidential' as restrictions upon access in light of the incremental move of the Common Foreign and Scurity policy (CFSP) from the second pillar to the first. The difficulty for the Council, as in the domestic context, is that it cannot prejudice its operation by divulging too many 'secrets'. However, the calls for greater transparency are bound up in the legitimacy debate on the nature of the EU, and the Council is one of the critics' main targets. The Nice Summit conclusions only reiterated the need for EU institutions to respond to written requests for information as quickly as possible, so essentially the Council is managing to resist calls for the further opening of its doors at present.

The survival of the Council?

While the introduction of new decision-making procedures, a limited increase in transparency, and in particular the extension of co-decision and qualified majority voting may have altered the manner in which the Council sometimes legislates, such developments have not radically transformed its overall character and position of authority within the EU. However, further enlargement poses some significant challenges to the future of the Council. Until now, it may be argued that a delicate balance exists between the national and supranational characteristics of the Council, and between the large and smaller member states. It is now crucial to adapt the Council in certain respects to retain this balance. Its role as final decision maker is unlikely to be threatened; indeed its authority could be strengthened by what was reflected at Nice. Existing members appear more concerned than ever as to how decisions are effectively to be reached with such a large number of representatives around the table. The qualified majority weighting and threshold that will be introduced in 2005 undoubtedly reflects this sense that consensus seeking may no longer be attainable, that new members may find the rules of the game difficult to adjust to in the Council, and that this may limit the Council's capacity for effective decision making.

At a more organisational level, some adjustments may have to be made to the Presidency. This has often been a target for reform; indeed discussion of reform emerges prior to every enlargement. However, the scale of pending accessions to the EU would mean that under the current system, a member state would hold the Presidency once every thirteen-and-a-half years in an EU of twenty-seven members. This would surely undermine the principles upon which the office of the Presidency was conceived, and which has worked to member states' satisfaction until now. It is likely that further changes will have to be made with the accession of applicant states if this balance is to be maintained, and there have been some discussions of changing the Presidency arrangements entirely. Member states agreed at the Amsterdam negotiations to appoint a High Representative for CFSP. Part of the reason for this was to try to improve the credibility of CFSP to member state audiences and the external world. Another motive was the issue of the Presidency and small states, and in particular applicant small states who might at least 'appear' to lack credibility on the international stage and thus perhaps undermine the ambitions of CFSP and its supporters. The appointment of the High Representative may in time undermine the role of spokesperson currently performed by the Presidency. It will not threaten the Presidency as a form of political leadership, but whether this can be provided by the Presidency in the long term remains to be seen.

A discursive document on reforming internal Council operating mechanisms was approved at the Helsinki European Council in December 1999, and is still under discussion. Most significant of the proposed suggestions include a reaffirmation that the role of the European Council should be to provide the general impetus and guidelines for the development of the EU, as opposed to the day-to-day policy making. This indicates a belief that the way in which the European Council has evolved is not sustainable in an EU of twenty-five members or more. To defer to so many heads of state or government as the problem solvers becomes less realistic with growth in numbers. An interesting agreement reached at Nice is that from 2002 at least one European summit meeting per year must be held in Brussels, and that when the EU reaches a total membership of eighteen, all European Council meetings are to be held in Brussels. This suggests that the European Council will revert to being more of a symbolic institution than it is now. Also in this document, there is a suggestion that the number of council formations be reduced to a maximum of fifteen, that joint sessions be avoided, and that the use of informal gatherings be limited to five per Presidency term. All these proposals indicate that the Council is thinking seriously about the ramifications to existing internal working methods in the light of enlargement.

The final challenge is that of 'flexibility' in Council membership, as promoted in the Treaties of Amsterdam and Nice, whose provisions on 'closer cooperation' between some but not all member states is likely to mean that in certain policy issues not all member states will be present at the relevant Council meetings. Such differentiated membership is inevitably going to have a confusing effect upon existing Council procedures. Until now, member state governments have been able to marry their national interests with their European commitment through the Council of Ministers, but the extent to which they will continue to be able to do this – or at least the manner in which they do so – is open to question. However, and despite reforms to the legislative process which have empowered the EP, the Council's dominant position within the EU institutional system remains. The challenge will be in adjusting its internal mechanisms to enable continued representation, efficiency and efficacy, and in a larger and far more diverse European Union.

Summary

- The Council of Ministers is the most important EU institution, in that it takes the final decision on legislative matters. It is a unique international forum in that it operates with the Community method while serving national interests.
- The cooperation and co-decision procedures increased the legislative input of the EP, and resulted in a shift in Council–EP dialogue. Yet in the Council, qualified majority voting is avoided where possible, and a consensus-seeking approach is preferred.
- The European Council provides member states with an additional platform on which to assert their national interests within a purely intergovernmental forum. The use of the European Council for problem solving has increased with the complexity of EU policy making.
- The Council's internal structure and operating mechanisms are a crucial aspect of ensuring its position within the EU framework, and for facilitating policy agreements. The Presidency often acts as a broker in negotiations, and Coreper and the working groups provide the necessary preparation and filtration of proposals for ministers.
- The Council faces a number of challenges with the accession of Central and East European states, including a threat to the rules of the game, the danger of overload and breakdown due to numbers and portfolios, the capability of the Presidency to continue acting as an effective problem-solving mechanism, its ability to resist further calls for greater transparency in its working methods, and its capacity to cope with a membership which differs according to policy area.

Test questions

1 Why has the Council remained the final decision-making body in the EU?
2 To what extent is the European Council distinct from the Council of Ministers?
3 How will further enlargement of the EU affect the working patterns of the Council?

Contact information

The easiest and quickest way of contacting the Council is via the Internet. Its homepage can be found at http://ue.eu.int. The site has useful information on the role and workings of the Council, specialist policy areas such as CFSP, details of its meeting schedule, and an online bookshop where you can order Council publications. There is similar information on the European Council. You can access all Council documents that have been released to the public through the press room link, and there are very useful links to all member state government sites, and to the current Presidency site. There is an internal directory of General Secretariat staff with their telephone, fax and e-mail address details. Finally, if you have a specific question, you can email public.info@consilium.eu.int.

If you do not have access to the Internet, the Council can be contacted by writing to Council of the European Union, Rue de la Loi 175, B-1048 Brussels, by telephoning (+32) 2 285 6111, or by faxing (+32) 2 285 7397.

Notes

1   Ratification of the Treaty on European Union meant that the Council of Ministers' official title was altered to Council of the European Union. In this chapter, the term *Council* will be used wherever possible to avoid possible confusion. However, where appropriate, the term *Council of Ministers* will refer to the pre-1993 period, and the *Council of the European Union* will be used for events since then.
2   For an overview of neofunctionalist integration theory, see Rosamond (2000).

Selected further reading

Although the Council plays such a crucial role in EU policy making, there are only a few published academic texts that deal with the Council of Ministers in its entirety, and all these have been published fairly recently, reflecting perhaps the growing recognition of the importance of the Council. These are as follows:

Hayes-Renshaw, F. and Wallace, H. (1997) *The Council of Ministers*. London: Macmillan.
Sherrington, P. (2000) *The Council of Ministers: Political Authority in the European Union*. London: Pinter.
Westlake, M. (1995) *The Council of the European Union*. London: Cartermill.

There are several academic studies of the European Council. The most useful of these are Bulmer, S. and Wessels, W. (1987) *The European Council*. London: Macmillan; Werts, J. (1992) *The European Council*. Amsterdam: Elseiver; and Troy Johnston, M. (1994) *The European Council. Gatekeeper of the European Community*. Boulder, Colo.: Westview Press. Although all these texts were published some time ago they retain their value, as they offer detailed analyses of what the European Council is, what it does, and how it fits into the Council's, and more broadly the EU's institutional framework.

References

Aggestam, L. (1997) 'The European Union at the Crossroads: Sovereignty and Integration', in A. Landau and R. Whitman (eds) *Rethinking the European Union. Institutions, Interests and Identities*. London: Macmillan.
Earnshaw, D. and Judge, D. (1997) 'The Life and Times of the European Union's Cooperation Procedure'. *Journal of Common Market Studies*, 35, 4: 543–64.
European Commission (2000) *Eurobarometer. Public Opinion in the European Union*. Report Number 53. Brussels: European Commission, October.
Hayes-Renshaw, F. and Wallace, H. (1997) *The Council of Ministers*. London: Macmillan.
Lewis, J. (1998) 'Is the Hard Bargaining Image of the Council Misleading? The Committee of Permanent Representatives and the Local Elections Directive'. *Journal of Common Market Studies*, 36, 4: 479–504.
Raunio, T. and Wiberg, M. (1998) 'Winners and Losers in the Council: Voting Power Consequences of EU Enlargements'. *Journal of Common Market Studies*, 36, 4: 549–62.
Rosamond, B. (2000) *Theories of European Integration*. London: Macmillan.
Shackleton, M. (2000) 'The Politics of Co-decision'. *Journal of Common Market Studies*, 38, 2: 325–42.

Sherrington, P. (2000) *The Council of Ministers: Political Authority in the European Union.* London: Pinter.

Sloot, T. and Verschuren, P. (1990) 'Decision-Making Speed in the European Community'. *Journal of Common Market Studies*, 29: 75–85.

Chapter 3

The European Commission

Michelle Cini

> **Key facts**
>
> The European Commission is the European Union's administration. However, to say this is to ignore the inherently political character of this hybrid institution. Indeed it is this political dimension that leads some commentators and practitioners to claim that the Commission is the EU's 'government-in-waiting'. The Commission is composed of a College of twenty Commissioners who are appointed by, though formally independent of, national governments. Each has at least one portfolio and heads at least one Commission service. These services are the Commission's departments, roughly equivalent to government departments at national level. They perform the functions associated with the Commission's role in the EU system, such as that of policy initiation or the management of Community programmes. However, these are turbulent times and a possible turning point for the Commission. Its role and functions have been challenged, among others by national governments and European parliamentarians; its internal organisation and working practices have been deemed inappropriate; and its organisational culture is now said to require root-and-branch reform.

The European Commission: composition and characteristics[1]

The origins of the European Commission lie with three European institutions: the High Authority of the European Coal and Steel Community which was set up in 1952, and the EEC and EURATOM Commissions, which were established in 1958. Yet while institutional questions certainly preoccupied the 'founding fathers' of post-1945 integration, they were not prioritised in the negotiations which preceded the signing of the Treaty of Rome in 1957. It should come as no surprise therefore that the treaty provisions dealing with institutional matters were rather vague both about how the Commission should be organised and about the functions it was to perform. Yet Article 155 did state that the Commission's primary responsibility was 'the proper functioning and development of the common market' and that in order to live up to that responsibility, the Commission was to ensure that the Treaty provisions and other measures adopted by the European institutions were applied. Moreover, it was clear that the Commission was to formulate recommendations and opinions on Treaty matters, whether or not it was explicitly called to do so; it was to have its own power of decision, allowing it to participate in the shaping of measures agreed by the Council and the European Parliament; and it was to draft rules to ensure that European legislation could be implemented.

From the late 1950s to the end of the 1960s, the EEC Commission President set about translating these rather sketchy provisions into clearly identifiable functions, as the institution sought to assert itself *vis-à-vis* national leaders. However, this did not transform the Commission into a consistently activist institution. Nor did it ensure that the powers and functions of the institution were streamlined – while there have been numerous internal reorganisations within the Commission since the end of the 1960s, there has until very recently been no attempt at overarching and comprehensive reform. Indeed, although the Commission has evolved over the decades since it was set up, its organisation has remained remarkably similar to the model which emerged over the course of the 1960s. Despite the continuity that has characterised the Commission, however, the institution has grown exponentially, not least as a result of the enlargements of the 1970s, 1980s and 1990s, each of which led to a flood of new nationals entering the Commission. Expansion of this kind has affected both the Executive and the Administrative Commissions, as Cram (1999) has called them. The former comprises the twenty European Commissioners (also known as 'members of the Commission' or collectively the 'College') together with their personal staffs or *cabinets*, whereas the Administrative Commission refers to the administrative services and the 16,000 or more staff within them.[2]

The Executive Commission can be conceptualised as the political head on the Administrative Commission's body. The analogy is appropriate to the extent that the Commission is an extremely hierarchical organisation. It is the College of Commissioners which takes decisions and the College and/or the President which sets the Commission's agenda. The Commissioners' posts are undoubtedly political, and this is reflected in the manner of their recruitment. They are appointed by national governments, with each member state selecting 'their' Commissioner(s), currently two in the case of the five larger EU states (the UK, France, Germany, Italy and Spain) and one each for the other ten members. After 2005, however, it was agreed in the Nice Treaty that all member states will send only one Commissioner, and an upper limit on the number of Commissioners has been set at twenty-seven. Thus, after further enlargement to Central and Eastern Europe, not every member state will be guaranteed a Commissioner, and the college – including the President – will be elected by the European Council using qualified majority voting. This is a potentially significant reform, for it may make 'penetration' of the Commission by individual member governments more difficult. Currently, it is only in the case of the very political choice of Commission President that a process of formal approval 'by common accord' is adhered to. All member states must agree for a new President to be selected, and so too must a majority of the Members of the European Parliament. This need for approval by the European Parliament will remain in future, but even though Commissioners are (Nice reforms notwithstanding) *de facto* national appointees, there is a formal requirement that they remain independent from national governments. Indeed, around the time of their appointment they are obliged to take an oath in the European Court of Justice to the effect that they will not accept instruction from any government. Informally, of course, close contacts with national governments are encouraged, and it is generally accepted that this is compatible with a Commissioner's independent role. However, if keeping a close eye on national political developments is an important part of a Commissioner's job, their primary responsibility rests with their portfolio, allocated often amidst controversy due to heavy lobbying by the member states of the new President at the start of the Commission's term of office (see Table 3.1 for the members of the 2000 Commission together with their portfolios).

Working closely with the twenty men and women who make up the Executive Commission are the personal offices of the Commissioners, the *cabinets*. These are composed of a relatively small number of staff, usually appointed by the

Table 3.1 The 2000 Commission

Commissioner	Nationality	Portfolio
Michel Barnier	French	Regional Policy
Frits Bolkestein	German	Internal Market
Philippe Busquin	Belgian	Research
David Byrne	Irish	Health and Consumer Protection
Anna Diamantopoulou	Greek	Employment and Social Affairs
Franz Fischler	Austrian	Agriculture
Neil Kinnock	British	Vice-President for Reform
Pascal Lamy	French	Trade
Erkki Liikanen	Finnish	Enterprise and Information Society
Mario Monti	Italian	Competition
Poul Nielson	Danish	Development/Humanitarian Aid
Loyola de Palacio	Spanish	Vice-President for Relations with the EP; Transport; Energy
Chris Patten	British	External Relations
Romano Prodi	Italian	President
Viviane Reding	Luxembourgeois	Education and Culture
Michaele Schreyer	German	Budget
Pedro Solbes Mira	Spanish	Economic and Financial Affairs
Günther Verheugen	German	Enlargement
Antonio Vitorino	Portugese	Justice and Home Affairs
Margot Wallström	Swedish	Environment

Commissioner either from within or outside the Commission. *Cabinets* can provide important support for their Commissioner. They allow a measure of policy expertise to be developed, while also allowing Commissioners to keep in touch with developments outside their own brief, important where policy domains overlap and national considerations are an issue. Since the 1960s, there has been substantial growth in the *cabinets*, not only in terms of their size, but also in their importance within the Commission as a whole. This has led to some tension, with officials frequently arguing that the *cabinets* are trespassing on functions that should be performed by the administration. The post-1999 reforms (see below) have sought to address some of these concerns.

The Administrative Commission is composed of officials, both permanent and temporary, who inhabit the institution's services. While Directorates-General (DGs) deal mainly with policy matters, the Commission's horizontal services offer support of an administrative or technical nature. The most important of these services are the Legal Service and the Secretariat-General, the latter providing a coordination function both within and beyond the Commission. Up until 1999 there were twenty-four DGs, all of them known by their number (e.g., DG IV was the agriculture department, and DGIX personnel). Immediately before Romano Prodi took over the Commission Presidency in 1999, he instituted a reform which cut the number of DGs to twenty-

Table 3.2 The Administrative Commission after 2000

General Services:

European Anti-Fraud Office	Publications Office
Eurostat	Secretariat General
Press and Communication	

Policies (internal):

Agriculture	Health and Consumer Protection
Competition	Information Society
Economic and Financial Affairs	Internal Market
Education and Culture	Joint Research Centre
Employment and Social Affairs	Justice and Home Affairs
Energy and Transport	Regional Policy
Enterprise	Research
Environment	Taxation and Customs Union
Fisheries	

External Relations:

Development	External Relations
Enlargement	Humanitarian Aid Office
EuropeAid – Cooperation office	Trade

Internal Services:

Budget	Legal Service
Financial Control	Personnel and Administration
Joint Interpretating and Conference Service	Translation Service

two, and relabelled them using a form of shorthand (the numbering system being considered too opaque and off-putting for outsiders). Thus the Competition DG is now known as DG COMP and the Environment DG is DG ENV (see Table 3.2).

The recruitment of Commission officials differs dramatically from the appointment of Commissioners, reflecting early intentions to construct a European public service (Coombes, 1970). To enter the Commission as a permanent *fonctionnaire* requires success in the open competition. While a position of this sort is prized, there are other ways of working within the Commission – for example, on a temporary contract as a national expert. In many cases, officials in this type of post are national civil servants spending a number of years in Brussels or Luxembourg on secondment. Both permanent and temporary officials perform a wide range of tasks within the Commission, ranging from the drafting of policy proposals to the management of programmes operating within the member states, or, indeed, outside the Union. What an official does depends in part on the particular service (with some more policy focused than others), but also on the grade of the officials. While Grade A staff are more likely to be involved in policy or decision making, those at Grade B tend to perform more of an executive function.

This brief introduction to the organisation of the European Commission throws up, if only implicitly, a number of characteristics which are important in pinning down the distinctiveness of this European institution. The first is its multinationality – both at the level of the College and within the administration. The second is the fact that the Commission is both a political and an administrative body. The third is that the

Commission comprises permanent civil servants, temporary officials and political appointees. These three characteristics are far from being the only distinctive features of the Commission, but they are, as Christiansen has pointed out, an important source of tension within the institution (Christiansen, 1996), a tension which needs to be acknowledged if any future reform of the Commission is to succeed.

Breaking with the past? Charting the evolution of the Commission

The history of the Commission: key events

Date	Event
1952	Establishment of the High Authority
1958	Establishment of the EEC and EURATOM Commissions
1966	The Luxembourg Agreement, marking the start of a less active phase in the Commission's history
1967	Merger of the Executives (the three 'Commissions')
1985	Appointment of Jacques Delors as Commission President, marking a new and more proactive stage in the Commission's evolution
1991	Maastricht Treaty agreed; considered a turning point in the climate of opinion *vis-à-vis* the Commission
1995	Appointment of Jacques Santer on a 'less but better' ticket
1997	Amsterdam Treaty reinforces the role of the Commission President in setting the Commission's agenda and in the appointment of the other Commissioners
1999	The forced resignation of the Commission (March) and the appointment of Romano Prodi as Commission President. A more high-profile reform agenda is announced
2000	Nice Treaty effectively sets maximum number of Commissioners at twenty-seven, and agrees that all Commissioners will in future be appointed using qualified majority voting. The principle that all member states should be entitled to a Commissioner is abolished, and the 'Big five' agree to give up one of 'their' Commissioners as from 2005

As has already been mentioned, the EEC Commission, now known as the Commission of the European Community (CEC), was established on the basis of provisions of the 1957 Treaty of Rome. At the time it was set up the EEC Commission reflected certain assumptions about 'good governance' which had been propagated by Jean Monnet, the first President of the European Coal and Steel Community's High Authority. Like the EEC Commission, Monnet's High Authority was something of a hybrid body, its conception drawn from a number of different sources, most notably the French *Administrations de Mission* and the International Authority of the Ruhr. The institution also drew on familiar characteristics of the French Administration: 'the divisional organization, the system of cabinets, the *habilitations* (internal delegation of tasks), the *statut du personnel*, and the role of the General Secretariat' (Featherstone, 1994: 155). While Monnet did not favour hierarchical bureaucratic structures, preferring a small, intimate and cohesive working environment, the High Authority nevertheless soon began to develop bureaucratic characteristics despite Monnet's best efforts. As Featherstone (1994: 156) notes, '[m]any of those features were carried over, albeit in modified form, to the EC Commission'.

The model was one based on a French planning approach which was strongly technocratic. This approach privileged the role of independent experts, who were to be outside the grasp of narrow, sectional vested interests. It sought, in effect, to take the politics out of what would inevitably be highly contentious (and political) decisions. There was, moreover, a strong corporatist strand in Monnet's thinking, with the 'social partners' and other interest group representatives involved in the formulation of policy. This was not intended to be interventionist in a *dirigiste* or 'top-down' sense; rather, it was a more fluid consensus-based form of policy making, though one which, at the end of the day, would still necessitate strong leadership. It was such thinking, set in a supranational context, that would later be labelled the 'Community Method' or 'Monnet Method'. This 'method' rested on the neo-functionalist logic of spill-over, a process built on technocratic and elitist decision making in which integration in one sector or policy domain would lead to integrative pressures in other, related areas. This subsequent progress in European integration would be seen to depend on a process of elite capture: the ability of the EC Commission to engage with key economic elites and to help them recognise their self-interest in supporting greater European unity (Featherstone, 1994: 155). The discourse underpinning the EEC Commission was one which emphasised efficiency, expertise, elites and functional interest intermediation; and which had little to say on the subject of democratic accountability and political representation.

With Walter Hallstein, a high-profile and well-respected West German politician as the first EEC Commission President, one could easily have predicted that the new institution would not be lacking in assertiveness, and this was indeed the case. Although it took several years before the Commission was fully up and running, by February 1959 it already had over a thousand staff, and by the end of that year five Commission departments were already in operation. As importantly, however, the Commission had already begun to prepare the ground which would allow it to perform the policy initiation function with which it had been endowed by the Treaty. This involved the collection of relevant economic data and the drawing up of basic studies. Given the underlying rationale of the EEC, economic matters dominated, with the main objective of the first decade of the EEC being the removal of tariffs and quotas by the six member states. As early as 1962, sufficient progress had been made in this area to allow the Commission to begin to shift its attention towards the goal of customs union (with a set of agreed EEC tariffs towards the outside world). Longer-term policy projects were also on the agenda at this point, not least the construction of common policies in areas such as competition and agriculture.

It was not long before the Commission had to face its first serious challenge, however. This took the form of a suspension on the part of the French President, General de Gaulle, of the enlargement negotiations (in a press conference held in January 1963) that had been initiated with the UK, among others. While this only indirectly affected the Commission, its reaction is noteworthy. Much to the dismay of some Commissioners, Hallstein chose to adopt a low profile at this time, stressing the unity of the Commission and the Community rather than protesting openly about De Gaulle's behaviour.

What was a 'crisis' for the Community turned out not to be so much of a crisis for the Commission, allowing it to continue with its activist policy-making approach after 1963 almost as if nothing had happened. It would be difficult to make the same claim for the 1965 crisis. While this was undoubtedly a crisis for the member states and for the EEC as a whole, it was also a turning point for the Commission. Now known as the 'empty chair' crisis, it took the form of a boycott of the European institutions and of European Community affairs by the French government, in order to forestall the introduction of majority voting (due to come into effect in January 1966), and to dampen the supranational activism of the European institutions – particularly the European Commission. While an informal (and uneasy) compromise was reached amongst the member states early in 1966, this was achieved at the expense of Commission activism. In the Luxembourg Agreement, to which all member states signed up (albeit reluctantly), a number of changes to the Commission–member state relationship were set out. For example, the Commission was in future to consult national governments through the permanent representatives before initiating new policies; it was not to make proposals public until the texts had been delivered to the member governments; there was in future to be closer cooperation between governments and the Commission, with restrictions placed on the institution's relationship with missions from non-member states and international organisations. While the details of the agreement might seem rather tame, having more to do with information policy than the explicit power and autonomy of the Commission, the Luxembourg Agreement was, and to a large extent still is, read as a major defeat for the Commission (Cini, 1996: 48–9).

While the events of 1965 to 1966 provoked a Commission crisis, there was no *de jure* break with the past. The Luxembourg Agreement was informal and legally unenforceable, and in itself could not compel the Commission to take a new path. It is only with the benefit of hindsight that it is convenient to see 1966 as a turning point, but other events after this date are equally important in contributing to what many have rightly interpreted as a new phase in the Community's and the Commission's history, though this is not to say that these are discrete events. These included the departure of Hallstein as Commission President, and the appointment of somewhat less high-profile Commission leaders after 1967; the second rejection of UK membership by de Gaulle also in 1967; the completion of the customs union in 1968 and the loss of purpose that followed that event; the economic turbulence of the early 1970s and the failure to introduce monetary union. There was no overnight conversion or step-change immediately after the Luxembourg Agreement. Rather, change was much more gradual and incremental than conventional wisdom about the European integration process might suggest.

Although the 1970s has often been defined as a decade of 'eurosclerosis' or 'eurostagnation', this characterisation of the era should not be overstated. Yet even if the Commission was actively involved in the key events of the decade, promoting new European policies (for example, on the regions and the environment), playing an active role in the enlargement process (culminating in the widening of the EC to include the UK, Ireland and Denmark), and pushing for direct elections to the European Parliament (which came eventually in 1979), it clearly did not seek, or was unable to play, the sort of leadership role that it had in the early 1960s. The Commission Presidents appointed after Hallstein were relatively weak or low profile (though Roy Jenkins was an exception) (see Table 3.3 for a list of presidents). This left the Community somewhat rudderless, until the Heads of Government and State stepped in to fill the leadership vacuum. The institutionalisation of the previously informal summit meetings from 1974 as the European Council was a turning point in this respect.

While the idea of reviving the common market goal which had been floundering since the end of the 1960s was not new, it took a new face in the European Commission to turn the idea into a workable set of policy proposals. This was the Commission doing what it did best: turning ideas into proposals to float before the member states. While there was little to suggest in 1985 that Jacques Delors' appointment marked a turning point in the history of the European Commission (and indeed the Community more generally), this is generally how his arrival in the Commission has since been interpreted. Although his first term in office was his most activist, throughout the ten years in which he remained at the helm of the Commission, he personified the institution for those outside (and in some cases for those working within the institution).

Table 3.3 Presidents of the European Commission

President	Nationality	Years
Walter Hallstein (EEC)	German	1958–67
Jean Rey	Belgian	1967–70
Franco Maria Malfatti	Italian	1970–72
Sicco Mansholt	Dutch	1972–73
François-Xavier Ortoli	French	1973–77
Roy Jenkins	British	1977–81
Gaston Thorn	Luxembourgeois	1981–85
Jacques Delors	French	1985–95
Jacques Santer	Luxembourgeois	1995–99
Manuel Marin (interim)	Spanish	1999
Romano Prodi	Italian	1999–

However, even though Delors' appointment was certainly a turning point in the history of the Commission, there was still no dramatic break with the past. What Delors was essentially doing was continuing the work that had begun during the 1960s. His style of leadership was certainly very different from his predecessors' and there was clearly an improvement in morale within the Commission after 1985. Where there were changes in the way the Commission operated, these came through the construction of informal networks of actors, often francophone, within the Commission. Once Delors had left the Commission, it became clear that he was leaving the institution in very much the same state in which he had inherited it ten years before.

It was left to Jacques Santer to have to face the consequences of Delors' lack of interest in internal reform. He did so by trying to make his own rather low-key style and his less political, more managerial approach to leadership an asset for the Commission. In practice, however, the Santer Commission has been damned for its lack of leadership; yet from the very start it had been understood that the appointment of Santer would mark a new phase in the Commission's evolution. This was inevitably going to be the case after ten years of Delors. Indeed, one might even suggest that all new Presidents tend to bring with them a change of style and policy priorities. However, rather than seeing Santer's appointment as a break with the past, it is his departure which now seems to mark the beginnings of a new phase in the Commission's history – one characterised by the planned reform of the Commission's internal organisation, working practices and culture. The events surrounding this potential critical juncture in the history of the Commission are worth reiterating as a result.

Both the European Parliament and the European Court of Auditors had long been critical of the Commission's efforts to manage efficiently the programmes and policies for which it was responsible. While an attempt by parliamentarians to censure the Commission in January 1999 (over the alleged mismanagement of the 1996 Budget, and indirectly over its mishandling of the van Buitenen case[3]) failed, it did so at some cost to the Commission, and triggered a series of events that would culminate in the Commission's resignation a couple of months later. Santer had been able to avert a vote of censure by the Parliament in January by agreeing to an independent inquiry which would investigate allegations of fraud, mismanagement and nepotism in the ranks of the Commission. The Committee of Independent Experts[4] limited their investigation to a number of cases which had been subject to as yet unproven allegations and rumours. These concerned the Tourism Unit; the MED (Mediterranean) programmes; ECHO (humanitarian aid); the LEONARDO DA VINCI programme (education); the operation of the Commission's Security Office; nuclear safety; and allegations of favouritism, particularly those concerning Edith Cresson and her entourage. From these specific cases, the experts drew a number of far-reaching conclusions summarised in their report which was issued on 15 March 1999.

The conclusions of the report were considered to be extremely damning, even though no fraudulent activities by the Commissioners themselves were identified. A number of general and pervasive weaknesses in the management, organisation and administrative culture of the Commission were highlighted, most notably: a loss of control of Commissioners over their departments (DGs); a lack of openness and transparency in the Commission's internal decision-making procedures; a failure to think through the implications of policy before it is proposed; the existence of internal problems, such as 'fiefdoms', which prevent the Commission from coping with new tasks; procedural problems associated with auditing and the investigation of fraud; procedural problems associated with calls for and the award of contracts; a failure by the Commission to transmit all relevant information to the European Parliament, or indeed to the Commission President and other Commissioners; favouritism and nepotism in appointments to Commission posts. The interpretation of the report by the Parliament and, more specifically, the intervention of Pauline Green, then leader of the Party of European Socialists (PES), during the Commission's late night meeting on 15 March, provoked the immediate resignation of the Commission, although the precise sequence of events that evening remains unclear.

To what extent, then, did the resignation really mark a break from the past? First, the events that took place immediately after the resignation are important. While one might have expected the Commissioners to leave office immediately, this did not happen. In fact, the College remained in place, ostensibly as a caretaker Commission until the new Commission – and Commission President – was chosen. While it was not quite business as usual (the Commissioners could not introduce new policy initiatives during this period), the aim was to ensure a smooth transition from one Commission to the next. Second, the leadership style and substance of the new Commission President, Romano Prodi, is also of relevance. While Prodi's appointment was welcomed with expectations that a cynic might consider to be a recipe for a fall, it was not long before he began to face criticism. While having put together a capable team of Commissioners, Prodi himself received a terrible press. Prodi, it seems, has increasingly come to resemble Santer in his leadership style. Third, and perhaps most pertinent, is the substance of the reform proposals sponsored by Prodi and managed by Neil Kinnock, the Commissioner in charge of reform. This is where we might really find some evidence of a break, but while the rhetorical evidence exists, the substance of the reforms does little more than pick up where the Santer Commission left off. As we shall see below, Santer himself was in the process of reforming the Commission, albeit at a rather slow pace and in a rather unassuming manner. The Prodi Commission's profile is much higher and the substance is different in parts, but it essentially continues the work which was initiated back in 1995.

Thus while it may be appealing to define the events of 1999 as a critical juncture in the history of the European Commission, this may be little more than wishful thinking – or perhaps more generously, a proposition that is intended to become a self-fulfilling prophesy. It is possible that the further we get from this event, the less like a dramatic sea-change in the history of the Commission this will appear. The story of the Commission's history remains one of continuity, incremental, gradualistic change, varying presidential styles and policy priorities, important events and turning points – but as yet there has been no dramatic break with the past. Nonetheless, the reforms to the appointment of the Commission and powers of its President made in the Nice and Amsterdam Treaties indicate that this situation must be monitored. The agreements by the member states effectively to elect the Commission President by qualified majority and also to increase the involvement of the European Parliament in the appointments procedure (see Burns, Chapter 4, this volume), to reinforce the

President *vis-à-vis* the other Commissioners (not least by giving him or her the formal right to sack an individual Commissioner after obtaining the agreement of the rest of the College), and to abandon the tradition of national 'entitlement' to a Commissioner indicate an increase in the 'supranational' character of the Commission, but also hint that the institution may be viewed by member governments as less crucial as a *political* actor than in the past.

The Commission in the EU system

The role of the Commission: key functions

The Commission performs a number of rather different functions. These can be categorised as follows: the Commission as the engine and voice of the Union; the Commission as European regulator; the Commission as European civil service; the Commission as European-level mediator; and the Commission as the external representative of the Union. The relative importance of these functions has varied across the life of the Commission, on the basis of: the institutional framework which was in place; the personalities and leadership capacity of individuals within the Commission; and the external environment – that is the climate of opinion amongst national governments, the European Parliament, and the media to the European Commission.

If there is as yet little evidence of a break with the past, there is no doubt that the Commission is continuing to evolve and change. Even if the functions performed by the institutions have remained much the same over the past few decades, the relative importance of those functions, and their legal and political characteristics have certainly been in flux. Before unpacking some of those changes, five functions performed by the Commission are discussed: namely, the Commission as the engine and voice of the Union; the Commission as European-level regulator; the Commission as European civil service; the Commission as European-level mediator; and the Commission as the external representative of the Union. It should be stressed however that these functions are in some cases overlapping, with the boundaries between them in practice often appearing indistinct and blurred.

The engine of the Union: As the engine or motor of the European Union, the Commission's *raison d'être* is clearly political. It has at least the potential (given conducive external circumstances and internal resources) to play a leadership role within the Union, though it has only been able to do so in short spurts within its history. There are at least three dimensions to this particular function.

The first dimension is somewhat formal. The Commission is responsible for initiating policy, that is, for making policy proposals. Under the first pillar of the European Union, the European Community pillar, it is the only body to have this responsibility. This involves the drafting of legislative proposals, consulting with interested parties on their content and implications, and ultimately presenting a draft to the Council of Ministers and the European Parliament. It also keeps a close eye on the proposal as it enters its legislative phase, though here – as is noted below – the Commission's function alters somewhat. While in the past this initiation role has tended to be considered the primary function of the Commission (and one which is has been rather good at performing), there has been a recent change of emphasis within the EU. Increasingly the Commission has been called on to play down this aspect of what it does, to concentrate on the more managerial aspects of policy making which in the past have tended to be ignored.

The second dimension of the Commission's function as engine of the Union is much softer and less legally defined. Alongside its initiation function, the Commission also has an initiative function. This might imply an agenda-setting dimension, but also includes research functions. The Commission has often acted as a research unit or think tank, as well as a policy maker, though its limited resources have meant that this function should not be over-emphasised. It is more important, perhaps, to consider the Commission not as the source of ideas but as a receptacle for them. It is clearly not the only institution to perform this function at the European level (the European Council, the European Parliament, and individual or groups of member states do so too), but it should not be discounted for this reason.

Finally, the third dimension of the Commission's function as engine of the Union points to the fact that the Commission has at various stages in the Community's history been the most vociferous and committed proponent of supranational European integration. In performing this function, the Commission has recourse to numerous strategies and tactics: creating packages so as to give the illusion of a fair deal (harder to do now that the member states are wise to this approach, and that there are more of them); engineering crises so as to construct threats in the hope of forging a new consensus; couching proposals in technocratic language to make them seem non-political; and postponing decisions when agreement is impossible, so as to reintroduce them at a more propitious time. Clearly, this has not been entirely detached from the institutional interests of the Commission, as enhancing integration has in the past been synonymous with enhancing the Commission's importance, prestige and autonomy. However, in the current climate, the Commission has often had to argue against its own institutional interest in favour of a broader European interest. Thus it is extremely difficult to draw a line between the Commission as motor of European integration, and the Commission as representative of the general interest. It is in this sense that it has often been stated that the Commission plays the part of a sort of sixteenth member state within the Union, as the only body holding and arguing for a general EU perspective. Even less tangibly, the Commission thus acts as a sort of 'conscience' of the Union.

To what extent does the Commission's function as motor of the European Union allow for an analogy to be drawn between *its* political functions and those of a national government? When the Commission performs this function, there are certainly some similarities to be drawn. For example, governments certainly perform leadership roles, as can the Commission. However, the comparison should not be overdrawn. After all, the extent to which the Commission is able to perform this function depends to a large degree on fluctuating external and internal conditions: the goodwill of the member states, and the leadership potential of the Commission President (Endo, 1999).

As well as performing the function of engine of the Union, the Commission also acts as a *European-level regulator*. As the EU watchdog, or the 'guardian of the Treaties', it must supervise and enforce the application of agreed Community legislation. This is an important but difficult task for the Commission, as to perform it well it needs to have a general overview of what is happening at national level, not just in terms of the transposition of European legislation into national law, but also in terms of the implementation of the legislation on the ground. The detection of incomplete or non-implementation is not easy, and the Commission is reliant on a wide variety of information sources, such as articles in the specialised press, complaints made by aggrieved member states, organisations and individuals, or self-notification requirements within regulations and directives. It is only in an area like competition policy that the Commission has powers of investigation or inspection. Moreover, when it comes to the related issue of enforcement, the Commission remains in a rather vulnerable position. While in enforcing European law the Commission has recourse to the Court, its duty to take miscreant states to task is restricted, not only by limited information, but also by its limited resources. Ironically it must rely to a great extent on the member states in performing this function, both in terms of the provision of information and in terms of their compliance with European law. Thus it is clear that this function of the Commission highlights the institution's ambivalent role within the EU system. While it must supervise the member states' implementation of the European rules, it also has to be politically astute enough to take a cautious line and back down when necessary.

A third function performed by the Commission is managerial or administrative. Thus the Commission acts as a sort of *European civil service*. This has increasingly been recognised as one of the Commission's most important tasks, coming close to the conventional role played by any civil service. Administering European policies already agreed by the Council and EP is much less glamorous a task than policy making, but it is nonetheless essential for the smooth operation of the Union. It has two interrelated dimensions: first, it involves laying the ground rules which translate Council and EP legislation into workable programmes and implementable policies. This is an executive task, which involves the Commission in filling in the (supposedly uncontroversial) details of legislation through a process of drafting administrative law. While the Commission was originally left much to its own devices when performing this function, increasingly the Council has been encroaching on the Commission's executive function. The proliferation of a network of supervisory committees (called 'comitology' in EU-speak) has clearly reduced the Commission's independence in this sphere. The second dimension of this function sees the Commission responsible for the day-to-day management of programmes and policies, and their budgetary implications. Controversially, the Commission has coped with the growth in this function (while facing tight resource constraints) by contracting out some of the programme work to consultants, without instituting adequate controls over this process (see, for example, Laffan on the Court of Auditors, Chapter 7, this volume).

A fourth function performed by the Commission is clearly an informal one, deriving as it does from the Commission's position in the policy process. It is inextricably tied to its policy-making function, and to its function as promoter of European integration, and involves the Commission acting as a sort of honest broker or *European-level mediator* among the member states and between member states and the other European institutions (especially the EP). Its objective is not only to facilitate European integration, but also the broader resolution of European problems, facilitating the smooth running of the Union in the process. While the Commission will have its own interest, and may seek to 'upgrade the common interest' during the legislative process (and the intergovernmental negotiations which form a part of it), this function highlights a rather different aspect of Commission activity, emphasising the institution's neutrality on the specifics of the policy, but at the same time its desire to reach an agreement. At times it is hard to see this as a separate function, though it is certainly worth emphasising it as such.

Finally, the Commission's fifth function is rather distinctive in that it relates to its negotiation with third parties outside the European Union of agreements such as trade and cooperation agreements, and those which ultimately lead to new accessions (i.e. to the enlargement of the Union). Thus the Commission acts as one of the *external representatives of the Union*. It performs this function on the basis of a mandate from the Council of Ministers, and as such has only a very limited freedom of manoeuvre within the negotiating process; and, while in these limited areas the Commission acts as the external face of the Union, there are more recently developed aspects of the EU's external dimension which do not allow for the Commission taking such a role, as in the Union's much more politically sensitive foreign and security policy.

We can see then that the European Commission performs a range of functions which have been divided into those that are largely political and those that are largely administrative. However, reliance on this rather illusive politics–administration dichotomy is easily open to the criticism that it merely describes what the Commission has the potential to do, rather than analysing what it actually does – and why. All the same, it does help us to add to our early conceptualisation of the Commission's evolution as an institution. Thus, rather than identifying a trend in the Commission's role within the EU system, or identifying periods of strength and weakness, activism and inactivism (as is ubiquitous in the press), it is more helpful to understand the Commission's development in terms of the fluctuating ascendency and decline of particular Commission functions. In other words, at any one time the relative importance of these functions will vary. That is not to ignore, in addition, the fact that the functions themselves have changed over time, not least as a consequence of institutional reforms introduced since the mid-1980s. A combination of three factors would appear to determine the relative importance of each of the Commission's functions: first, institutional factors, and particularly the rules which govern the role the Commission performs; second, the personality and leadership qualities of key actors within the Commission; and third, the external environment, in this case the climate of opinion as regards the Commission's role, as filtered through the member states, the European Parliament and the media.

After Nice: challenges and prospects

What, then, are the key challenges facing the European Commission in the early years of the twenty-first century? While there are clearly specific policy challenges arising out of the still growing competences (economic and monetary policy, or justice and home affairs, for example) and territorial expansion of the European Union, this section focuses more generally on a broader challenge facing the Commission: that if the Commission is to survive as an effective and legitimate player in EU affairs it must reform itself. While internal reform may not be a sufficient condition for survival, it is without a doubt a necessary one. This final section considers both the demands and expectations being placed upon the Commission and how the Commission is responding to these pressures.

Earlier in this chapter I noted that the Commission was tied to a particular conception of good European governance: one which rested on the so-called 'Monnet' or 'Community method' of European integration. This had become embedded institutionally within the organisation and practices of the Commission as the institution established itself in the 1960s. Since the Maastricht Treaty of 1991, however, a transformation in the dominant discourse of European governance has occurred. While this shift has its origins in the period well before 1991, Maastricht has become a symbol of a discourse change that has undermined the elitist, technocratic institutional assumptions, institutionalised within the Commission in the 1950s and 1960s. We are talking here not only about the Treaty process, but also the ratification problems which followed, not least the Danish rejection of that Treaty in a referendum in June 1992. The events of 1992 made the EU appear distanced from the lives of ordinary people within the Union, even if it was clear that it was in fact more involved in those lives than ever before. Recognition of growing concern over democratic, implementation and management deficits, about secrecy, fraud and mismanagement in the work of the European institutions and in the operation of its policies, prompted a reaction on the part of the EU – both from national governments and European institutions (Metcalfe, 1992; Laffan, 1997). The adoption of the subsidiarity principle and its subsequent elaboration was part of a process of change which was intended to make the EU more acceptable to the European public, as was: the avowed shift in priorities away from policy initiation and policy making towards implementation and evaluation; the introduction of more participatory strategies in the making and implementation of certain policies, most notably regional and environmental; and the assertion by the EU institutions that openness and transparency were to become the norm. This was a conscious and deliberate act on the part of a coalition of pro-European national and European elites who sought to 'save' the Union at time when its very existence seemed threatened (Cini, 2000).

The change was radical in that it involved a shift to a more inclusive discourse which brought together as a package the principles of accountability and effectiveness. Understanding the accountability elements within the new discourse is important, for the concept of accountability is used here as shorthand for a wide range of ideas, of which parliamentary democracy is just one. The new discourse also encompasses a recognition of the importance of transparency in decision making and probity in the allocation of the EU budget. It acknowledges the necessity of bridging the chasm between state and society through participatory strategies, which implies the involvement, at the policy formulation stage, of those actors affected most by European legislation. Accountability also refers in this context to a preference for decisions taken wherever possible at the lowest level of government (the subsidiarity principle), thus favouring decentralisation over central control. This emphasis on accountability is closely linked to concerns about effectiveness. This responds to the perceived managerial and administrative failure of the Commission (in particular) to deliver good governance. In challenging the assumptions inherent in the old discourse that a technocratic approach to public administration and policy making is the most appropriate way of achieving organisational effectiveness, the new discourse draws conclusions about the compatibility of accountability and effectiveness which are likely to impact considerably on the future reform of the EU generally, and on the reform of the Commission more specifically. Thus the new discourse explains the challenges facing the Commission. While the challenge of democracy responded to the perception that the political (policy-making) role of the Commission had allowed the institution too great an autonomy, the challenge of effectiveness arose from an acknowledgement that the Commission's managerial skills left a lot to be desired.

The Commission has responded to this changing discourse by means of a commitment to reform. We have already covered some of these reforms in the above section. These specifically addressed what tends to be called 'institutional reform'; that is, reform which is negotiated intergovernmentally during times of treaty revision. While it is true that the institutional reform process has at least on the surface addressed accountability and effectiveness concerns, it has to be admitted that in practice it is much more about power politics – especially in the case of the Treaty of Nice agreed at the end of 2000. While by no means claiming that the internal reform process, which has been taking place within the Commission in stages since the mid-1990s, is apolitical, it is somewhat divorced from the intergovernmental process associated with intergovernmental conferences and treaty revisions. The Commission is, on a day-to-day basis, to a large extent allowed to 'get on with it': the politics involved, while not to be understated, is of a qualitatively different nature. The reforms made in the Nice Treaty should help this reform, as the College will be less subject to influence by individual member states, and the managerial powers of the President *vis-à-vis* the rest of the College have been reinforced.

It is perhaps rather odd to emphasise the continuity between the Santer and Prodi Commissions on the reform front. Yet while the internal reform process introduced by Santer in 1995 is generally considered to have failed to take hold within the Commission, Prodi did, in many respects, pick up from where Santer left off, even if the rhetoric is somewhat different. Together with his Reform Commissioner, Neil Kinnock, the new President has attempted to institute reforms that will 'modernise' the Commission. These were proposed in a White Paper in March 2000 on the basis of a study of the Commission's organisation and working practices undertaken towards the end of the Santer Commission.

While these reforms have sought to respond to the challenge of democracy and accountability on the one hand, and efficiency and effectiveness on the other, there is no certainty that they will succeed in bringing the Commission's culture in line with what is now the dominant discourse of EU governance. More important perhaps is the question of competence, and the continuing tensions that exist over the level at which policies in Europe should be made and implemented – the European, the national or the regional/local level. Of course, this question stretches well beyond the Commission, but the Commission's future role will certainly be determined by this debate as much as by debates on democracy and effectiveness. Ultimately, what this amounts to is an acknowledgement, however unoriginal, that we are still far from any consensus on what the European Union should look like in the future and what its purpose should be. It is only when (if ever) the core actors of the Union begin to adhere to a shared vision of whatever sort that a clear picture of the Commission will emerge. Until then, it would seem, the institution is likely to continue on its well-worn, path-dependent course.

Summary

- The European Commission has both administrative and political characteristics and functions, causing some to label it a hybrid institution.
- The Commission has evolved incrementally, even if the history of the Commission points to various phases, marked by crises and turning points.
- These changes have not constituted breaks with the past, but a shifting of the relative importance of the Commission's functions over time.
- The reforms of 1999 and beyond are the first comprehensive planned transformation of the Commission. However, even here there is little to suggest that this will constitute a real break with the past.
- Even if this is so, the major challenge facing the Commission is tied up in the reform process, raising the question of the capacity of the Commission to adapt to the new demands and expectations being placed upon it, in light of a change in the discourse of European governance that has been in evidence since the early 1990s.

Test questions

- What are the key functions performed by the European Commission? How is the relative importance of these functions shifting?
- What is the 'Monnet method' or 'Community method' and how does it help to explain the problems now facing the Commission?
- What is the biggest challenge facing the Commission? Do you think the Commission is likely to be able to respond adequately to this challenge?

Contact information

The European Commission
200 Rue de la Loi
Brussels B-1049
Belgium
Telephone: 00 32 2 299 11 11

For Commission email addresses, go to:
<http://europa.eu.int/geninfo/mailbox/index_en.htm>

Notes

1   The role and powers of the Commission are highly complex and discussed on pp. 52–4 of this chapter.
2   The total number of Commission staff varies depending on who, precisely, is included. This figure is rather inclusive, covering not only those based in the Commission's offices in Brussels and Luxembourg, but also staff in research centres.
3   Paul van Buitenen, an assistant internal auditor in the Commission, leaked a report alleging mismanagement and fraud within the Commission to the Parliament. He was subsequently suspended on half-pay for breaching staff regulations on the release of confidential documents.
4   The Committee comprised five independent experts, who were given six weeks to report on activities at the level of the Commissioners. It would have until September to address the Commission's services.

Selected further reading

After decades in which the Commission was virtually ignored, other than in policy-related studies, there are now a number of good introductory texts covering such aspects of the Commission as its history, organisation, working practices, and its relations with other institutions and actors.

Nugent, N. (2000) *The European Commission* (Basingstoke: Palgrave).
   An excellent introduction to the European Commission, readable and up-to-date.

Stevens, A. (2001) *Brussels Bureaucrats?* (Basingstoke: Palgrave).
   A focused study of the EU's public administration, with much interesting material on the Commission.

Edwards, G. and Spence, D. (1997) *The European Commission* (London: John Harper Publishing).
   A detailed edited volume on the Commission containing a wide range of perspectives and approaches.

Cini, M. (1996) *The European Commission* (Manchester: Manchester University Press).
   A solid introduction to the Commission as of the mid-1990s.

References

Christiansen, T. (1996) 'A Maturing Bureaucracy? The Role of the Commission in the Policy Process', in J. Richardson *European Union: Power and Policymaking* (London: Routledge).
Cini, M. (1996) *The European Commission: Leadership, Organisation and Culture in the EU Administration* (Manchester: Manchester University Press).
Cini, M. (2000) 'Organisational Culture and Reform'. Robert Schuman Centre Working Paper, EUI, Florence.
Coombes, D. (1970) *Politics and Bureaucracy in the European Community* (London: George Allen and Unwin).
Cram, L. (1999) 'The Commission', in L. Cram, D. Dinan and N. Nugent (eds) *Developments in the European Union* (Basingstoke: Macmillan).
Endo, K. (1999) *The Presidency of the European Commission under Jacques Delors: The Politics of Shared Leadership* (Basingstoke: Macmillan).

Featherstone, K. (1994) 'Jean Monnet and the "Democratic Deficit" in the European Union'. *Journal of Common Market Studies*, 32, 2, pp. 149–70.

Laffan, B. (1997) 'From Policy Entrepreneur to Policy Manager: The Challenge Facing the European Commission'. *Journal of European Public Policy*, 4, 3, pp. 422–38.

Metcalfe, L. (1992) 'After 1992: Can the Commission Manage Europe?' *Australian Journal of Public Administration*, 51, 1, pp. 117–30.

Chapter 4

The European Parliament

Charlotte Burns

Key facts

The European Parliament (EP) is the only directly elected EU institution. European elections have been held every five years since 1979. There are currently 626 Members of the European Parliament (MEPs), drawn from the fifteen member states of the Union and representing over 140 different political parties. The EP decides its own organisational structure and internal rules, which are formally outlined in its rules of procedure. The Parliament organises its work through a system of standing and temporary committees. Its formal powers fall into five main areas: amending legislation; controlling the budget; exercising powers of scrutiny and control over the executive; appointing personnel to other institutions; and, finally, the EP is the only institution which has the right to dismiss the Commission. The Parliament has eleven official languages and three seats of office, in Luxembourg, Brussels and Strasburg.

The European Parliament: composition, powers and functions

The European Parliament was established in 1951 as one of the original institutions of the European Coal and Steel Community (ECSC). The General Assembly, as the Parliament was then known, was supposed to lend democratic legitimacy to an institutional structure otherwise dominated by national governments and unelected Commission officials. However, members of the General Assembly were not directly elected but rather were national parliamentarians, appointed by their respective national assemblies. The role and powers of the EP have changed significantly since 1951. The Parliament is now directly elected and as such provides the Union's institutional structure with its only strand of direct democratic legitimacy. The EP also now enjoys a wide array of powers that allow it to influence policy; indeed, the Parliament acts as a co-legislator with the Council in numerous policy areas. A key consequence of the increase in the Parliament's powers has been a shift in the Union's inter-institutional balance of power, away from the Commission towards the Parliament.

Nonetheless, as will be argued below, the Parliament is still weaker than the Commission and Council in several important respects. This disparity in power has contributed towards the EU's democratic deficit. This deficit is further compounded by the EP's declining popular legitimacy. Thus the EP's fortunes have been mixed. It has been the beneficiary of institutional reforms, but its powers are still not commensurate with those of the Commission and Council. It is the only democratically elected EU institution, but less than half those eligible to vote did so in the 1999 European Elections.

EP Elections are held every five years and there are currently 626 MEPs. The number representing each state is decided on a sliding scale according to population size; thus Germany has the most and Luxembourg the fewest (see Table 4.1). Members are selected as candidates by their national political parties. EU citizens

Table 4.1 Number of MEPs per country

Country	No. MEPs
Germany	99
UK	87
France	87
Italy	87
Spain	64
Netherlands	31
Greece	25
Belgium	25
Portugal	25
Sweden	22
Austria	21
Denmark	16
Finland	16
Ireland	15
Luxembourg	6
Total	626

Source: Article 190 (TEC)

resident in another member state are entitled both to vote and to stand for office in European and municipal elections in that country.

Once elected, most MEPs affiliate themselves to transnational party federations, or political groups. Following the 1999 elections there were seven political groupings in the Parliament, and twenty-six MEPs chose to remain unaffiliated (See Table 4.2). Each political group is composed of members from different countries and parties who nevertheless share the same broad ideological convictions. Thus the PPE is a right-of-centre Christian Democrat Group, which includes MEPs from all fifteen EU states, drawn from thirty-three different political parties and movements. The PSE is a left-of-centre political grouping also with members from all fifteen states, but drawn from fewer (nineteen) different political parties (www.europarl.eu.int).

Table 4.2 Political groups after 1999 Elections

Political groups	Size
Group of the European People's Party (PPE)	233
Group of the Party of European Socialists (PSE)	180
European Liberal, Democratic and Reformist Group (ELDR)	51
Group of Greens/ European Free Alliance	48
Confederal Group of the European United Left/Nordic Green Left (GUE)	42
Group of Europe of Nations	30
Europe of Democracies and Diversities (EDD)	16
The non-attached members	26
Total	626

Source: www.europarl.eu.int

All activities within the Parliament revolve around the political groups, which control appointments to positions of responsibility and set the EP's calendar and agenda. Their importance is best illustrated by 'the powerlessness of those non-attached members . . . who are highly unlikely . . . ever to hold a powerful post within the Parliament or become a rapporteur' (Corbett *et al*. 2000: 59).[1] In short, it makes sense for MEPs to affiliate with the larger political groupings if they wish to hold any position of influence. There are four key posts of importance in the EP: President, Vice-President (VP), Quaestor and Committee Chair. Elections for these posts are held every two and a half years, at the beginning of the EP's term of office and again half-way through. The duties and responsibilities of each post are spelled out in the Parliament's *Rules of Procedure* (European Parliament 1999). The President provides the Parliament with its leadership both internally and externally and is responsible for: opening and closing the Parliament's sittings; chairing plenary debates; and representing the Parliament on official occasions (Rule 19). The fourteen Vice-Presidents help the President carry out her duties when she is not available.[2] The VPs also take part in the work of the Bureau, one of the Parliament's management bodies, which deals with internal financial, organisational and administrative matters (Rules 20 and 22). The five Quaestors are responsible for administrative and financial matters that concern the members individually (Rule 25). Finally, the Committee Chairs provide leadership and are responsible for chairing meetings of the Parliament's seventeen standing committees (Rules 150–67).

The Parliament's committees are its most important bodies. They meet in Brussels, and are responsible for drafting and adopting reports for consideration and adoption at the Parliament's plenary session, which is held in Strasburg once a month.[3] The committees carry out the EP's detailed policy work and are responsible for its formal input into the legislative process (Collins *et al*. 1998). They have a cross-party membership, which reflects the strength of the political groups in the Parliament as a whole. The role of Committee Chair varies, depending upon the person occupying the position. Some Chairs are very proactive and shape the style of their committee; they seek to raise its profile and build up relationships with Commission officials and lobbyists, thereby establishing networks of contacts that revolve around the committee and increase its policy-making role and profile. However, the legislative role of a committee depends upon its policy competencies and the extent of the Parliament's powers in those areas.

The EP has five key formal powers. First, it has the right to amend legislation. The EP and Council are now often described as co-legislators and are regarded as equals in numerous areas of policy making. Second, the Parliament provides one arm of the Union's bicameral (i.e. two-chamber) budgetary authority, the other arm being the Council. As such, the EP has the right to decide with the Council how the Union's budget should be distributed and spent. The EP also has the right to approve the way in which the Commission has discharged (i.e. spent) the budget, which falls under its third area of powers: scrutiny and control of the executive. In addition to its right of discharge, the EP has the power to ask questions of the Commission and Council, as well as to convene Committees of Inquiry to investigate maladministration in the implementation of Community law (Shackleton 1998). Fourth, the Parliament has powers of appointment in relation to a number of institutions including the Commission. Finally, the EP is the only EU institution that has the right to dismiss the Commission, a power formally known as the right of censure.

The exercise of these powers falls almost exclusively within the first, European Community (EC), pillar of the EU. Under the second pillar, covering Common Foreign and Security Policy (CFSP), the EP's role is very limited. The Council Presidency is obliged to consult the Parliament on the main aspects and choices of the CFSP, and to make sure that the EP's views are taken into consideration. The EP is also supposed to be kept informed about developments, and may ask questions and hold an annual debate on the implementation of the CFSP. The Parliament's role under the third pillar, covering Justice and Home Affairs (JHA), is similarly circumscribed; the Parliament is only consulted on actions taken by the Council on closer police and judicial cooperation. However, it is worth noting that many of the provisions originally covered by the third pillar were transferred by the Treaty of Amsterdam (ToA) to the first pillar, under which the EP can exercise significant legislative influence.

Many of the EP's powers have been recently acquired, and the Parliament's evolution since 1951 is explored immediately below. It will be argued that the EP's powers have increased, particularly since 1979, due to the entrepreneurship of MEPs and the desire of some Council members to make the Union's institutional structures more democratic. However, there have been limits to the expansion of the EP's power, imposed by those members of the Council who view the chamber with suspicion. As a consequence the Parliament remains weaker than the Commission and Council. Moreover, the EP is currently facing a crisis in its popular legitimacy.

History and evolution of the European Parliament: from talking shop to legislature

Date	Event
1951	General Assembly established by the Treaty of Paris, with limited power to hold the High Authority to account. The Assembly is comprised of national parliamentarians.
1957	Under the Treaties of Rome, the General Assembly becomes common to all three Communities – the ECSC, EEC and Euratom – and is given a consultative role in adoption of legislation.
1970	Treaty changes give EP budget powers.
1975	Treaty changes give EP further budget powers.
1979	First Direct Elections to the European Parliament and in December EP rejects the budget for the first time.
1980	Isoglucose Ruling gives EP power to delay legislation.
1984	The Draft Treaty on European Union (DTEU) spelling out EP's agenda for institutional reform is adopted.
	Second Direct Elections.

1986 Single European Act extends EP's legislative powers to include co-operation and assent procedures.

1989 Third Direct Elections.

1992 Maastricht Treaty extends range of areas covered by cooperation and assent procedures and again extends EP's powers with introduction of co-decision procedure, rights of appointment and improvement in EP's powers of scrutiny.

1994 Fourth Direct Elections.

1997 Amsterdam Treaty streamlines and extends scope of application of the codecision procedure and gives EP right to confirm choice of Commission President.

1999 Commission resigns in face of censure vote from Parliament.
      Fifth Direct Elections.

2000 Nice IGC.

Prior to the 1979 Elections the EP's powers were fairly limited. Under the terms of the Treaty of Paris (ToP), which established the ECSC, the General Assembly's only power was the right to adopt a motion of censure against the High Authority (later to become the Commission). The Treaties of Rome (ToR) gave the Parliament the right to be consulted on Commission proposals before they were adopted by the Council. However, the EP's most significant early powers were conferred by the Budget Treaties of 1970 and 1975. Under the terms of these Treaties the Parliament was given the right to increase, decrease and redistribute expenditure in the Community budget; reject the budget; grant discharge to the Commission for its execution of the budget; and to be consulted on appointments to the Court of Auditors (Corbett *et al.* 2000). However, the EP did not take full advantage of its powers until after the shift to universal suffrage. In short, before it was directly elected, the EP was little more than a consultative forum with some monetary muscle.

Since 1979, the role of the Parliament has been transformed by a series of reforms to the original treaties; by the Single European Act (SEA) in 1986, the Treaty of Maastricht (ToM) in 1992, and the Treaty of Amsterdam (ToA) in 1997. The SEA increased the EP's legislative powers by introducing the assent and cooperation procedures. The assent procedure allowed the Parliament the right to approve a planned Council measure, in a single reading, with a simple majority of members. The procedure was used to adopt association agreements with other countries and to agree to the accession of new states to the Union. The cooperation procedure gave the Parliament two readings of legislation, and the power to reject proposals with an absolute majority, although a unanimous Council could overturn the rejection. The procedure applied only to ten Treaty Articles. However, they included important areas such as single market legislation under Article 95 (TEC) (ex Article 100a) (Corbett *et al.* 1995). The introduction of the cooperation procedure therefore significantly increased the Parliament's legislative clout.

The Treaty of Maastricht extended the application of the cooperation and assent procedures to cover a wider range of areas, and also introduced the co-decision procedure. Under co-decision the Parliament acts as a genuine co-legislator with the Council; the approval of both institutions is necessary for legislation to be adopted. The EP has three readings of legislation, an absolute right of veto, and the right to conciliation. The conciliation procedure is triggered after the EP's second reading if the Council cannot accept the Parliament's amendments. The process involves a Conciliation Committee made up of delegations of equal size from both the Council and EP, which negotiate a compromise they are both prepared to accept. The Commission is also present and acts as a facilitator to agreement. If either institution fails to adopt the compromise text negotiated by the Conciliation Committee, the legislation falls. However, according to the terms of the Maastricht Treaty, the EP's powers under co-decision were limited in two important respects. First, in the event that the Conciliation Committee could not reach agreement, the Council had the power to reimpose the position it had adopted after the EP's first reading, the so-called 'Common Position'. The Parliament was then faced with the choice of adopting the Common Position as it stood, or rejecting the whole law and receiving the blame for doing so. Second, in two areas (culture and research), the Council acted by unanimity. Where unanimous voting applies it is difficult for the Council to change its position, as all members must agree; therefore the Council tends to be more intransigent in those areas, and it is consequently more difficult for the Parliament to achieve its goals. Thus the use of unanimity voting in areas covered by co-decision acted as a considerable check on the EP's influence. Furthermore, co-decision only applied to fifteen areas under the Treaty. However, notwithstanding these weaknesses, the introduction of co-decision did give MEPs the unconditional right to reject legislation and the right to negotiate face-to-face with members of the Council.

Furthermore, the ToM not only extended and increased the Parliament's legislative powers but it also improved the EP's powers of scrutiny, by giving it the right to establish Committees of Inquiry to investigate alleged contraventions or misadministration in the implementation of Community law (Shackleton 1998). It gave the EP new powers of appointment, so that the Parliament now has the right to appoint the EU Ombudsman directly, as well as being consulted on nominees for President of the European Monetary Institute and the Executive Board of the European Central Bank. Finally, the Treaty increased the Parliament's control over the Commission by bringing the terms of office of the two institutions into line with one another, giving the EP the right to a vote of confidence on the incoming Commission, and the right to a consultative vote on the nominee for Commission President (Westlake 1998). The Treaty of Amsterdam (ToA), agreed in 1997, streamlined the co-decision procedure and removed the Council's power to reimpose its Common Position. It also further extended the application of co-decision to cover thirty-eight areas under the Treaty. However, four areas are still subject to unanimity voting in the Council.[4] The ToA also turned the EP's consultative vote of confidence on the Commission President into a legal confirmation.

Thus, since 1979, the EP has been transformed from a consultative forum into a co-legislator with the Council, and now enjoys extended powers of control over the Commission. As the EP's powers have increased, MEPs have become more confident about using them, as was demonstrated in 1999 when the Parliament forced the

Santer Commission to resign *en masse* over allegations of malpractice in the discharge of the Community budget (for details see Corbett *et al.* 2000: 243–4). There are two sets of reasons which explain the Parliament's transformation: first, the behaviour of MEPs and EP officials, who have been proactive in seeking the expansion of the Parliament's powers; second, the willingness of the Council to introduce direct elections and subsequently delegate new powers to the Parliament in successive Treaty reforms.

Turning first to the behaviour of actors in the EP, it has consistently been argued by MEPs that the Parliament's powers should be increased in order to address the democratic deficit. Prior to the first direct elections the EU's democratic legitimacy was derived from the mandate of national governments in the Council of Ministers and the fact that national parliaments had agreed to delegate certain policy-making powers to the supranational level (Neunreither 1994). However, in most EU countries national parliaments had little opportunity to scrutinise or influence either the decisions taken by their national executives or the content of EU legislation. Thus national governments were not held accountable for their actions at EU level by their national parliaments. Furthermore, there was no democratically elected institution at the European level which could control and scrutinise the actions of either the Commission or Council. This absence of direct control and accountability characterised what has become known as the democratic deficit. The introduction of direct elections went part of the way towards addressing the deficit by introducing a strand of direct democratic legitimacy to the Union (Neunreither 1994). MEPs were directly elected by citizens of the member states, and were able to scrutinise and amend legislation and the budget, as well as try to hold the Commission and Council to account. Yet, as discussed above, the EP's early powers were very limited, and therefore since the first direct elections MEPs have been proactive in seeking to consolidate and increase the power and influence of the European Parliament. Three examples of the types of activity in which they have engaged are given below.

First, MEPs have always used their powers to the full; for example, the EP rejected the draft budget in 1980, forcing the Commission to bring forward a second draft. In 1983 the Parliament rejected a supplementary budget providing compensatory payments to the UK as part of Council's package to settle the dispute over the UK's budgetary contributions (Corbett 1998). In 1985 it adopted a budget which surpassed expenditure that the Council was prepared to accept by more than 600 million ECUs. In 1987 the Commission and EP took the Council to Court on the grounds that it had failed to bring forward a draft budget by the deadline required in the Treaty (Corbett *et al.* 2000). The Parliament refused to grant a discharge to the budget in 1984 and spectacularly forced the Commission to resign in 1999 over irregularities in the budget. The Parliament has also made ample use of its power to amend legislation, seeing approximately 2000 of its amendments adopted under the cooperation procedure between 1987 and 1993 (Corbett *et al.* 1995), and having 74 per cent of its second reading amendments adopted under the co-decision procedure between 1993 and 1997 (Shackleton 2000), incorporated in some form into EU legislation.

Second, MEPs have used their own rules of procedure as a means to introduce practices that have informally augmented the EP's influence. For example, in 1980 when the Court of Justice ruled in the isoglucose cases[5] that a Council regulation was void because it had been adopted before the Parliament had had the opportunity to offer its opinion (Kirchner and Williams 1983), the EP adopted a new rule of procedure, which allowed it to delay giving its opinion on legislation. Thus the Parliament was able to hold up the legislative process and had a strong bargaining position to fall back on in disputes with the Council, at least in cases where legislation was urgent (Corbett 1998). In other areas the EP has introduced rules of procedure that have allowed it to adopt legislative reports on its own initiative, i.e. without waiting for a proposal from the Commission; to establish Committees of Inquiry before it was formally awarded the right to do so in the ToM; and to hold a debate and vote of confidence on the incoming Commission, again before it was given the formal right to do so in the Treaty of Maastricht. Furthermore, since 1994 the EP has taken it upon itself to hold congressional-style hearings to quiz prospective Commissioners on their suitability for the post (Peterson and Bomberg 1999). Thus the EP has taken the initiative to establish informal practices that enhance its influence, many of which have subsequently been given formal recognition in the Treaty.

Third, the Parliament has been a proactive campaigner for institutional reform. In 1982 the EP established an Institutional Affairs Committee, which was entrusted with the task of drafting a new constitutional framework for the EC (Lodge 1984). The Committee produced the Draft Treaty on European Union (DTEU) in 1984, one of the many factors that eventually led to the Single European Act (Corbett 1998). In the run-up to each intergovernmental conference (IGC) the Institutional Affairs Committee's rapporteurs have prepared detailed reports on the Parliament's position on institutional reform, and have advanced the case for further reform with national governments, parliamentarians and NGOs alike (Corbett 1998). The EP's status as a stakeholder in the process of institutional reform was formally recognised by the inclusion of MEPs in the IGC reflection groups established to prepare for the Amsterdam and Nice Summits.

Thus the Parliament has been proactive in seeking to consolidate and extend its powers. However, as noted by Moravcsik and Nicolaides (1999: 69), 'activity is not influence'. The entrepreneurship of EP actors provides only part of the explanation for the institution's growing importance. All the formal increases in the EP's power have to be agreed by a unanimous Council in Treaty negotiations; therefore any explanation must take into account the Council's reasons for delegating increased powers to the Parliament. One key reason for the EP's success is that it has some strong allies in the Council who have consistently lobbied on its behalf, namely Germany, Italy and the Benelux states (Belgium, The Netherlands and Luxembourg) (Moravcsik 1999). These states argued for the introduction of direct elections and subsequently pushed for increases in the EP's powers, in order to address the Union's democratic deficit. However, there are also some governments, notably the UK, Denmark and France, that have traditionally opposed any increase in the Parliament's influence (Moravcsik 1999). Indeed, French President Charles de Gaulle consistently blocked any move to a directly elected EP throughout the 1960s (Dinan 1999). When the decision to move to direct elections was eventually taken in 1974, it was regarded as a means to balance the demands of the two sides in the Council (Dinan 1999). Subsequent treaty reforms benefiting the EP have been the result of similar trade-offs and compromises, which is why it has often taken years for reforms to make their way from proposal to practice.

For example, the EP proposed the introduction of co-decision in the DTEU in 1984, but the procedure was not introduced until 1992. Even then, despite the support of the German government, opposition from other states (France, the UK and Denmark) meant that the final version of co-decision included in the Treaty gave the EP less influence than either the Germans or the Parliament had originally envisaged; and the extent of the procedure was limited to those areas already covered by co-operation, a few areas where the Community's powers were limited, and areas where decision making was uncontroversial (Moravcsik 1999). In addition, as noted above, even though co-decision applied, the framework for research and technological development, and policies relating to culture, required unanimity voting in the Council, which, as all members must agree, makes it more difficult for the Council to change its position. Consequently, the Parliament is less likely to be successful in those areas. Finally, Moravcsik (1999) argues that the Council was only prepared to agree to the introduction of the co-decision procedure because it did not involve a transfer of power from nation states to the European Parliament, but rather involved a transfer of power from the Commission to the Parliament, thereby weakening the Commission.

The Commission has long been an advocate of increased EP powers, since it has viewed the Parliament as a vehicle for the popular legitimation of its policies (Corbett 1998). However, with each Treaty reform the Parliament's powers of control over the Commission have been increased and, as will be argued below, the Parliament has increasingly displaced the Commission in policy making. Therefore a key effect of increases in the EP's powers has been a shift in the inter-institutional balance of power away from the Commission towards the European Parliament. Indeed, the Santer Commission's resignation may have symbolised a watershed in relations between the two institutions. According to Moravcsik (1999), this shift in power has been the product of design rather than accident, as governments in the Council prefer transferring power from the Commission to the Parliament, to transferring powers from the national to supranational level.

Thus, while there is no question that the EP's powers have increased, the Parliament has often been subject to the vagaries of intergovernmental bargaining. Reforms have therefore been less radical and proceed at a slower pace than the EP would like. Furthermore, many reforms have simply entailed giving those informal practices already established by the EP a legal basis under the Treaty. There is also a suspicion that some reforms have been seen in the Council as a means to weaken the Commission as much as a tool for strengthening the Parliament. Moreover, while the introduction of direct elections and subsequent increases in the EP's powers have gone some way towards addressing the democratic deficit, the Parliament still remains weaker than the Commission and Council. The EP has virtually no power under the second and third pillars. Even under the first pillar, unanimity is often still required in Council, and also applies under four areas covered by the co-decision procedure, thereby weakening the EP's legislative impact. The consultation procedure, under which the EP is weakest, still applies to thirty Treaty Articles; and, one of the EU's most important policy areas, the single currency, is covered by cooperation rather than co-decision. While the EP's power of control over the Commission has been extended by the reforms of the ToM and ToA, the resignation crisis of 1999 illustrated a key deficiency, namely the fact that the Parliament can only censure the whole Commission rather than individual Commissioners.[6]

Table 4.3 Average turn-out for European elections

Year of election	Average turnout across EU (%)
1979	63.0
1984	61.0
1989	58.5
1994	56.8
1999	49.4

Source: Corbett *et al.* (2000): 25

To compound these remaining institutional weaknesses, the Parliament has also seen a drastic decline in its popular legitimacy since the first direct elections. Turnout for European elections has consistently fallen, reaching its lowest level yet in 1999 (see Table 4.3). Thus even though the EP's powers have substantially increased since 1979, the Parliament's perceived legitimacy – or at least its ability to resonate with voters – has declined over the same period, a fact that undermines its calls for further powers.

The European Parliament and policy making in the EU

The Parliament's role in policy making

The EP now enjoys significant policy-making powers. Through the development of informal practices in the field of co-decision the Parliament has developed a shared culture with the Council (Shackleton, 2000), which is increasingly leaving the Commission on the legislative sidelines. The EP has also pushed successfully for increased transparency in decision making. However, the Parliament's ability to shape policy under co-decision is dependent upon the ability of the political groups to secure the requisite number of votes in order to adopt amendments, which may be a challenge for the current EP.

Despite its remaining weaknesses, the Parliament does now play a central policy-making role. MEPs have the right to amend legislation in most areas of competence under the first, EC, pillar, where it has the power of co-decision with the Council in thirty-eight policy sectors. Unlike politicians in many national parliaments, individual MEPs can see their amendments incorporated word for word in the final text of legislation. Moreover, the Parliament's ability to reject legislation under the cooperation and co-decision procedures means that the Commission and Council are increasingly likely to consider the EP's reaction to legislative proposals when deciding their own positions. The extension of the EP's formal policy-making power has given rise to two key developments: first, the growth of a shared culture between the Council and Parliament in the field of co-decision, which has increasingly excluded the Commission from decision making (Shackleton 2000); second, increased transparency in decision making when secondary legislation is adopted.

Let us turn first to the relationship between the Council and Parliament. Mike Shackleton, a senior EP official, has argued that since the introduction of co-decision the Council and Parliament have developed a shared culture based on a set of inter-institutional norms and conventions (Shackleton 2000). A central plank of this shared culture has been the development of a process of informal meetings between the Council and Parliament to supplement formal conciliation. As conciliation meetings may have up to fifty people present at any one time, they are ill suited to detailed negotiation of policy. Consequently, the EP and Council have developed a system of smaller informal meetings called trialogues, at which the key actors from the Council and Parliament come together, with the Commission present as a facilitator, in order to discuss the areas of disagreement (Garman and Hilditch 1998; Shackleton 2000). This system has been successful because it allows for a frank exchange of views otherwise impossible in the larger and more formalised forum of a conciliation meeting. The system of trialogues has been developed so effectively that most negotiations now take place in this forum, and the conciliation meetings, if they are necessary at all, are reserved only for those issues where the two sides really cannot agree.

Informal contacts between the two institutions have further intensified since the entry into force of the Amsterdam Treaty, which introduced provisions allowing legislation to be adopted earlier in the process. Prior to these changes, it was still very rare for either Council or EP officials to be aware of the other institution's position on proposed legislation. However, there are now multi-layered contacts between the Council and Parliament at secretariat level, as well as between MEPs and representatives from the Council Presidency. Using informal channels of communication, the two sides exchange information and seek compromise proposals in an attempt to reach agreement as early as possible (interview with EP official, 08 March 2000).

Two implications arise from this new shared culture between the Council and Parliament. First, the EP has shown itself to be an institution with which the Council can work, thereby strengthening the Parliament's claim for further extension of the co-decision procedure to encompass new areas (Shackleton 2000). Second, the Commission is increasingly excluded from decision making (Shackleton 2000). Under the procedures of consultation, cooperation and co-decision in its early days, the Commission was perfectly placed to act as an informal agenda setter; an innovative policy actor or entrepreneur, able to set the substantive agenda through its ability to define issues and present proposals which can rally consensus among other actors (Pollack 1997). The Commission's influence as an agenda setter is highest when there are informational asymmetries between the institutions, i.e. when the institutions have imperfect information about the preferences of the other institutions with which they are negotiating (Pollack 1997). The Commission attends meetings both in Council and Parliament and therefore has unique access to information about what each side is thinking. Thus the Commission has traditionally played the role of interlocutor between the two institutions. It has also been perfectly placed to exploit informational asymmetries between the two sides in order to make proposals that it prefers, but which can also rally consensus. However, the introduction of co-decision and the willingness of Council and Parliament to talk directly to one another, thereby reducing informational asymmetries between them, has deprived the Commission of its role as interlocutor and reduced its informal agenda-setting influence within the policy-making process. Thus the EP, in showing willingness to use informal methods of communication and through expanding its informal role under co-decision, has shunted the Commission to the legislative sidelines. If the Council's intent when introducing co-decision was to shift power from the Commission to the Parliament (see above), then it appears the strategy has been successful.

The second development arising from the EP's increased policy-making powers has been the reform of the notoriously opaque and complex comitology system. The term *comitology* was coined to describe the proliferation of committees and types of procedures used to adopt implementing measures (Corbett *et al.* 2000). As in other legislative systems, EU legislation often needs to be updated. For example, legislation authorising food ingredients may require amendment after its adoption in order to authorise new ingredients. In the EU, the Commission is responsible for adopting such implementing measures or, as it is also known, secondary legislation. However, the Commission is obliged to work with committees comprised of national civil servants. These committees have existed since the 1960s, but the system was standardised in 1987 when three key types of procedure for adopting secondary legislation were established (Corbett *et al.* 2000).[7] The respective roles of the Commission, the relevant committee and the Council of Ministers were determined by the choice of procedure used to adopt the implementing measure.

First, there was the advisory committee procedure under which the Commission sent a draft measure to the relevant committee, which offered an opinion to the Commission. The Commission was required to take the utmost account of the committee's opinion. Second, under the management committee procedure, a qualified majority of the relevant committee could refer the Commission's draft to the Council. Finally, there was a regulatory committee procedure, under which implementing measures were automatically referred to the Council of Ministers unless a qualified majority in the committee supported the measure. Under one variant of this procedure, the Council could block a measure by a simple majority.

A key feature of the comitology system was the complete absence of the Parliament from any of the procedures. The EP did not even have the right to be informed that the Commission was drawing up an implementing measure, despite the fact that in many instances such secondary legislation can be both commercially and politically sensitive (Corbett *et al.* 2000). It is consequently not surprising that the EP was opposed to the comitology system for several reasons: first, the Parliament viewed the system as overly bureaucratic and complex; second, it was unhappy that it was not informed about comitology measures; third, the EP objected to the fact that it had no opportunity to comment upon or shape their content (Corbett *et al.* 2000); finally, underpinning the Parliament's opposition was the overriding objection that comitology allowed national administrations to circumvent the EP and undermine its legislative role (Bradley 1997). In short, the Parliament felt that comitology was fundamentally undemocratic and un-transparent.

Following the introduction of the co-decision procedure in 1993, the EP's objections to comitology mounted. The Parliament argued that it should have equal rights to delegate and scrutinise implementing measures for laws adopted under co-decision, as the primary legislation had been adopted jointly by the Council and Parliament. Comitology became an inter-institutional battleground between the EP and Council and dominated many of the early conciliation meetings. The EP even rejected a piece of legislation over the issue in 1994. Eventually, to prevent institutional deadlock on the issue, the Council agreed to draw up an informal inter-institutional agreement, the *modus vivendi*, which conferred some limited rights upon the Parliament and referred the issue of comitology to the Amsterdam IGC, at which the Commission was asked to bring forward a proposal for an agreement between the institutions (Corbett *et al*. 2000). After lengthy negotiations a new decision was adopted in June 1999.[8]

This new comitology decision reduced the types of procedure that can be used to adopt secondary legislation and explicitly stated the criteria used to determine the choice of committee. It provided for the EP to receive more information about the composition and agendas of committees, and to be informed when draft measures are transmitted from Commission to Council. The EP will also receive drafts of implementing measures for legislation adopted under co-decision. Furthermore, the Council can no longer block measures by a simple majority and the EP can contest the content of some measures, but only if the provisions fall outside the scope of the implementing measure. Under the terms of this new comitology decision, the EP is still not on an equal footing with the Council; furthermore it now faces the problem that it has insufficient staff and resources to be able to deal effectively with all the information it receives (Corbett *et al*. 2000). Nevertheless, the Parliament has to some extent been able to open up the comitology system and insert itself into a process from which it was completely excluded, and by so doing the EP has been able to bring previously inaccessible, yet often important, information into the public domain.

Thus, through its new policy-making powers, the EP has been able to shift the inter-institutional balance of power further in its favour, away from the Commission, through the development of increased informal contacts with the Council. It has also been able to improve transparency in decision making through the reform of comitology. Yet, ironically, in many respects these two developments contradict each other. The EP's participation in small-scale informal meetings behind closed doors may be a more efficient way of doing business under co-decision, but it is far from transparent. It may be that the price for the Parliament of moving away from the Commission and working more closely with the Council is that it is being sucked into the Council's often secretive and un-transparent ways of doing things. The EP must then decide which is more important: efficient or transparent decision making.

One final point worth raising on the issue of the EP's policy-making powers is the fact that the Parliament has to overcome a significant internal obstacle in order to take full advantage of them. To see its second reading amendments under the cooperation and co-decision procedures included in legislation, the EP must achieve an absolute majority vote of 314 members. Yet, as Table 4.2 shows, no one political group within the Parliament is large enough to command an absolute majority; therefore, to get amendments adopted, the groups need to form coalitions with one another. The majority requirement has a twofold effect. First, within the political groups, the leaderships need to be able to negotiate a compromise that all their members are prepared both to accept and to vote for; second, that agreement also has to be acceptable to potential coalition partners.

In the 1994 to 1999 Parliament a 'grand coalition' existed between the PPE and PSE whereby the two groups cooperated closely to carve out compromises that their respective memberships could accept, in order to achieve the requisite number of votes and take full advantage of the EP's legislative powers. However, following the 1999 elections, when for the first time the PPE won more seats than the PSE, this agreement broke down. In addition, the PPE now comprises members from thirty-three different political parties and movements, which will make it difficult for the group to forge agreement between its own members (Dinan 2000), let alone be able to negotiate a stable coalition with other groups. Therefore a major challenge for the 1999 to 2004 Parliament is to find enough votes to reach the majority requirement in order to make the most of its policy-making powers.

Looking to the future: the Nice intergovernmental conference and beyond

As the Nice Summit came so soon after the entry into force of the Amsterdam Treaty, and because its aim was to settle Amsterdam's leftovers, the agenda for the IGC was inevitably circumscribed. Discussion at the summit focused upon the questions arising from enlargement, such as the re-allocation of voting weights in the Council, the size of the Commission, and the redistribution of seats for the EP (see Table 4.4). The Parliament's aims for the summit included, *inter alia*: the extension of qualified majority voting (QMV) and co-decision to all areas under the first pillar; the improvement of the EP's powers of control over the Commission; the full merger of the third pillar into the first, where policies would be subject to QMV and co-decision; and to secure an expanded role for itself under the second pillar (CFSP). However, the Nice outcome was disappointing for the EP, although some important steps forward were achieved. The Parliament has been given the right to consult the Court of Justice on the legality of agreements made between the Union and third states or international organisations under Article 300 (TEC). It has also been given equal status with the Commission and Council to challenge the legality of an act in the Court of Justice, and may now also charge a member state with a breach of fundamental rights under Article 230 (TEC). However, there was only a limited extension of QMV and co-decision, which means that many policy areas are still subject to unanimity voting in the Council, and the consultation procedure still widely applies. A new rule was brought in under Article 217 (TEC) allowing the Commission President to censure individual Commissioners, a power that the EP would prefer to hold itself; but at least now the Parliament will be able to bring pressure to bear on the Commission President to get rid of individual Commissioners.

The new allocation of seats will expand the EP's size beyond the 700 maximum agreed at Amsterdam to 732, and the new allocation has broken the convention that the number of seats given to a state should be roughly proportional to its population size. Belgium and Portugal have smaller populations than the Czech Republic, yet both countries have been given more seats. Similarly, Hungary has a larger population than Belgium but has fewer seats.

Given the limited steps taken forward at Nice, the EP's long-standing goals will remain the same, namely to extend co-decision and QMV to a wider number of areas,

Table 4.4 Allocation of MEPs agreed at the Nice Summit

Current member states	Number of MEPs
Germany	99
UK	72
France	72
Italy	72
Spain	50
Netherlands	25
Greece	22
Belgium	22
Portugal	22
Sweden	18
Austria	17
Denmark	13
Finland	13
Ireland	12
Luxembourg	6
Candidate countries	
Poland	50
Romania	33
Czech Republic	20
Hungary	20
Bulgaria	17
Slovakia	13
Lithuania	12
Latvia	8
Slovenia	7
Estonia	6
Cyprus	6
Malta	5
Total	732

Source: *Financial Times*, 12 December 2000

to incorporate more policies into the first pillar and to extend its powers of control over the Commission. However, in the short term, the Parliament's priorities must be to consolidate its existing powers to ensure that it can exercise its legislative influence by gaining absolute majorities for its amendments and, perhaps most importantly, to improve its profile amongst European citizens in a positive and clear-cut way. The EP is supposed to be a standard-bearer for democracy in the Union, yet, as discussed above, turnout for European Elections has consistently declined. The enlargement of the Union and the entry of a new cohort of MEPs from diverse political and national backgrounds make the resolution of this problem more pressing. MEPs will be representing larger numbers of constituents and will become further removed from the citizens whom they are supposed to represent. Therefore, as the EU expands eastwards, concerns about democratic participation will only intensify.

A number of solutions to the problem of the EP's declining popular legitimacy have been suggested. Some argue that more interest would be generated if the composition of the Commission depended upon the outcome of European elections (Corbett *et al.* 2000). Others suggest that because most citizens associate more closely with their national parliaments than with EU institutions, national parliaments should start scrutinising EU legislation in a more thorough way, and the EP should improve its relations with these bodies (Neunreither 1994). It has also been argued that the solution lies in the entrenchment of European citizenship, which could be harnessed through the extension of existing measures such as transnational rights to vote and stand for election in other EU countries, and the creation of European political parties, trade unions and a genuinely European media, so that the reporting of EU affairs is no longer refracted through a prism of national prejudices (Chryssochoou 2000). Whatever solution or combination of solutions is chosen, the EP must find a way of improving its public profile to prevent the further erosion of its popular legitimacy in the coming years, as the Parliament's calls for increased powers to reduce the democratic deficit are seriously undermined by the lack of public participation in its election.

Summary

- The European Parliament is the only elected EU institution. Established in 1951 as an unelected forum with little power, it has been transformed over the years to become a co-legislator with the Council, with considerable powers of control over the Commission.
- The change in the EP's status has taken place due to its own entrepreneurship and the support of the expansion in its powers from key actors in the Council of Ministers committed to improving the democratic accountability of the EU's institutional structures. However, the Parliament still remains weaker than the Council and Commission and its democratic legitimacy has been undermined by the decline in turnout for European elections.
- The Parliament is now central to policy making under the first pillar, and through the exercise of its powers under co-decision has developed a shared culture with the Council, which is increasingly excluding the Commission from decision making. The Parliament has also used its policy-making role to press for reforms to the comitology system. However, the EP must be able to find an absolute majority in order to use its legislative powers to the full, which may be a challenge in the current Parliament.
- The EP's future priorities are to achieve co-decision and qualified majority voting in all areas of policy making covered by the first pillar, to incorporate policies under the third pillar into the first, to extend its role under the second pillar and to extend its powers of control over the Commission. The EP must also improve turnout for European elections.

Test questions

1   How and why have the EP's powers expanded since 1979?
2   What has been the impact of the increase in the EP's policy-making powers?
3   What are the future challenges for the EP?

Contact Information

The best way to contact the Parliament is via its website, www.europarl.eu.int. The website is available in eleven languages and contains a plethora of information about the Parliament's structure and activities, including details of the plenary and committee agendas. It also contains information about MEPs including their individual contact details, in addition to which there are detailed pages covering the political groups. You can also download reports from the site's legislative observatory on the activities page. There are National EP Information Offices in each member state, the contact details of which may also be found on the EP's website on the useful addresses page.

You may also contact the Parliament by conventional methods, at one of its three seats of office:

Plateau de Kirchberg, L-2929 Luxembourg, Tel +352 4300 1
Rue Wiertz, B-1047 Brussels, Tel +32 2 284 21 11
Allée du Printemps, BP1024 F-670670 Strasburg Cedex, Tel +33 3 88 17 40 01.

Notes

1   The term *rapporteur* refers to the person responsible for writing the EP's reports.
2   The current President of the European Parliament is French PPE member Nicole Fontaine.
3   The Parliament also now holds plenary sessions in Brussels, but it is required to hold at least twelve of its sessions in Strasburg. In addition, the Parliament has offices in Luxembourg which house some administrative staff.
4   Citizenship, freedom of movement for workers, measures concerning the self-employed, and culture.
5   Cases 138 and 139/79, *Roquette Freres v Council* and *Maizena Gesellschaft v Council*.
6   In fact, the EP did not actually have to vote, since the Commission resigned as a collective upon learning that the vote of censure would be carried.
7   Council Decision (87/373/EEC), 13/07/87 OJL 197 18/07/87, p. 33.
8   Council Decision (1999/468/EC), 28/06/99, OJL 184 17/07/99, pp. 23–6.

Selected further reading

Corbett, R., Jacobs, F. and Shackleton, M. (2000) *The European Parliament* (4th edn): (London: John Harper Publishing).

This book provides an excellent and detailed introduction to the Parliament from an insider perspective. It is a first stop for anyone interested in knowing more about the EP.

Corbett, R. (1998) *The European Parliament's Role in Closer Integration* (Basingstoke: Macmillan).

Corbett provides an interesting account of the EP's role in institutional reform.

Shackleton, M. (2000) 'The Politics of Co-Decision'. *Journal of Common Market Studies*, 38, 2, pp. 325–42.

Shackleton provides a clear and enjoyable explanation and discussion of the Parliament's powers under co-decision.

References

Bradley, K. (1997) 'The European Parliament and Comitology: On the Road to Nowhere?' *European Law Journal*, 3, 3, pp. 230–54.

Chryssochoou, D. (2000) *Democracy in the European Union* (London: IB Tauris).

Collins, K., Burns, C. and Warleigh, A. (1998) 'Policy Entrepreneurs: the role of European Parliament Committees in the Making of EU Policy'. *Statute Law Review*, 19, 1, 1–11.

Corbett, R. (1998) *The European Parliament's Role in Closer Integration* (Basingstoke: Macmillan).

Corbett, R., Jacobs, F. and Shackleton, M. (1995) *The European Parliament 3rd Edition* (London: Cartermill International).

Corbett, R., Jacobs, F. and Shackleton, M. (2000) *The European Parliament 4th Edition* (London: John Harper Publishing).

Dinan, D. (1999) *Ever Closer Union* (Basingstoke: Macmillan).

Dinan, D. (2000) 'Governance and Institutions: Resignation, Reform and Renewal'. *The European Union Annual Review 1999/2000, Journal of Common Market Studies*, 38, pp. 25–41.

European Parliament (1999) *Rule of Procedure 14th Edition* (Luxembourg: Office for Official Publications of the European Communities), June.

Garman, J. and Hilditch, L. (1998) 'Behind the Scenes: An Examination of the Importance of the Informal Processes at Work in Conciliation'. *Journal of European Public Policy*, 5, 2, pp. 271–84.

Kirchner, K. and Williams, K. (1983) 'The Legal, Political and Institutional Implications of the Isoglucose Judgments 1980'. *Journal of Common Market Studies*, 22, 2, pp. 173–90.

Lodge, J. (1984) 'European Union and the First Elected European Parliament: The Spinelli Initiative'. *Journal of Common Market Studies*, 22, 4, pp. 377–402.

Moravcsik, A. (1999) *The Choice for Europe* (London: UCL Press).

Moravcsik, A. and Nicolaides, K. (1999) 'Explaining the Treaty of Amsterdam; Interests, Influence and Institutions'. *Journal of Common Market Studies*, 37, 1, pp. 59–85.

Neunreither, K. (1994) 'The Democratic Deficit of the European Union: Towards Closer Co-operation between the European Parliament and National Parliaments'. *Government and Opposition*, 29, 3, pp. 229–314.

Peterson, J. and Bomberg, E. (1999) *Decision-Making in the European Union* (Basingstoke: Macmillan).

Pollack, M. (1997) 'Delegation, Agency, and Agenda-setting in the European Community'. *International Organization*, 51, 1, pp. 99–134.

Shackleton, M. (1998) 'The European Parliament's new Committees of Inquiry: Tiger or Paper Tiger?' *Journal of Common Market Studies*, 36, 1, pp. 115–30.

Shackleton, M. (2000) 'The Politics of Co-Decision'. *Journal of Common Market Studies*, 38, 2, pp. 325–42.

Westlake, M. (1998) 'The Parliament's Emerging Powers of Appointment'. *Journal of Common Market Studies*, 36, 3, pp. 431–44.

Chapter 5

The European Central Bank

David Howarth

Key facts

Created by the Treaty on European Union, the European Central Bank (ECB; the European bank) came into existence on 1 June 1998. It is the only EU institution to be based in Frankfurt am Main, Germany. On 1 January 1999, the ECB gained control over European monetary policy (including interest rates and money supply) for the Euro-Zone. The ECB consists of the Executive Board and the Governing Council: the first comprises the President, Vice-President and four monetary policy experts, all appointed for minimum non-renewable eight-year terms; the second comprises National Central Bank (NCB) governors, who in turn are appointed by member state governments for a minimum renewable period of five years. The ECB's autonomy from any instruction both from EU institutions and from member states is guaranteed by the TEU (Art. 108 (ex Art. 107) EC) and all participating NCBs must be 'independent' of national governments. In pursuing its monetary policy, the ECB's sole goal (Art. 105) is to maintain 'sound money' (low inflation) in the Euro-Zone. It has the power to express opinions on its own initiative on the economic policies pursued by the twelve Euro-Zone member states. All decision making takes place on the basis of simple majority voting, with each member possessing one vote.

The ECB: composition, powers and functions

Composition

The Treaty on European Union (TEU) called for the creation of the ECB prior to the start of Stage Three of Economic and Monetary Union (EMU).[1] The ECB principally consists of the Executive Board and the Governing Council. The Executive Board comprises the President, the Vice-President, and four monetary policy and banking experts.[2] They are appointed for minimum non-renewable eight-year terms by the European Council after it has consulted the European Parliament and the Governing Council of the ECB (the Council of the European Monetary Institute (EMI) for the first appointments in 1998). The first Executive Board members (with the exception of the President) were given terms of different length so that future members can be given staggered terms in order to ensure the continuity of policy making. According to the Treaty, the Executive Board is appointed purely on the grounds of recognised standing and professional experience in monetary or banking matters (Art. 109a, Art. 112 EC). In theory, the Board is not supposed to be representative of the participating member states. However – as the designation of the first Board in May 1998 demonstrated – some governments have placed great emphasis on the inclusion of a member from their country, and four of the six current members are citizens of the most populous participating member states with the largest economies (Germany, France, Italy and Spain).

The Governing Council comprises all the members of the Executive Board and the 'Eurosystem' NCB governors – that is of those EU member states which participate in the Euro-Zone (see Table 5.1). NCB governors are appointed by governments for minimum renewable terms of five years. In order to improve the efficiency of its decision making, the Governing Council has divided itself up into working groups on matters including forecasting and econometric modelling. Like the Executive Board, all decision making in the Governing Council takes place on the basis of simple majority voting. Each member, including the NCB governors, possesses one vote, regardless of the population and GNP of the Member State.[3] In the event of a tie, the President casts the deciding ballot. However, so far, decision making has been based on consensus and no voting has taken place. The President of the Council of Economic and Finance Ministers (Ecofin) (the Minister of Finance of the member state holding the EU Council Presidency) and a member of the Commission attend the Governing Council and can submit motions to it (Art. 113(3) (ex 109b) EC). However, they have no voting rights. The Governing Council normally

Table 5.1 Current members of the ECB Governing Council (as of 1 January 2001)

Executive Board members and responsibilities

Willem F. Duisenberg (The Netherlands),
President of the ECB: Directorates External Relations, Secretariat and Language Services, Internal Audit.
Christian Noyer (France),
Vice-President of the ECB: Directorates-General (DGs) Administration and Personnel, Legal Services.
Eugenio Domingo Solans (Spain),
expert member: DGs Information Systems, Statistics, Directorate Banknotes.
Sirkka Hämäläinen (Finland),
expert member: DG Operations, Directorate Controlling and Organisation.
Otmar Issing (Germany),
expert member (chief ECB economist): DGs Research, Economics.
Tommaso Padoa-Schioppa (Italy),
expert member: DGs International and European Relations, Payments Systems.

National Central Bank Governors

Jaime Caruana	(Spain)
Antonio Fazio	(Italy)
Klaus Liebscher	(Austria)
Lucas D. Papademos	(Greece)
Yves Mersch	(Luxembourg)
Maurice O'Connell	(Ireland)
Guy Quaden	(Belgium)
Vitor Manuel Ribeiro Constâncio	(Portugal)
Jean-Claude Trichet	(France)
Nout Wellink	(Netherlands)
Ernst Welteke	(Germany)
Matti Vanhala	(Finland)

meets in Frankfurt, although it was agreed that starting in 2000 there would be at least two meetings a year in another member state of the Euro-Zone. The President or three members of the Governing Council can call a meeting at any time.

The ECB is at the summit of the European System of Central Banks (ESCB), created by the TEU, which consists of the NCBs of all fifteen EU member states (including those not participating in the Euro-Zone). The governors of the non-participants – currently Britain, Denmark and Sweden – are not entitled to take part in decision making on the single monetary policy. However, a third body, the General Council, was created to deal with matters concerning the entire ESCB, and thus consists of the governors of all ESCB (EU) central banks in addition to the President and Vice-President of the ECB. Like the Governing Council, voting in the General Council takes place according to simple majority with each member possessing one vote. The expert members of the Executive Board are entitled to attend meetings of the General Council, although they have no voting rights. General Councils are held once a quarter on the same days as Governing Council meetings.

The ECB administrative and operational staff is divided into nine Directorates-General (DGs): administration and personnel, legal services, information systems, statistics, operations, economics, research, international and European relations, and payment systems. The DGs fall under the responsibility of one of the five members of the Executive Board other than the President. Several directorates stand on their own outside the framework of the Directorates-General (for example, prudential supervision, banknotes, and controlling and organisation). A total of 770 policy staff from the fifteen member states of the ESCB – including those not participating in EMU – work for the ECB.

The ECB is normally considered to be one of the most independent central banks in the world (Kaufmann 1995; Hirst and Thompson 1996; de Hann 1997; Elgie 1998; Elgie and Thompson 1998), both in terms of economic independence – the ability to use the full range of monetary policy instruments without restrictions from the government – and political independence – the ability to make policy decisions without interference from governments.[4] To guarantee this independence, numerous provisions have been included in the TEU, and the Protocol on the Statute of the ESCB and of the ECB appended to the TEU. For example, minimum terms for members of the Executive Board and NCB governors are established. Removal from office is only possible in the event of incapacity or serious misconduct, with the European Court of Justice granted competence to resolve any disputes. This issue of political independence will be discussed further below in the context of the debate on the ECB's accountability.

Powers and functions

The basic power of the ECB is to define and implement the monetary policy of the Euro-Zone. According to the TEU and the Statute of the ESCB and of the ECB (Art. 105),

> [t]he primary objective of the Eurosystem [is] to maintain price stability. Without prejudice to [this] objective, the ESCB shall support the general

economic policies in the Community and act in accordance with the principles of an open market economy with free competition, favouring an efficient allocation of resources.

The Executive Board of the ECB implements monetary policy in accordance with the guidelines and decisions laid down by the Governing Council and, in doing so, gives necessary instructions to the NCBs. The ECB can intervene in the market (open market operations) to secure its policy objectives. It can also issue opinions on the actions taken by the other EU institutions and the member states in pursuit of 'sound money'. The Executive Board also executes those powers which have been delegated to it by the Governing Council.

Although the ECB does not possess overall power to make regulations, it can make them to the extent necessary to implement specific tasks (Art. 110 (1) (ex 108a (1)) EC), notably with regard to the operation of the ESCB (see Craig 1999). Some of the ECB's regulatory power also depends upon what the Council of Ministers grants to it (for example, regarding the establishment of the minimum and maximum reserves to be held by national credit institutions with the ECB). The ECB possesses the limited power to impose fines or periodic penalty payments for failure to comply with obligations contained in its regulations and decisions (Art. 110 (3) (ex 108a (3)) EC); for example, with regard to the setting of reserves credit institutions should hold with the ECB or the prudential supervision of credit institutions. While the possibility exists for the ECB to be taken to the European Court of Justice (ECJ) or Court of First Instance (CFI) on matters pertaining to its management of the ESCB (Craig 1999), the ECB can itself have recourse to the courts (as stated in Article 230 (3) (ex 173 (3)) EC), in particular with regard to inter-institutional disputes – for example, if the Council fails to consult the ECB on matters where it is expected to do so.

The Governing Council has three main responsibilities. First, it adopts the guidelines and makes the necessary decisions to ensure the maintenance of price stability (Art. 12 ESCB Statute). This involves defining price stability and the policy instruments to be used in maintaining it; it also entails a broadly based assessment of the forecast for price developments and risks to price stability in the Euro-Zone (see ECB 1999). Second, the Governing Council formulates the monetary policy of the Eurosystem, including decisions relating to intermediate monetary objectives, key interest rates and the supply of reserves throughout the system. Third, the Governing Council establishes the necessary guidelines for the implementation of these decisions (EMI 1997a, 1997b; ECB 1998b).

The General Council has assumed responsibility for the tasks previously performed by the European Monetary Institute (EMI) which must still be assumed by a body that includes both ESCB NCBs participating in the Euro-Zone and those that are not. These tasks include the preparations for setting the irrevocable exchange rates of the currencies joining the Euro-Zone in the future (as in the Greek case in 2000). The General Council also contributes to several ECB functions including: the collection of statistical information and the preparation of the ECB's quarterly and annual reports and weekly consolidated financial statements; the setting of rules for standardising the accounting and reporting of operations undertaken by the NCBs; and the establishment of the conditions of employment of ECB staff.

It should be noted that the NCBs also perform several operations vital to the operation of the Euro-Zone; notably, they conduct foreign exchange operations and ensure the smooth operation of payment systems (including TARGET). The NCBs also hold and manage the official foreign reserves of the member states (of which they can supply up to 40 billion euro to the ECB). In addition, NCBs hold the capital of the ECB (just under 4 billion euro).

Brief history and evolution of European monetary authority

Date	Event
1964	First regular meetings of the Committee of Governors of the central banks of EEC member states.
1979	The creation of the European Monetary System (EMS) which involves the possible creation of a European Monetary Institute (EMI).
1990	Start of Stage One of the EMU project. Principle of independent European central banks is agreed.
1991	European Council agrees a timetable for the move to EMU, and the creation of the EMI and the ECB.
1994	(1 January) Start of Stage Two of EMU. Replacement of the Committee of Governors by the EMI.
1995	(December) The European Council meeting in Madrid adopts the 'change-over scenario' to the single currency drafted by the EMI.
1996	(December) The European Council meeting in Dublin agrees to the terms of the 'Stability and Growth Pact' (ratified by the Amsterdam European Council of June 1997).
1998	Announcement of which member states will participate in Stage Three of EMU. Creation of the European Central Bank. Agreement at Vienna European Council to allow ECB President to attend G7 meetings.
1999	(1 January) Start of Stage Three of EMU. ECB starts to manage the euro.
2000	(22 September) The first joint intervention with Americans and Japanese to support declining euro.
2000	(December) ECB starts to publish Eurosystem forecasts.
2001	(1 January) Greece joins the Euro-Zone and the ECB Governing Council.

The ECB itself has had a relatively short history, but its antecedents, the Committee of Governors of the Central Banks of the EEC, the European Monetary and Cooperation Fund (EMCF) and the European Monetary Institute (EMI), played an important role in the management of European monetary policy and the move to EMU. EEC central bank governors – notably in the EEC's Monetary Committee (Kees 1994), the Delors Committee (1988–89) and the EMI of the second stage of the EMU project – formed part of an 'epistemic community' which provided the intellectual and institutional backing to the underlying principles of EMU (sound money and finance and central bank independence) (Dyson 1994; Verdun 1999).[5] In 1964, EEC central bankers began to meet separately in the Committee of EEC Governors following Bank for International Settlements (BIS) meetings in Basle. In its October 1970 report, the Werner Committee – set up to examine the practical steps to EMU – recommended the creation of an ECB and an EC organisation of national central banks. The creation of the European Monetary Cooperation Fund (EMCF/ FECOM) in 1973 was the major institutional legacy of the EMU discussions and provided the central bank governors with their first collective task since the European Payments Union (EPU) of the late 1940s: the management of a small percentage of European reserves pooled to help maintain stability in the first European monetary mechanism, the 'Snake', established in April 1971. These reserves were expanded with the creation of the European Monetary System (EMS) in 1979. During the negotiations on the EMS, the German government accepted French demands that the EMCF be strengthened and transformed into an EMI in order to promote the use of the fledgling European currency, the ECU. However, this agreement was informal and, in the context of widely diverging French and German economic policies following the 1981 election victory of the French Socialists, the central bank governors quietly shelved plans to create the EMI. Throughout the 1980s, the French were the most active proponents of expanding the powers of the EMCF as a device to promote the use of the ECU, which was seen as a way to challenge the supremacy of the German mark (Howarth 2000).

In March 1988, Hans Dietrich Genscher, then West German Minister of Foreign Affairs, submitted a memorandum on the creation of the ESCB including an independent ECB. At the June 1988 Hanover European Council, it was agreed to create a committee of central bank governors, chaired by the Commission President Jacques Delors, to examine the practical steps leading to EMU. Following the recommendation of the Delors Report (March 1989), the European Council granted the Committee of Governors additional responsibilities from the start of Stage One of EMU on 1 July 1990 (laid down in a Council Decision dated 12 March 1990). The NCB governors were to hold consultations on, and promote the coordination of, the monetary policies of the member states, with the aim of achieving price stability. They were also responsible for preparing for Stage Three of EMU by identifying the major issues and establishing a work programme by the end of 1993. Most of the governors campaigned publicly for independent central banks, prior to the heads of government or state accepting independence in principle at the December 1990 Rome II European Council. During intergovernmental negotiations on EMU in 1991, the German vision of a minimalist EMI in Stage Two prevailed. Control over monetary policy would be transferred to the European level only with the creation of the single currency at the start of Stage Three. At the Maastricht European Council, the heads of government or state reached an agreement on a timetable to move to Stage Three either in 1997 or 1999. The Treaty on European Union included the protocols on the Statute of the ESCB and of the ECB and on the Statute of the EMI.

At a special October 1993 European Council, the European partners agreed to place the EMI and thus the future ECB in Frankfurt. The French had favoured Lyon. However, Chancellor Kohl insisted upon Frankfurt on the grounds that a German location was needed in order to assuage the large number of Germans hostile to the loss of the deutschmark and the transfer of monetary power to the European level, and also to address the fear that the ECU (as it was then still called) would be much weaker than the mark and that the ECB would have difficulty maintaining low inflation.[6]

As called for in the TEU (Art. 109e (1), (116 EC)), the transitional EMI replaced the Committee of Governors on 1 January 1994, marking the start of the second stage of the EMU project. Alexandre Lamfalussy, the Belgian former head of the BIS, became the first President of the EMI. The Institute possessed essentially the same powers as the Committee of Governors: it was a forum for strengthening central bank cooperation and monetary policy coordination and making the necessary preparations for the establishment of the ESCB, the conduct of the single monetary policy and the creation of a single currency in Stage Three of EMU.

Still, with the convergence criteria and a deadline in place, the EMI Board's monthly debates and regular reports on monetary policy and economic performance and convergence assumed greater importance than those of the former Committee of Governors and helped nudge member states towards compliance.[7] Although the final decision on which member states adequately met the convergence criteria and thus could join EMU remained the responsibility of the European Council, the EMI's March 1998 report (EMI 1998) was considered the more objective and authoritative statement on the suitability of member state participation.[8]

The EMI also performed a series of essential tasks: preparing the chronological sequence of events for the changeover to the euro (adopted by the European Council at Madrid in December 1995), the future monetary and exchange rate relationships between the Euro-Zone and other EU countries, the regulatory, organisational and logistical framework necessary for the ESCB (including the ECB) to perform its tasks in Stage Three, including the TARGET cross-border payment system (EMI 1995; ECB 1998a), the collection of EU-wide statistics, and the design series for the euro banknotes (agreed formally by the European Council). On 2 May 1998, the ministers of finance and central bank governors of participating member states, representatives of the Commission and the President of the EMI agreed that the existing Exchange Rate Mechanism (ERM) bilateral central rates of the participating currencies would be used in determining the irrevocable conversion rates for the euro.

One of the major controversies in the lead-up to EMU concerned the selection of the first ECB President. In May 1996, the NCB governors – with the approval of the heads of government or state – selected Wim Duisenberg, the experienced governor of the Bank of Netherlands, as the final President of the EMI. He was generally expected to become the first president of the ECB. However, the TEU granted the European Council the power to select the ECB president. At the December 1997 Luxembourg European Council, the political leaders failed to agree upon Duisenberg because the French President, Jacques Chirac, insisted upon the appointment of the Governor of the Bank of France, Jean-Claude Trichet. A compromise was finally engineered at the 25 May 1998 extraordinary Brussels European Council. Duisenberg would stay on. However, to meet Chirac half-way, the Dutchman agreed to step down after mid-2002 to make way for Trichet.[9] In the meantime, the French would be adequately represented on the Executive Board, with the appointment of Christian Noyer, the former head of the French Treasury, as ECB Vice-President. The incident increased the perception that the ECB's independence would be difficult to safeguard from the influence of member states. Moreover, the compromise was almost certainly illegal when viewed against TEU provisions because Article 112(2)(b) EC (ex 109a(2)(b)) requires that the term of the President's office last eight years (Craig 1999).

On 1 June, in accordance with Article 123 EC (ex 109L), the EMI was replaced by the ECB and the Executive Board began its term. With the preparatory work successfully completed prior to June 1998, the ECB devoted the remaining seven months of the year to the final testing of systems and procedures and to establishing the rules of procedure of the General Council. There remained a few points of controversy, notably with regard to the external representation of the euro: whether or not the ECB President should be present at G7 meetings. At the December European Council in Vienna, it was agreed to allow the ECB President to attend along with the President of Ecofin (to be precise, the Euro-group which consists of the ministers of finance of the member states participating in the Euro-Zone) and assisted by the Commission.

On 1 January 1999, EMU was officially launched: control over European monetary policy, including interest rates and monetary mass, was transferred to the ECB, the parities of the participating currencies were fixed irrevocably, all new public debt was to be issued in euros, and the TARGET payment system was put into operation. In addition to managing European monetary policy, the ECB/ESCB has continued preparations for the introduction of euro notes and coins at the start of 2002 at the latest, and the removal of national notes and coins by 1 July 2002 at the latest. The ECB has also clarified its rules of procedure on the operation of the ECB (April 1999), the Executive Board (October 1999), and the imposition of fines for failure to comply with obligations contained in its regulations and decisions (September 1999 and February 2000). In Helsinki in November 1999 and Vienna in December 2000, the representatives of the ECB Executive Board, the then eleven Eurosystem NCBs and the central banks of the twelve countries applying for EU membership, met together in seminars to review the central banking issues involved in the accession process, identify the main problem areas and enhance cooperation between the Eurosystem and applicant NCBs.

Developments over the first two years of EMU have highlighted several issues, discussed in more detail below, concerning the operation of the ECB and its role in the European policy-making process. The most publicised issue has been the dramatic decline in the value of the euro in relation to the dollar (from $1.16 to under $0.90 in mid-2000) and other leading world currencies, prompting Duisenberg's 5 May 2000 statement in defence of the ECB's actions and the 22 September 2000 joint intervention with the Americans, Japanese and other national central banks to prop up the weak currency. Basing interest rate policy solely on monetary aggregates, the ECB has claimed that it will not raise interest rates in order to defend the euro but only to address the inflationary impact of the drop of the European currency. With low levels of inflation in the Euro-Zone during the first two years of EMU, the ECB Governing Council avoided raising interest rates substantially in order to defend the euro (indeed the ECB lowered rates in April 1999 despite the weakness of the European currency).

There has been considerable debate about the cause of the decline. Some commentators point to economic factors or the problems of promoting a 'virtual currency' (i.e. the current absence of notes and coins). Some have focused on the failure of European governments to pursue sufficiently ambitious structural reforms in order to demonstrate sustainably low deficits and surpluses. Other observers have focused on what they perceive to be the public relations incompetence of Duisenberg and other Executive Board members. Still others have focused on the organisation of European monetary authority. Not surprisingly, the French have led those who blame the euro's drop on the lack of strong political leadership in the Euro-Zone (a political counterweight to the ECB; a European equivalent to the American Secretary of the Treasury). Some observers have also focused upon the inadequate transparency of ECB decision making to date (discussed below). Political leaders have generally refrained from directly criticising the ECB to avoid contributing to the decline, although Duisenberg's competence has been increasingly questioned.

A powerful supranational institution: the ECB in the EU policy-making system

The contribution of the ECB to EU policy making

The ECB and NCBs of the ESCB/Eurosystem are independent of other EU institutions, national governments and other bodies. Nonetheless, monetary policy is not made in a vacuum. First, other EU institutions have a limited say on aspects of European monetary policy and the ECB will use other institutions to forward its own policy goals. Second, a degree of loose coordination has been established (and is gradually being reinforced) between the ESCB and fiscal and macroeconomic policy-making authorities at the EU and national levels in order to achieve an appropriate policy mix and the kind of structural reforms that will ensure the maintenance of price stability in the medium to long term. The ECB has most of the responsibility for managing the single currency. However, it can only make an economic success of the euro – and thus maintain public support for it – within the context of tight coordination with other EU institutions and national governments. Adequate transparency in ECB policy making will be vital to ensure effective coordination. As a non-majoritarian institution, there remains considerable sensitivity about the ESCB's lack of democratic legitimacy, which its constituent parts have sought to address.

The provisions of the TEU have created a distinct institutional setting for monetary policy making, with the ECB at its core and a unique policy-making style which can be labelled 'supranational'. The Treaty gives some of the other institutions – notably the EU Council of Ministers, the European Council and the European Parliament – specific responsibilities with regard to monetary policy. However, the ECB interrelates informally with a large number of other actors with distinct roles at both the EU and national levels.

The ECB/ESCB does not control all aspects of European monetary policy. The Council (the Council of Economics and Finance Ministers, Ecofin) is given several powers over monetary policy and the management of the ESCB.[10] Notably, it is responsible for establishing target zones with third currencies (as temporarily existed with the dollar in 1986–87) and setting exchange rates between the euro and other EU currencies participating in the second-generation Exchange Rate Mechanism (ERM II) (the Danish krona and, until the start of 2001, the Greek drachma). However, when performing these tasks, the Council must consult the ECB and respect the goal of price stability. With the constant drop in the value of the euro, this power has been of importance to the Danes and Greeks whose currencies were revalued within the ERM II. The Council of Ministers retains its power to set the rate at which new currencies merge into the euro – as with the drachma – while the European Council makes the final decision on entry. Ecofin (or to be precise the Euro-group) and the Economic and Finance Committee of the Council are also playing an increasingly important role as the interlocutors of the ECB in the coordination of monetary and economic policies (discussed below). The President of the ECB possesses the right to attend Council meetings when the Council is deliberating on matters relating to the objectives and tasks of the ESCB (Art. 113(2) (ex 109b(2)) EC).

The European Central Bank also maintains direct relations with the European Parliament (EP), notably in terms of *ex-post-facto* reporting and questioning. The EP must be consulted on appointments to the ECB Executive Board. It receives and debates the ECB's annual report and requests that the President and other Executive Board members appear before its committees (notably the Committee on Economic, Monetary Affairs and Industrial Policy and the Subcommittee on Monetary Affairs) (Art. 113 (ex 109b) EC) (see e.g. ECB 2000b). In these relations, the ECB pursues several goals. The wide-ranging review of the ECB by the EP's committees can ensure that the Bank's technical decisions are subject to scrutiny from beyond the ESCB. This review can increase awareness and widen support for the Bank's underlying policies and principles. Regular meetings with the EP's committees can also help to personalise the ECB and build public support for its actions. Overall, however, the EP has little say over the ECB's management of monetary policy. As Dyson (2000: 69) notes, the model of ECB–EP relations 'is no match for . . . US Federal Reserve–Congress relations'. The ECB is not responsible to the EP or other EU institutions: none has the power to dismiss ECB Executive Board members on the grounds of unsatisfactory performance according to fulfilment of the Bank's own goals (as in New Zealand) (Taylor 2000).[11]

Coordination at the European level in the areas of fiscal and macroeconomic policy – which can of course affect price stability, and are thus of concern to the ECB – is leading to the creation of a form 'of collective governance among core actors from several institutions and bodies in a multifaceted network which is constituted by mutual participation patterns' (Wessels and Linsenmann 2001; see also Boyer 1999; Wicks 1999; Wyplosz 1999). The nature of policy making in these fields thus differs considerably from the 'supranational' policy making in monetary matters, where the ECB is dominant. The European Bank's role in both the 'hard' – binding

– coordination of fiscal policy (Art. 105 EC and the Stability and Growth Pact) and 'soft' – largely unbinding – coordination of macroeconomic and employment policies (Art. 99 and 128 EC) is important, yet more subtle and not yet fully fleshed out.[12]

According to the TEU, the ECB is expected to be involved in a 'constructive dialogue' with the other institutions engaged in this coordination – crucially the Council. Opportunities for constructive dialogue are invariably increased by the right of one ECB Executive Board member (normally the President) to attend Council/ Euro-group meetings where matters pertaining to the tasks of the ESCB are discussed. Two members of the ECB Executive Board also attend meetings of the Economics and Finance Committee, where the negotiations on the details of macroeconomic policy coordination take place. The presence of the President of Ecofin/the Euro-group and a member of the Commission at ECB Governing Council meetings – and their right to submit motions – also contributes to the constructive dialogue (Art. 113(3) (ex 109b) EC) (Everson 1999).

The precise role of the ECB in these policy areas varies. In the 'hard' coordination of fiscal policy, the ECB contributes to policy making in the Euro-group aided by the presence of its President (Eijmffinger and de Haan 2000). The European Bank consults informally with the Commission alone and formally with national and Commission officials in the Economic and Financial Committee, who are given the power (Art. 104 EC) to watch over national budgets. The Stability and Growth Pact (agreed at the December 1996 Dublin European Council) gives the Commission – not the ECB – the power to express opinions to Ecofin to adopt recommendations, requirements and ultimately impose sanctions if the obligatory annual national fiscal and structural plans are deemed insufficient (Artis and Wrinkler 1997). However, the ECB will also have its say on national plans, notably in the Euro-group and through the Economic and Financial Committee (which must also be consulted), and informally. What the ECB thinks about national plans will invariably have as much influence on Council pronouncements as the Commission's opinion – if not more. The manipulation of interest rates – or the threat of doing so – is the ECB's most effective sanction of inadequate member state policies. Likewise, the ECB President can appear before the European Parliament to defend the continued imposition of Stability and Growth Pact rules and (one day) even recommend the use of fines, however politically problematic this might be.

The interest rate weapon is likewise a source of influence in the context of the 'soft' (largely unbinding) coordination on economic and employment policies. In addition to its links with the Euro-group (Ecofin) and the Economic and Financial Committee, the ECB has input in the macroeconomic dialogue (the Cologne process) initiated by the Germans during their 1999 EC Presidency as a means to improve the interaction between monetary, budgetary and fiscal policy and wage developments in order to achieve stronger growth and higher employment. Despite the gradual development of 'economic government', the lack of binding EU rules in these areas means that coordination on macroeconomic and employment policies will remain 'soft' for the foreseeable future despite pressures for continued convergence. In this context, the links between Eurosystem NCBs and national governments remain vital in terms of establishing the precise policy mix that is best for each country, in the context of the maintenance of sound money policies, and for the Euro-Zone more generally. However, the ECB will increasingly take centre stage in the coordination of NCB efforts.

Moreover, coordination is a two-way process: it is meant to shape national government policy making as well as the formulation of ECB monetary policy (via the NCBs). Much of the coordination is informal and indirect (as in most countries where the central bank is independent). Indeed, a major feature of ECB decision making is its reliance upon the much greater analytical resources available in the NCBs. This encourages a combination of collaborative and competitive work (Goodfriend 1999; Mayes 1998, 2000). Moreover, because the NCBs are also independent they are free to maintain different approaches and views. The exchange of different NCB analyses is essential to the formulation of ECB policy, given that the Euro-Zone currently lacks statistics of its own and a track record of established behaviour. Despite the often heated debate over appropriate policy, members of the Governing Council are expected to speak with one voice to the outside world, a convention which appears broadly successful to date.

In the light of the likely developments of national fiscal and structural policies, the NCB governors and Executive Board members debate appropriate monetary policy. The ESCB has been very forthright to date in setting out the difficulties that governments face (see e.g. ECB 2000a). At the same time, discussions in the ESCB have been rather general in nature, as the ECB published its own Euro-Zone-wide forecasts and simulations for the first time in its December 2000 *Monthly Bulletin* (ECB 2000c). This publication should improve coordination by helping the Commission and national governments set the guidelines for fiscal, employment and structural policies. It should also improve ECB policy-making transparency which – linked with the accountability of the ECB – is a major concern both of economists and of political scientists.

The transparency and accountability debates

The precise nature of ECB transparency and accountability is a matter of some debate. The Treaty on European Union supplements the considerable degree of institutional independence granted to the ECB by extensive provisions concerning transparency and accountability. Articles 253–6 (ex 190–2) EC oblige the ECB to give reasons for monetary policy decisions, publish these reasons, provide access to documents and the like. Article 110(2) (ex 108a(2)) EC stipulates that this duty applies to regulations and decisions made under Article 110 EC. Article 110(2) EC notes that, while the ECB is under no obligation to publish recommendations, opinions and decisions, it may choose to do so. The NCBs of the Eurosystem currently produce full forecasts at six-monthly intervals. As noted above, the ECB began to publish full annual forecasts in December 2000. The ECB also publishes its *Monthly Bulletin*, which can be used to provide updates on policy developments, while the press conferences that follow Governing Council meetings can be used to announce policy changes if the ECB thinks that the ECB and NCB forecasts have become too out of date to be useful.

Economists – concerned about the dangers of separating monetary from fiscal and macroeconomic policy (the 'assignment problem') – have tended to focus on policy-making transparency and accountability as a way of helping the ECB maintain price stability by improving coordination with national fiscal and macroeconomic policy makers (Dornbusch *et al.* 1998; Issing 1999; Favero *et al.* 2000; Mayes 2000). There is considerable disagreement as to precisely what the ECB should publish and how often it should do so. Most central banks publish only a discussion of published indicators. Very few publish disagreements and voting records. Those which do so will either produce a single set of indicators or supplement them with simulations or a discussion of 'risks' or discuss the range of possible outcomes on the basis of an agreed distribution of risks. Because the ECB Governing Council does not meet long or often enough – even with special allowance for teleconferencing – it cannot agree upon the kinds of detailed texts produced by NCBs. The Governing Council has opted for a form of *ex-ante* transparency that involves the establishment of a 'map' that sets out the rules by which the ECB makes monetary policy and reacts to fiscal and macroeconomic policy developments and external shocks. However, in order to improve transparency and meet the demands of many observers (including *Business Week* 2000), a great deal more information must be made available, even if there are limits to the commitments to specific measures (rather than general strategies) that any central bank can make (Mayes 2000).

When political scientists focus on the issue of transparency and accountability, they do so in the context of a concern for the lack of democratic control over monetary policy making and democratic legitimacy of the EMU project more broadly (see Gormley and de Hann 1996; Teivainen 1997; Elgie 1998; Verdun 1998; Taylor 2000; Verdun and Christiansen 2000). They are concerned about the exceptional strength of the ECB's policy mandate and independence, the absence of counter-balancing EU institutions and the weakness of democratic accountability.[13] Verdun and Christiansen (2000: 163) discuss the problematic nature of the establishment of a powerful ECB prior to the emergence of a fully fledged EU political community, and notably the institutions of representative democracy, in which the bank's decisions, or, more significantly, the procedures for taking such decisions can be grounded. The ECB lacks the societal embeddedness that legitimises the policy making of other non-majoritarian institutions such as independent national central banks and supreme courts.

The legitimacy problem has placed increased focus on the matters of accountability and transparency. Monetary policy decisions will affect member states differently due to different national economic cycles (despite some convergence) and differently structured economies. Given the lack of financial transfer payments to compensate those parts of the Euro-Zone suffering from asymmetrical shocks, limited labour mobility and the strong constraints placed on the use of national fiscal instruments, the ECB's response to these shocks will be of considerable importance. The risk remains strong that some member states may come to feel disadvantaged by ECB monetary policy, that the legitimacy of the bank will then be called into question, and the pressure will increase on governments to speak out. Doubts about the ECB's legitimacy increase the need for Executive Board members to give frequent interviews, press conferences and speeches about goals and instruments. NCB governors need to do the same at the national level. Likewise, the decision to hold two Governing Council meetings a year in other member states was designed to improve the visibility of the ECB. The ECB must also be careful in its public criticism of member state economic policies, leaving this mostly to the Commission and the Euro-group – as in February 2001 with regard to Ireland. More generally, the maintenance of an effective and positive working relationship with the Euro-group is vital to the ECB's public image.

Many call for strengthened links between the ECB and the EP to improve the democratic legitimacy/accountability of the ECB. Favero *et al.* (2000) argue that the European Parliament should have a greater say in the appointment of the members of the Executive Board *and* the weight of the Board versus NCB governors could be increased (see also Taylor 2000). However, this is inherently problematic given that the EP, despite being directly elected, is neither well understood nor well liked by many Europeans (see Burns, Chapter 4, this volume). Moreover, the strong opposition of several Euro-Zone member state governments to increased EP involvement in European monetary affairs makes this unlikely. There is concern that increased EP meddling would damage the appearance of independence and the credibility of ECB monetary policy. Other observers, led by the French government, argue that the democratic legitimacy problem can be partially resolved by creating a stronger and more visible political counterweight to the independent ECB – the European equivalent to the American Treasury Secretary (Boyer 2000). This could come through the reinforcement of the Euro-group – a priority of the French Council Presidency in 2000 – through, for example, the eventual creation of a high-profile permanent representative to help manage economic policy coordination and act as the ECB's leading political interlocutor – an objective of the 2001 Belgian Council presidency (Howarth 2001).

Enlargement and the future of the ECB

Neither the 1996–97 nor the 2000 IGCs focused much attention on the impact of enlargement upon the operation of the ECB and the Eurosystem. The lack of urgency is in part due to the two-step process by which the applicant countries will join the Euro-Zone. While they must respect the convergence criteria and make the necessary institutional preparations to accede to the EU, they will initially join the Single Market and the ERM II and only accede to the Euro-Zone at a later stage. Nonetheless, the impact of enlargement looms large principally because it highlights existing problems with the operation of the Governing Council. As it stands now, many observers question if the Eurosystem's structure – notably a Governing Council of eighteen – is conducive to efficient policy making, or even policy coordination (Favero *et al.* 2000). The Governing Council can change its own practices if it finds problems in decision making. There is much scope for its procedures to evolve – such as the creation of more working groups – and the work of the Governing Council can involve more activity at the ECB or through the NCBs. However, the size problem still matters.

Favero *et al.* (2000) amongst others suggest that the problem could be resolved by emulating the American Federal Reserve Board, by increasing the power of the Executive Board in relation to the NCB governors and rotating Governing Council places amongst the member states. However, such a recommendation ignores the unique character both of the Eurosystem as a 'federal' banking system and of the EU as a political entity. First, the centre (the ECB) is considerably less dominant in the

Eurosystem than in the American system. The NCBs retain considerably more power than American state banks and the governors have final say – thanks to their majority in the Governing Council – over the allocation of functions. Any reform to strengthen the Executive Board at the expense of the Governing Council would be challenged on grounds of legitimacy. The arrangements of the American Federal Reserve Board were developed just over sixty years ago, around 160 years after the creation of the United States as a country, and long after the conclusion of the Civil War successfully asserted federal government authority. There is obviously no parallel situation in the EU.

Buiter (1999) recommends – even without enlargement – restricting the size of the Governing Council to nine members and the Executive Board to four. Officially, each NCB Governor is there in a personal capacity as an experienced expert on central banking, not as a national representative *per se*. In theory, therefore, a rotation of governors (either all or only the less populated member states) would be adequate: a particular group of them should be as representative of informed opinion as all of them. However, the Governors are *de facto* national representatives because they each come from one of the member states and are most familiar with their own national systems. It would be difficult, but perhaps not impossible, for Governors to present the perspective of other member states as effectively as their own. One possibility might be to group the smaller member states together so that they share one seat on the Governing Council, or three member states (for example, The Netherlands, Belgium and Luxembourg) could share two seats. The Governors would be required to maintain close links with the Governors and central banks of their partner states. The decision at the Nice Summit to move to the future rotation of Commission places – yet to be devised but 'based on the principle of equality' and reflecting demography and geography – once the number of EU Member States reaches twenty-seven sets a precedent which might be followed for the ECB Governing Council.

Summary

- On 1 January 1999, the launch of the euro made the ECB one of the most powerful EU institutions, affecting the lives of all people living in the member states of the Euro-Zone.
- The ECB possesses considerable independence, both from other EU bodies as well as national governments.
- The European Bank will have to manage with considerable technical skill and political sensitivity its role in monetary policy making, as well as the 'hard' and 'soft' coordination of fiscal and macroeconomic policies with other EU institutions and national governments.
- The bank's technical legitimacy can be enhanced; the clarification of the ECB's policy strategy 'map' will be vital in this regard.
- Efforts to strengthen the democratic legitimacy of European monetary policy making have focused less on the role and powers of the ECB – given the desire to preserve the bank's independence and credibility – and more on the reinforcement of the coordination role and profile of the ECB's political interlocutor in the Euro-group.

- It remains to be seen if the European Bank can cope with (and if European governments can manage) the political fallout created by economic recession and uneven internal shocks in the Euro-Zone without the support of a more interventionist 'economic government' at EU level (McKay 1999a, 1999b, 2000).

Test questions

1 What is the relationship between the Executive Board and the Governing Council of the ECB in the management of Euro-Zone monetary policy?
2 Outline the role of the ECB's monetary authority predecessors in the process of European monetary integration.
3 How do economists and political scientists approach the issues of ECB legitimacy, transparency and accountability?

Contact information

Address: European Central Bank, Kaiserstraße 29, D-60311 Frankfurt am Main, Germany. Tel: 49 69 1344 0; Fax: 49 69 1344 6000.
Postal address: Postfach 16 03 19, D-60066 Frankfurt am Main, Germany.
Email address: info@ecb.int
Web address: http://www.ecb.int/

Notes

1 The move to Stage Three of EMU involved the irrevocable fixing of the exchange rate parities between participating currencies. The replacement of national currencies by the single European currency was to follow.
2 Article 11.1 of the Statute of the European System of Central Banks (ESCB) allows the European Council to appoint as few as four members.
3 On most matters concerning the ECB's capital, qualified majority voting applies. Votes in the Council are weighted according to the national central banks' subscribed capital in the ECB, and Executive Board members possess no votes (Art. 10.3).
4 Elgie and Thompson (1998: 74–6) provide a precise list of variously weighted indicators of political and economic independence. Although scholars often disagree on the best manner in which to measure independence, they concur that the ECB is one of the most independent central banks.
5 Epistemic communities are 'networks of professionals with recognised expertise and competence in a particular domain' who define problems, identify compromises and supply 'expert' arguments to justify political choices (Haas 1992: 3).
6 As another compromise to assuage the wary Germans, at the Madrid December 1995 European Council the name of the European currency was changed from ECU – which the Germans thought sounded too French – to the more linguistically neutral euro.
7 The EMI's reports were decidedly more negative than those of the Commission, emphasising the additional effort required in most member states to meet the convergence criteria.
8 Of the countries that wanted to participate, only Greece was deemed to have failed to have satisfied the convergence criteria. The EMI report ended years of speculation on Italian participation.

9   Dinan 1999: 477. Duisenberg subsequently announced on 31 December 1998 that he did not recognise, or intend to abide by, this compromise. However, faced with growing criticism of his competence, it became increasingly likely that Duisenberg would step down in 2002.

10   For example, the Council has the power to define the basis for the minimum and maximum reserves to be held by national credit institutions with the ECB, and the maximum permissible ratios between these reserves, as well as the appropriate sanctions in the case of non-compliance (Art. 19.2, ESCB Statute, referred to in Craig 1999).

11   However, there is a judicial mechanism for dismissing an individual member of the Executive Board in Article 11.4 of the protocol on the Statute of the ESCB: 'if a member of the Executive Board no longer fulfils the conditions required for the performance of his duties or if he has been guilty of serious misconduct, the Court of Justice may . . . compulsorily retire him'. Nonetheless, the onus rests with the Governing Council or the Executive Board of the ECB to apply to the ECJ on such matters.

12   These three types/modes of governance have been described by several authors; see e.g. Wessels and Linsenmann 2001.

13   Through his comparison of the ECB to two other main paradigms of central banking independence, the US Federal Reserve System and the 'New Zealand model', Taylor (2000) offers proposals for strengthening the democratic and cooperative elements in the Maastricht model, while respecting the treaty constraints and the objectives of the key players.

Selected further reading

Verdun, A. and Christiansen, T. (2000) 'Policies, Institutions and the Euro: Dilemmas of Legitimacy', in C. Crouch (ed.) *After the Euro: Shaping Institutions for Governance in the Wake of European Monetary Union*, Oxford: Oxford University Press, pp. 162–78.
   A good overview of the issue of ECB independence and problematic democratic legitimacy.

Buiter, W. (1999) 'Alice in Euroland', *Journal of Common Market Studies*, 37, 2, pp. 181–209.
Issing, O. (1999) 'The Eurosystem: Transparent and Accountable or "Willem in Euroland"', *Journal of Common Market Studies*, 37, 3, pp. 503–19.
   The article by Buiter and the response by Issing provide an excellent summary of the debate on ECB transparency and accountability.

Dyson, K. (2000) *The Politics of the Euro-Zone, Stability or Breakdown?*, Oxford: Oxford University Press.
   Provides an excellent overview of the role of the ECB in the EU fiscal and macroeconomic policy processes.

Loedel, P. and Howarth, D. (2002 forthcoming) *The European Central Bank, the New European Leviathan?*, Basingstoke: Palgrave.
   The first detailed book-length study of the ECB.

References

Artis, M. and Wrinkler, B. (1997) 'The Stability Pact: Safeguarding the Credibility of the ECB', London: Centre for Economic Policy Research, CEPR Working Paper no. 1688.
Boyer, R. (1999) *Le Gouvernement Economique de la Zone Euro*, Paris: La Documentation française. Report of the 'groupe de réflexion' of the French Planning Commission presided over by Boyer.

—— (2000) 'The Unanticipated Fallout of the European Monetary Union: The Political and Institutional Deficits of the Euro', in C. Crouch (ed.) *After the Euro: Shaping Institutions for Governance in the Wake of European Monetary Union*, Oxford: Oxford University Press, pp. 24–88.

Buiter, W. (1999) 'Alice in Euroland', *Journal of Common Market Studies*, 37, 2, pp. 181–209.

Craig, P. (1999) 'EMU, the European Central Bank and Judicial Review', in P. Beaumont and N. Walker, *Legal Framework of the Single European Currency*, Oxford: Hart, pp. 95–119, pp. 395–426.

de Hann, J. (1997) 'The European Central Bank: Independence, Accountability, and Strategy: A Review', *Public Choice*, 93.

Dinan, D. (1999) *Ever Closer Union*, Basingstoke: Macmillan, esp. Chapter 16.

Dornbusch, R., Favero, C. and Giavazzi, F. (1998) 'Immediate Challenges for the European Central Bank', *Economic Policy*, 26, April, pp. 17–52.

Dyson, K. (1994) *Elusive Union: The Process of Economic and Monetary Union in Europe*, London: Longman.

—— (2000) *The Politics of the Euro-Zone, Stability or Breakdown?*, Oxford: Oxford University Press.

Eijmffinger, S. and de Haan, J. (2000) *European Monetary and Fiscal Policy*, Oxford: Oxford University Press.

Elgie, R. (1998) 'Democratic Accountability and Central Bank Independence: Historical and Contemporary, National and European Perspectives', *West European Politics*, 21, 3, pp. 53–76.

Elgie, R. and Thompson, H. (1998) *The Politics of Central Banks*, London: Routledge.

European Central Bank (ECB) (1998a) *TARGET: The Trans-European Automated Real-Time Gross Settlement Express Transfer System*, Frankfurt: ECB, July.

—— (1998b) *The Single Monetary Policy in Stage Three: General Documentation on ESCB Monetary Policy Instruments and Procedures*, Frankfurt: ECB, September.

—— (1999) 'The Stability-Oriented Monetary Policy Strategy of the Eurosystem', *Monthly Bulletin*, January, pp. 39–50.

—— (2000a) *Annual Report 1999*, Frankfurt: ECB.

—— (2000b) Hearing before the Committee on Economic and Monetary Affairs, European Parliament, 20 March.

—— (2000c) *Monthly Bulletin*, December.

European Monetary Institute (EMI) (1995) *The TARGET System*, Frankfurt: EMI, May.

—— (1997a) *The Single Monetary Policy in Stage Three: Specification of the Operational Framework*, Frankfurt: EMI, January.

—— (1997b) *The Single Monetary Policy in Stage Three: Elements of the Monetary Policy Strategy of the ESCB*, Frankfurt: EMI, February.

—— (1998) *Convergence Report*, Frankfurt: EMI.

Everson, M. (1999) 'The Constitutional Law of the Euro? Disciplining European Governance', in P. Beaumont and N. Walker *Legal Framework of the Single European Currency*, Oxford: Hart, pp. 119–141.

Favero, C., Freixias, X., Persson, T. and Wyplosz, C. (2000) *One Money, Many Countries: Monitoring the European Central Bank 2*, London: CEPR.

Goodfriend, M. (1999) 'The Role of a Regional Bank in a System of Central Banks', Federal Reserve Bank of Richmond Working Paper no 99-4.

Gormley, L. and de Haan, J. (1996) 'The Democratic Deficit of the European Central Bank', *European Law Review*, April, pp. 95–112.

Haas, P. (1992) 'Epistemic Communities and International Policy Coordination', *International Organization*, 46, 1, pp. 1–35.

Hirst, P. and Thompson, G. (1996) *Globalisation in Question*, Oxford: Polity Press.

Howarth, D. (2000) *The French Road to European Monetary Union*, Basingstoke: Palgrave.

—— (2001) 'The French Council Presidency and "European Economic Government"', paper presented at the UACES conference 'France and Europe: The French EU Presidency 2000 in Perspective', Loughborough University, 9 March.

Issing, O. (1999) 'The Eurosystem: Transparent and Accountable or "Willem in Euroland"', *Journal of Common Market Studies*, 37, 3, pp. 503–19.

Kaufmann, H. M. (1995) 'The Importance of Being Independent: Central Bank Independence and the European System of Central Banks', in C. Rhodes and S. Mazey (eds) *The State of the European Union. Building a European Polity?*, Boulder, CO: Lynne Rienner, pp. 267–92.

Kees, A. (1994) 'The Monetary Committee as a Promoter of European Integration', in A. Bakker, H. Boot, O. Sleipen and W. Vanthoor (eds) *Monetary Stability through International Cooperation*, Dordrecht: Kluwer.

McKay, D. (1999a) 'The Political Sustainability of European Monetary Union', *British Journal of Political Science*, 29, pp. 510–41.

—— (1999b) *Federalism and European Union: A Political Economy Perspective*, Oxford: Oxford University Press.

—— (2000) *Designing Europe: Institutional Adaptation and the Federal Experience*, Oxford: Oxford University Press.

Mayes, D. G. (1998) 'Evolving Voluntary Rules for the Operation of the European Central Bank', *Current Politics and Economics of Europe*, 8, 4, pp. 357–86.

—— (2000) 'Independence and Co-ordination – The Eurosystem', paper presented at the UACES 30th Anniversary Conference and 5th UACES Research Conference, Central European University, Budapest, 6–8 April, Panel 11.

Taylor, C. (2000) 'The Role and Status of the European Central Bank: Some Proposals for Accountability and Cooperation', in C. Crouch (ed.) *After the Euro: Shaping Institutions for Governance in the Wake of European Monetary Union*, Oxford: Oxford University Press, pp. 179–202.

Teivainen, T. (1997) 'The Independence of the European Central Bank: Implications for Democratic Governance', in P. Minkkinen and H. Patomaki (eds) *The Politics of Economic and Monetary Union*, London: Kluwer, pp. 164–206.

Verdun, A. (1998) 'The Institutional Design of EMU: A Democratic Deficit', *Journal of Public Policy*, 18, 2, pp. 107–32.

—— (1999) 'The Role of the Delors Committee in the Creation of EMU: An Epistemic Community?', *Journal of European Public Policy*, 6, 2, pp. 308–28.

Verdun, A. and Christiansen, T. (2000) 'Policies, Institutions and the Euro: Dilemmas of Legitimacy', in C. Crouch (ed.) *After the Euro: Shaping Institutions for Governance in the Wake of European Monetary Union*, Oxford: Oxford University Press, pp. 162–78.

Wessels, W. and Linsenmann, I. (2001) 'EMU's Impact on National Institutions. A Gouvernement Économique in the Making: Towards Vertical and Horizontal Fusion?', in K. Dyson *The European State in the Euro-Zone*, Oxford: Oxford University Press.

Wicks, N. (1999) 'Will EMU Lead to European Economic Government?', London: Centre for European Reform.

Wyplosz, C. (1999) 'Economic Policy Coordination in EMU: Strategies and Institutions', mimeo of the Graduate Institute of International Studies, Geneva, presented to the Franco-German economic forum in Bonn, 12 January.

Part III

'POLICING THE SYSTEM': THE OVERSIGHT INSTITUTIONS

Chapter 6

The European Court of Justice and the Court of First Instance

Jo Hunt

Key facts

The EU has two supranational judicial bodies: the European Court of Justice (ECJ) and the Court of First Instance (CFI) (together, the 'Community judicature'). The ECJ, which was established in 1951 under the ECSC Treaty, became the Court of the European Communities with the coming into force of the Treaty of Rome in 1958. The Court of First Instance, meanwhile, which is described as being 'attached' to the ECJ, was established in 1988. It is the task of the Courts to ensure that the rule of law is observed. Both Courts comprise fifteen judges, one from each member state, and the ECJ is also assisted by eight advocates general, who have the role of presenting independent opinions in all cases brought before it. The ECJ has jurisdiction to hear all direct actions brought by the Community institutions or by member states, including challenges to the legality of Community acts, and actions against member states for non-compliance with EC law. In addition to this adjudicative role, the ECJ also has an important interpretive function, assisting the member states' courts in their application of EC law. This is done through the delivery of preliminary rulings on the meaning and validity of EC law. In the exercise of its functions, the ECJ has handed down decisions which are considered to have had a crucial impact on the evolution of the EC legal order, and on the integration process more generally. These decisions have sometimes strayed from the literal text of the provisions it is called upon to interpret, and the ECJ has been criticised for stepping outside the conventional limits of the judicial role. The decisions of the lower profile CFI have aroused less political controversy. The CFI has jurisdiction to hear direct actions brought by non-state actors, such as individuals and companies, against the acts of the institutions, including claims for damages as well as all staff cases. The efficiency of the judicial system as a whole is compromised by the very heavy workload of each Court.

The European Court of Justice and the Court of First Instance: composition, powers and functions

Under Article 220 EC Treaty, the European Court of Justice of the European Communities (ECJ, the Court) is given the task of ensuring that 'in the interpretation and application of this Treaty, the law is observed'. More particularly, the ECJ's key functions are threefold: it polices the use of the decision-making powers of the Community institutions, ensuring that the institutions are playing by the rules (through judicial review); it seeks to ensure that member states abide by their legal obligations under Community law (through enforcement actions); and it offers interpretive assistance and advice to national courts on the meaning of Community law (by means of the preliminary ruling procedure). In addition to these main areas of its jurisdiction, the Court can also be called upon to issue opinions on the conformity with the Treaty of proposed international agreements involving the EC. While the Court is therefore rightly described as an oversight institution, it should be recognised that through its policing of the system, the Court has established norms and principles which govern the operation of the Community polity. This 'constitutionalisation' of the Treaty by the ECJ will be addressed below.

The Court's first incarnation was as the Court for the European Coal and Steel Community, established in 1951. It became the Court of Justice of the European Communities with the coming into force of the EEC Treaty in 1958. Its seat is at the Palais de Justice, on the Kirchberg plateau, Luxembourg. The ECJ is currently composed of fifteen judges, with convention decreeing that one is drawn from each member state.[1] Judges are appointed by the member state governments for a renewable six-year period, though appointments are staggered, with half of the seats coming up for renewal every three years. Article 223 EC Treaty provides that the members of the Court are appointed 'by common accord of the Governments of the Member States', which in practice involves each government putting forward its nomination, which must then be endorsed by all other member state governments. Once at the Court, however, it is most definitely not the task of the judges to represent the interests of 'their' member state government. Indeed, Article 223 EC Treaty stipulates that members of the Court must be 'persons whose independence is beyond doubt'. Members of the Court need not have held a judicial position prior to appointment, as the pool from which they may be drawn includes not only those qualified for 'appointment to the highest judicial offices in their respective countries', but also 'juriconsults of recognised competence'. This can cover those in non-judicial legal practice, legal advisers and legal academics. Among the current ranks of ECJ judges are many who have combined legal practice and judicial appointments with academic positions. There are now also two women judges, the ECJ's first having been appointed in October 1999.

The Court is assisted in its work by eight advocates general, who have the task of making 'independent and impartial submissions' in all cases coming before the ECJ (Article 222 EC Treaty). Advocates general have the same status at the Court as the judges. They are appointed in the same way as the judges, and must fulfil the same conditions of appointment. According to convention, there is one advocate general from each of the big five member states (Germany, the UK, France, Italy and Spain), with the remaining posts rotating amongst the smaller states. Each judge and advocate general is assisted by a small team of legal secretaries, referred to as their *cabinet*, with administrative support provided by the Court's Registry. Heading the Court, and charged with the task of directing judicial business, is the Court's President, appointed by a secret ballot of the judges of the ECJ for a renewable three-year period.

It is rare to find all fifteen judges of the ECJ sitting together to hear a case. The sheer number of cases coming before it each year simply precludes this possibility.[2] It is far more common to find the Court sitting in chambers of either three or five judges. The full Court is reserved for only the most significant of cases. Cases involving a member state government or one of the Community institutions will usually be heard either by the full Court or by a 'small plenum' of eleven judges. The standard procedure before the ECJ involves first the appointment to the case of an advocate general, as well as a *judge-rapporteur*, from within the ranks of the judges of the ECJ. The *judge-rapporteur* has particular responsibility for the case, with the appointed judge and his or her *cabinet* undertaking much of the research for and preparation of the Court's response. By the time the advocate general and *judge-rapporteur* are appointed, the language of the case will have been selected. This may be any of the eleven official languages, and Irish. The judges themselves work in

French. Following the submission of written pleadings by all parties to the action, the *judge-rapporteur* will present a Report for Hearing summarising the main facts and issues. On completion of this written round, the parties may present oral submissions before the Court. Next it is the turn of the advocate general to present an opinion, which will comprise a review of the facts of the case, the submissions of the parties, and the relevant law. The advocate general's opinion concludes with a suggested course of action for the Court to follow. Upon the public delivery of this opinion, the Court will meet in private to decide the case, with a draft judgment prepared by the *judge-rapporteur* as their starting point. Once agreement has been reached (by a majority), a single collegiate judgment will be delivered in open court. No record is made of any minority or dissenting opinion.

In 1988, the Council responded to the request of the Court and established the Court of First Instance (the CFI),[3] primarily with a view to taking some of the pressure off the increasingly overloaded ECJ, but also in order to establish a specialised forum which would be better suited to hearing cases involving complex factual situations. The CFI, which was not initially recognised as a Community institution in its own right, instead being 'attached' to the ECJ,[4] is also composed of fifteen judges, who are appointed in the same way as the judges of the ECJ. The conditions of appointment to this Court are again independence, and 'the ability required for appointment to judicial office' (Article 225 EC Treaty). No advocates general are assigned to this Court, although a judge of the CFI may take on the role where it is deemed necessary. As with the ECJ, the CFI sits in plenary session only in the most important of cases, and most commonly sits in chambers of three or five. Since 1999, it has also been possible for cases to be heard by a single judge of the CFI. The CFI has jurisdiction to hear only certain categories of cases, from which there will lie an appeal in law to the ECJ. These categories have increased over the years, and there are calls for the jurisdiction of the CFI to be extended still further. The Treaty of Nice will, if ratified, allow the CFI to hear certain categories of actions brought under the Article 234 EC Treaty preliminary rulings procedure.

The preliminary rulings procedure currently accounts for around half of the actions coming before the ECJ each year. Until the Treaty of Nice is ratified, the ECJ will continue to have the sole competence to hear these actions, which provide an 'organic connection' between the national courts and the Community Court (Shaw 2000: 422). Through the preliminary rulings procedure, national courts may seek interpretive guidance from the ECJ on matters of Community law coming before them, including the validity of legal acts of the institutions. The ECJ will duly interpret the relevant provision of EC law, and the referring Court must then apply the law in the case before it. The Court's ruling will also, of course, provide guidance to all other courts throughout the Community. For the ECJ, this procedure 'is essential for the preservation of the Community character of the law . . . and has the object of ensuring that in all circumstances the law is the same in all States' (Case 166/73 *Rheinmuhlen-Dusseldorf* [1974] European Court Reports 33 at p. 43). Its significance has been immense – almost all of the 'constitutionalising' decisions to be considered below were brought before the Court under Article 234. As a general rule, any national court or tribunal may bring an action, and courts of last resort are under an obligation to do so (for exceptions to this rule, see Case 283/81 *CILFIT* [1982] European Court Reports 3415, and see also the limitations imposed on lower courts' power to refer in the context of Title IV EC Treaty). Following the coming into force of the Amsterdam Treaty, the ECJ has also obtained a limited right to deliver preliminary rulings in relation to certain aspects of the Police and Judicial Cooperation pillar.

The ECJ is also the only Community Court currently competent to hear enforcement actions against member states for non-compliance with Community law. These may come before it following the instigation by the Commission of the Article 226 enforcement procedure. Enforcement actions can also reach the ECJ under Article 227, which gives member states the power to instigate actions against each other – though this is, in practice, little used. In both cases, should the Court find there has been a breach of Community law it will issue a declaratory judgment, with which the member state must comply. Failure to do so may lead to the imposition of a fine (Article 228 EC Treaty). Both the ECJ and the CFI have a role to play in the task of the judicial review of the acts of the Community institutions, however. Both courts are empowered to review the legality of the legal decisions taken by the institutions, with the ECJ having jurisdiction for cases brought by a Community institution, or one of the member states, and the CFI hearing cases brought by private individuals, companies and the like. In addition to its judicial review function, the CFI also has jurisdiction to hear all staff cases brought by employees of the Community institutions, competition law cases brought by private companies, and all actions for damages brought by private parties under Article 288 EC Treaty. The decision to transfer jurisdiction for certain categories of case to the CFI rests not with the ECJ but with the Council. The Council must also approve the Rules of Procedure of the Court, which, along with the Statute of the Court and the relevant Treaty articles, formally regulate the operation of the Community's judicial bodies.

History and evolution of the Community judicature

Date	Event
1951	ECJ is established as the Court of the ECSC.
1957	ECJ becomes the Court of the European Communities.
1963	ECJ delivers the *Van Gend en Loos* judgment and establishes direct effect, enabling individuals to invoke Community law directly before national courts.
1964	ECJ delivers the *Costa* judgment, and establishes the principle of supremacy of EC law over national law.
1988	A second judicial body – the CFI – is established in an attempt to reduce the ECJ's workload.
1991	ECJ develops the principle of state liability in the *Francovich* ruling.
1992	ECJ given power to fine member states for infringement of EC law, but is excluded from operating in the CFSP and JHA pillars.

1993	German Constitutional Court delivers the *Brunner* judgment, and questions ECJ's 'kompetenz-kompetenz'.
1997	Amsterdam Treaty extends the ECJ's jurisdiction to certain aspects of the third pillar (now 'Police and Judicial Cooperation').
2000	Nice Treaty provides jurisdiction for CFI to hear certain Article 234 references for preliminary rulings. A range of other measures are adopted designed to speed up the workings of the courts.

The history of the European Court of Justice is in large measure the history of the Community legal order, and it is the nature of its legal order which most clearly differentiates the EC from an international organisation. Throughout the course of its existence, the Court has taken a leading role in developing and refining key elements of this legal order, searching for ever more effective ways of ensuring that the law is observed. In so doing, the Court has made what some may see as bold and audacious claims, not only about the nature of Community law, but also as regards its own powers, competences and position within the EU polity.

A key task of this section is to chart the way in which the Court has built upon the powers given to it under the Treaty, and ascribed itself roles which were perhaps not envisaged by the member state governments when they first set up the Treaty system. This expansion and entrenchment of its role has been the by-product of the ECJ's development of core doctrines which structure the relationship between national and EC law. Through the introduction of the principles of, most notably, direct effect and supremacy of EC law, the ECJ is regarded as having 'constitutionalised' the Treaty, transforming it from a set of horizontal legal arrangements between sovereign states into 'a vertically integrated legal regime conferring judicially enforceable rights and obligations on all legal persons and entities, public and private, within EC territory' (Stone Sweet 1998: 306). In developing this constitutional doctrine, the Court has necessarily been involved in a process of constitutional self-positioning (Weiler 1993). From the comfortable position of relative obscurity and 'benign neglect' (Stein 1981) it enjoyed for the first twenty-five years or so of its existence, the Court has now moved into the spotlight. It has become the subject of increasing critical attention and, more recently, apparent attempts to rein in its power.

When the EC Treaty was first established, it appeared to bear most of the hallmarks of a conventional international organisation. One innovative structural feature, however, was that contained in current Article 234 EC Treaty (former Article 177 EC Treaty), the preliminary rulings procedure. As was described above, this provision provides a point of connection between national courts and the ECJ, allowing them to refer to the ECJ questions concerning the interpretation, and validity, of Community law. The significance of this Article in the construction of the Community legal order has been immense. For a variety of reasons (which will be addressed below), national courts have on the whole proved ready and willing partners in the Article 234 process. At the very least, they have provided the ECJ with a steady stream of references, granting it opportunities to deliver judgments – the Court, of course, can only perform its functions when called upon to act by others (be they national courts, the member states or other Community institutions) as it has no power to deliver opinions or rulings by its own, independent motion. To the Treaty drafters, Article 234 may have appeared quite innocuous. The use made of it by the ECJ, through its purposive, 'teleological' method of interpretation of the Treaty, has, however, transformed this Article into a most powerful tool, a 'quasi-federal instrument for reviewing the compatibility of national law with Community law' (Mancini and Keeling 1994 as cited in Mancini 2000: 40). This *de facto* power of review and control over the acts of the national authorities has emerged alongside the ECJ's explicit Treaty-based competence to enforce Community law directly against infringing member states, available under Articles 226–8 EC Treaty. However, while the latter actions must be brought directly before the Court by the Commission, or by another member state, the Article 234 procedure is brought, indirectly, by individuals. This then provides an additional channel through which Community law can be enforced: one which accords a role to national courts, and to individuals within those jurisdictions which is not explicitly provided for under the Treaty.

The first step in this process of constitutionalisation was the creation of the doctrine of direct effect – the principle that Community law may create rights which may be legally enforced by individuals before their national courts. This doctrine was first introduced in the 1963 case of *Van Gend en Loos*, a reference from a Dutch court, which was brought before the ECJ under Article 234 in the course of an action concerning the levying of an import duty, in apparent contravention of the current Article 25 EC Treaty. According to the ECJ, the importing company could directly invoke the Treaty provision before the national courts, despite the fact that the national authority had not yet introduced it through secondary legislative means. In arriving at this conclusion, the ECJ differentiated between the traditional international law and the 'new legal order' of the EC: 'for the benefit of which the states have limited their sovereign rights, albeit within limited fields, and the subjects of which comprise not only Member States, but also their nationals. Independently of the legislation of Member States, Community law therefore not only imposes obligations on individuals but is also intended to confer upon them rights which become part of their legal heritage' (Case 26/62 [1963] European Court Reports 1 at p. 12). In developing this doctrine, the ECJ was creating new roles not only for the national court, and for individuals, but also for itself. As de Witte has argued, the 'crucial contribution . . . [of *Van Gend*] was that the question whether specific provisions of the Treaty (or later, secondary Community law) had direct effect was to be decided centrally by the Court of Justice, rather then by the various national courts according to their own views on the matter' (de Witte 1999: 181).

Thus, through *Van Gend*, we see the Court claiming an authority for itself, and for Community law which was nowhere mentioned in the Treaty. A decision of comparable significance was taken in 1964, in the *Costa* case, in which the ECJ declared that EC law has primacy over all conflicting national laws. As a result of this doctrine of supremacy, national courts are required in all circumstances to give effect to Community law, if necessary disapplying conflicting national law. This requirement holds, regardless of the status of the national law in question – as the ECJ held in *Internationale Handelsgesellschaft*, 'the validity of a Community measure or its effect within a Member State cannot be affected by allegations that it runs counter to either fundamental rights as formulated by the constitution of that state or the principles of a national constitutional structure'(Case 11/70 [1970] European Court Reports, 1125). It is in this way, and through a combination of the doctrines of direct effect and supremacy, that the Court crafted a *de facto* power of review of national legislation which individuals can themselves instigate through action before the national courts. Member state compliance with their EC law obligations is thus now subject to policing 'from above' by the Commission, and 'from below' by individuals within their own legal orders.

So far, this chapter has concentrated on the contribution of the ECJ to the establishment of the Community legal order. Crucially, of course, the Court needed to enlist the support of the national judiciary in the operation of this legal order, and, for the most part, this support has been forthcoming. Indeed, so successful was it in quantitative terms that the system became overloaded by Article 234 references. The establishment of the CFI was motivated in great part by a need to reduce the case-load of the ECJ, though the situation has improved little, if at all, since that time. According to the 1999 figures, some 255 requests for preliminary rulings were lodged in that year, and national courts will have to wait, on average, some twenty-one months until these requests can be answered by the ECJ (ECJ 2000).

The number of references being made, of course, says nothing about the use these rulings are put to when they are returned to the national courts, or, more fundamentally, whether the various national judiciaries accept the principles of supremacy and direct effect. While detailed empirical accounts of the day-to-day application of EC law by national courts are few and far between (for an exception, see Chalmers 2000), it would appear that, for the most part, the national courts have accepted the constitutional pronouncements of the ECJ. *Why* this should be so has been the subject of speculation. Some accounts highlight the strategic actions of the ECJ, detailing the way in which the Court actively sought to foster the support of national judiciaries, not least through the many 'seminars, dinners, regular invitations to Luxembourg and visits around the Community' (Burley and Mattli 1993) organised by the ECJ. It is also argued that the national courts are prepared to participate in the system quite simply because it is in their interests so to do – that through it, they are empowered. This is particularly the case in relation to lower courts, which could find themselves in a position to exercise quite extensive powers of judicial review through cooperation with the ECJ (Weiler 1994; Alter 1996, 1998). No less significant for these 'political' accounts is the impact of that which Weiler terms the 'compliance pull' of legal formalism. The courts – Community and national alike – are members of the same professional community, they communicate through the language of law, and are conditioned to operate in accordance with the formal requirements of legal reasoning and logic.

While the lower courts appear to be cooperative partners, there has been a more hesitant acceptance of the ECJ's key constitutional pronouncements from certain of the higher courts. In certain member states, for example, there has been something of a reluctance by the national constitutional courts to accept uncon-ditionally the principle of supremacy of Community law. In short, the degree to which the EC legal order may be described as autonomous and supreme depends on one's vantage point – the views of the ECJ will be somewhat different from those held by certain of the member state constitutional courts. A clear example of a more conditional acceptance of the ECJ's image of the EC legal order as autonomous and supreme was provided by the German Constitutional Court's decision in *Brunner* ([1994] 1 Common Market Law Reports, 57), in which it ruled on the compatibility of the (then proposed) Maastricht Treaty with the German constitution. Observations made by the German Court in this case challenged the ECJ's so-called *kompetenz-kompetenz* – that is, its authority to determine the extent of the Community's competence. As will be seen below, the Court, in the exercise of its judicial review function, has had occasion to rule upon whether an act of the institutions falls inside or outside the Community's competence. In performing this task, the ECJ has developed the doctrine of the implied powers of the Community institutions which recognises that, even in the absence of an explicit mandate for action in the Treaty, the institutions should be considered to have been granted such powers as are necessary to achieve their tasks under the Treaty. Arguably, the Court has done more than simply identify the pre-ordained outer limits of competence, but has itself determined them. According to the German constitutional court, the Community can act only within the scope of the powers ascribed to it, and the power to mandate any extension to these competences does not lie with the ECJ.

The *Brunner* decision was a stark example of the more openly critical environment in which the ECJ now operates. As the ramifications of the 'constitutionalising' decisions began to emerge, the ECJ became the subject of scrutiny on the part of national administrations. In the run-up to the Maastricht Treaty (TEU), a number of member states considered tabling proposals which would severely constrict the power of the Court, including the removal of the right of all but the highest national courts to request preliminary rulings (Mancini and Keeling 1995). In the event, while this particular proposal was not adopted, the TEU did exclude the ECJ from having jurisdiction in relation to matters arising under the new Common Foreign and Security pillar and the Justice and Home Affairs (now Police and Judicial Cooperation) pillar. The TEU also gave rise to the so-called Barber Protocol (Protocol number 2), in which the member state governments effectively reinterpreted a decision by the ECJ handed down in the field of occupational pensions – and fired a warning shot at the Court's activism (Curtin 1993).

On the other hand, the Maastricht Treaty did grant new powers to the Court, most notably the power to fine member states for the continued infringement of Community law following a finding that the member state has failed to fulfil its Community law obligations under Article 226/227 EC Treaty. The Court, supported by the Parliament, had been demanding such a power for many years in order to render more effective the enforcement of EC law. Equally, both institutions had recognised the potential usefulness of a Community rule of state liability, which would enable individuals themselves to claim compensation against member states for non-compliance (Tallberg 2000). Both the power to fine and the principle of state liability were considered by the member state governments in the context of the 1991 IGC, although only the former was adopted. Nevertheless, convinced of its necessity, the ECJ went on to introduce such a principle through its case law, establishing it in the November 1991 decision of *Francovich* (Case C-6, 9/90 *Francovich v. Italian State* [1991] European Court Reports I-5357) – despite the objections made by a number of governments submitting observations before it.

The deep-seated opposition from certain member states to the ECJ's decision in *Francovich*, and to its activism more generally, gained an outlet in the IGC which led to the Treaty of Amsterdam. Proposals came both from the UK and France seeking not only to limit the implications of *Francovich*, but also to limit the role and competence of the Court in other ways. In the event, the requisite unanimity among member state governments was not forthcoming, with the smaller states in particular standing by the Court (Tallberg 2000). Nevertheless, certain constraints were built into the system by the Amsterdam Treaty – for example, Article 68 EC Treaty limits the power to make requests for preliminary rulings to only the highest of national courts in relation to questions arising under new Title IV EC Treaty, which covers visas, asylum and immigration. While some have seen this as an unjustified restriction of the Court's jurisdiction, its introduction under the Amsterdam Treaty was accompanied by an extension of the ECJ's jurisdiction beyond the Community pillar, with a restricted power now available in relation to certain aspects of the Police and Judicial Cooperation pillar (subject to member state acceptance of jurisdiction, Article 35 TEU).

With the Court now operating in a more complex, critical and ambiguous environment, it is clear that the age of benign neglect is over. However, while the last decade witnessed more critical attention being directed at the Court, the member states may be seen to have been guilty of neglect of a different sort – that is, of a failure to intervene positively to assist the Court in the administration of its tasks. As the ECJ made clear in the run-up to the Nice IGC, a failure on the part of the member states to address the near-crisis point it had reached in terms of its ability to handle its ever-increasing case-load threatened to undermine the rule of law upon which the EU is founded (ECJ and CFI 1999). This warning has been taken seriously, and the Nice Treaty makes some significant contributions to alleviating the problems faced by the courts. Most notably, the Nice Treaty provides the possibility for not only the ECJ, but also the CFI (which is now designated as a body in its own right, no longer 'attached' to the ECJ) to have jurisdiction to hear Article 234 references for preliminary rulings. The Nice Treaty provides an enabling clause for this division in competences to come about; its activation will require the adoption at some future date of new provisions in the Courts' Statute. The Statute and Rules of Procedure (which together supplement the general principles in the Treaty in regulating the courts' operation) are now more easily amended (the Rules of Procedure by qualified majority voting), providing the opportunity at least for a more flexible and speedier response to the needs of the courts. Outside the Treaty negotiations, amendments were made to these documents in November 2000 that provide for a fast-track procedure which can be followed as and when the President of the Court sees fit. In addition, funds are being made available to finance the appointment of more translating staff. It would appear that the member state governments are taking seriously and attempting to address the administrative problems faced by the Community judicature. It of course remains to be seen how far these changes in fact alleviate these problems, and the extent to which the current financial and political commitment shown to the Court is maintained.

The contribution of the Community judicature to the EU policy process

The Community courts and the EU policy-making process

The Community courts play a crucial oversight role in the policy process. They have the power to annul decisions taken in contravention of the formal rules operating in the decision-making arena. The courts' contribution goes beyond this, however. For example, the 'constitutional' decisions reviewed above have had a considerable impact upon the enforceability of the legal outputs of the policy-making process, and have thus conditioned the policy environment, and considerations of what is possible through Community level policy making. The ECJ also makes a significant contribution to substantive policy development, through its 'interpretation' of the law, bringing new meanings to existing policy commitments, suggesting new developments, and provoking change. While some authors have portrayed the Court as a policy actor with its own preferences and strategies, this image comes into conflict with the traditional 'legalist' conception of the Court as a neutral, impartial arbiter.

There are many ways in which the ECJ may be seen to contribute to the policy process at the supranational level. The above discussion has already shown that the Court has played a crucial role in establishing a legal order which seeks to ensure that the policy commitments entered into by the member state governments and expressed as EC legislation are given full effect at national level. As well as handing down decisions which create the framework for the exercise of citizens' Community law rights, the Court has also played a highly influential role in determining the content of those rights. As a cursory review of any policy area will make clear, the Court is unavoidably involved in substantive policy development. This occurs most clearly through the responses it provides to the constant stream of requests for preliminary rulings on the meaning of both primary and secondary Community legislation.[5] For example, while primary and secondary Community legislation may lay down principles such as equality for men and women in the workplace, or of non-discrimination against migrant EC workers, the Court is involved in determining the precise content of these obligations, with sometimes dramatic consequences for the member states and their nationals. The Court's interpretation of the concept of 'worker', for example, has drawn in ever wider categories of EU citizens who may benefit from social rights and advantages on equal terms with nationals of the state in which they are resident. Both part-time workers (Case 53/81 *Levin v. Staatssecretaris van Justitie* [1982] European Court Reports 1035) and job seekers (Case 2-292/89 *R v. Immigration Appeal Tribunal, ex parte Antonissen* [1991] European Court Reports I-745) have been included in these categories through decisions of the Court. In 1998, the ECJ appeared to push the outer boundaries of this concept yet further, if not jettison it completely, with its ruling in the *Martinez Sala* case (Case C-85/96 *Martinez Sala v. Freistaat Bayern* [1998] European Court Reports I-2691). This decision could be interpreted as developing a general right to non-discrimination for lawfully resident EU citizens, independent of the performance of any economic activity (see the discussion in Fries and Shaw 1998).

The Court's decisions may have direct and immediate policy consequences, as with, for example, the *Kreil* case, which has required Germany to lift its ban on women serving in the armed forces (Case C-285/98 *Tanja Kreil v. German Federal Rupublic*). Alternatively, its decisions may in turn contribute to further policy development through Community legislative channels, in that these decisions may highlight deficiencies in the law, and regulatory gaps, or simply suggest policy solutions (Alter and Meunier-Aitsahalia 1994). In short, the Court should be recognised as being tied into every stage of the policy process, with this process recognised as an open-ended one within which policy problems emerge, and solutions are provided and refined, through a series of ongoing interchanges between legal and political institutions (see further Wincott 1996; Dehousse 1998).

In this section, however, the particular focus will be on the series of checks and balances that the courts operate within the policy process. Through this system, the ECJ in particular plays a crucial role in policing, and indeed determining, the rules of the game which must be followed by the policy participants located within the political sphere. Its power of oversight over the policy process is such that it may potentially overturn decisions agreed upon by a majority of member state governments. This power is exercised in the context of the courts' judicial review function, which enables parties to come before it to challenge the legality of the acts of the Community institutions. While the CFI has jurisdiction to hear cases brought by private parties, interest groups and the like,[6] the ECJ is competent to hear those challenges brought by member state governments and the Community institutions. This function, exercised for the most part in proceedings brought under Article 230 EC Treaty, gives the courts the power to annul the acts of the institutions on the grounds of lack of competence, infringement of an essential procedural requirement, infringement of the EC Treaty or of any rule of law relating to its application, or misuse of powers. Many of the actions brought under Article 230 involve quite detailed, technical questions regarding the procedural propriety of Community (often administrative) acts, concerning, for example, the observation of time limits, or the submission of documents in proceedings. Others, however, appear avowedly political in nature, as the institutions or the member states seek to re-open the decision-making process, using legal channels to articulate political dissatisfaction. As Jo Shaw has shown, such actions may be constitutional in nature, raising as they do 'fundamental questions about the division of competence, inter-institutional balance, and principles such as democracy, institutional accountability and legitimacy' (Shaw 2000: 491). The ECJ then is required actively to address these questions, with potentially profound implications for the participants in the policy-making process.

Such challenges may, for example, be directed against the legal base upon which acts have been introduced. Legal bases, of course, determine which of the decision-making routes are to be used, and thus the relative role and powers of the institutions. The process of their selection is thus both strategic and politically sensitive, and there is clearly the potential for discontent amongst the policy participants. In these situations, the Court may be called upon to decide whether the 'right' legal base was used. The ECJ has stated that the choice of legal base should be guided by 'objective factors which are amenable to judicial review, including, in particular the aim and content of the measure', and its own test for assessing whether the 'right' legal base has been used involves it considering the 'centre of gravity' of the disputed measure. If the Court accepts a challenge as well founded (that is, if the institution or member state concerned successfully transposes its political discontent into convincing legal argument) then a successful Article 230 procedure will provide the applicant with an opportunity to, in effect, redefine its role in the policy process. However, while the Commission, Council and the member state governments are granted standing to bring actions against any legal act adopted by any of the institutions, such standing was not originally extended to the Parliament. Initial attempts by the Parliament to come before the Court were rejected, the ECJ ruling that the Parliament's interests were adequately protected by the Commission's role as Guardian of the Treaties (Case 302/87 *Parliament v. Council (Comitology)* [1988] European Court Reports 5615). Repeatedly petitioned by the Parliament, however, the ECJ changed tack, and read into this Article the right of Parliament to bring annulment actions, but only in situations where it is seeking to protect its own prerogatives, that is, its place in the inter-institutional balance (Case C-70/88 *Parliament v. Council (Chernobyl)* [1990] European Court Reports I-2041). This decision was later formally endorsed by the member state governments at Maastricht, when Article 230 was amended so as to include a limited right of standing for the Parliament. This will become a full right on a par with the privileged applicants on the coming into force of the Nice Treaty.

Thus, Article 230 can involve litigation between institutions attempting to redress a perceived imbalance in the inter-institutional division of powers. Increasingly, it is also being invoked by member state governments in an attempt to control the exercise of Community competence and to act as a check upon its extension. Actions of this type have become more frequent and more politically sensitised with the extension of qualified majority voting, with disaffected member state governments turning to Article 230 as a channel for 'diplomacy by other means' (Cullen and Charlesworth 1999). The inclusion of the constitutional principle of subsidiarity in the EC Treaty has also provided the member states with new ammunition to use against unwelcome Community law (de Burca 1998). Recent high-profile examples of such legal base actions include the UK's (predominantly unsuccessful) challenge to the Working Time Directive (Case C-84/94 *UK v. Council (Working Time Directive)* [1996] ECR I-5755]), and the German government's entirely successful challenge to the 1998 Tobacco Advertising Directive (Case C-376/98 *Germany v. Parliament and Council* judgment of 5 October 2000). The Court overturned the latter directive on the grounds that the legal basis used for its adoption did not provide the member states with the competence to introduce such a measure. It is impossible to read the Court's tobacco judgment without calling to mind the warnings which came from the German Constitutional Court in the *Brunner* case, in which, it has to be remembered, the Constitutional Court refused to recognise the ECJ as having the authority to mandate any extension to the competences ascribed to the institutions under the Treaty and defined therein.

Of course, in the Tobacco judgment, the Court overruled a decision which the majority of member states had indicated they were content with, and in this regard it may be seen as going against the policy preferences of the member states. This decision would appear to go against a recent trend identified by a number of eminent commentators, who see the Court as having entered a more conservative phase, and one which pays greater deference to the autonomy of the member states in their capacity to conduct their public policies (Mancini and Keeling 1994, Dehousse 1998: 148). As Dehousse argues, however, the Court has maintained a bold approach in matters relating to the fundamental principles underlying the EC's legal architecture (Dehousse 1998: 153), as witnessed in cases such as *Francovich*. The Tobacco judgment can be absorbed within this category of cases, as at issue there was the very rule of law in the Community, the point being that the member states cannot ignore the legal constraints imposed upon them by the Treaty as and when they see fit. The case of *Martinez Sala* meanwhile is perhaps less easy to accommodate with this image of a more conservative Court, though it is of course simply one judgment from among the thousands handed down over the past decade.

To the extent that a new conservatism may be discernible, one is led to enquire why the Court may have put aside its early activism. Is it a response to the more critical attention being levelled at it? Is the Court responding to the political context within which it operates, and reflecting these political pressures? This image of a 'political' court is very apparent in the work of those such as Garrett, who has argued that the Court consciously seeks to reflect the wishes of the dominant member states when it is framing its decisions (Garrett 1995). Others however, would strongly deny such a political quality to the Court's decisions, presenting the Court as a legal institution, performing a judicial role, and operating in accordance with the basic norms of that role. These include, for example, the expectations that legitimate judicial institutions will apply the law in an objective, neutral manner, automatically arriving at the 'right' decision in the case before it on the basis of deductive inference. The reality of the situation, of course, falls somewhere between the extremes of, on the one hand, a Court slavishly tracking the political preferences of the member state governments, and, on the other, of a Court wholly insulated from political pressure. Clearly, the Court is aware of, and at times responds to, the political context, but at the same time it works within the language and logic of the law and the legal role: these factors also contribute to the Court's autonomy and legitimacy. Burley and Mattli (1993) have argued that the ECJ's success in avoiding political censure, particularly in relation to its 'constitutionalising' work, owed much to the fact that the manner in which it rendered its decisions – that is, in accordance with the requirements of legal reasoning – enabled it to hide behind the mask of legal formalism, and provided it with a protective shield against political pressures. In recent years, however, the sustained attention directed at the Court has involved the peeling back of this mask, which has left the Court in a somewhat vulnerable position.

The future of the judicial system of the EU

The ECJ of today is generally characterised as a more conservative Court than in the past. It operates in an environment of greater scrutiny, and the recent succession of IGCs, and the threats of reform therein, have perhaps contributed to a heightened sensitivity on the part of the Court to the political context within which it operates. As the outcomes of these IGCs have shown, however, the Court has not necessarily suffered a *reduction* in its formal power and status. While it is true that with the Maastricht Treaty the member states embarked on a policy of containment, excluding the Court from operating in the second and third pillars, the Amsterdam Treaty opened the door for the Court to be involved in the Police and Judicial Cooperation pillar. The Nice Treaty, though, makes no further extension to the jurisdiction of the Court, and so as yet the Courts of the European *Community* have not become the Courts of the European *Union*. Such a transformation will come about only with the positive political intervention of the member state governments, as and when they deem it appropriate to accept the Court into highly sensitive areas of policy cooperation.

Within its existing areas of jurisdiction, it is to be expected that increasingly the Court will find itself drawn in to arbitrate disputes between the players in the Community policy process. Mention has already been made of the growing tendency for the 'losers' in the decision-making process to turn to the Court in an attempt to undo policy outcomes with which they are dissatisfied. With the extension of qualified majority voting into more policy areas under the Nice Treaty, it can only be expected that the potential for such disputes to arise will intensify. It is unlikely that such challenges will come from the member state governments alone, given the enhanced powers the Parliament has to bring judicial review actions granted to it by the Nice Treaty. Working within this highly politicised environment, the Court will undoubtedly find itself exposed to increasing critical attention as it conducts the necessary 'marginal balancing of competing legitimate interests' (Shapiro 1999: 344).

Quite apart from the pressures such inter-institutional litigation places on the ECJ in political terms, there are very real concerns about the capacity of the Community judicial system to handle the increase in such litigation. In view of the new areas of jurisdiction introduced by the Amsterdam Treaty, and the prospect of further enlargement of the EU, it is clear that the Courts' case-load is unlikely to diminish. Quite simply, the system is nearing breaking point, and the extent of the crisis warrants a determined, bold response from the member states and from the Courts themselves. The recent amendments, including the introduction of fast-track procedures, the possibility of a sharing of the Article 234 workload between the two Courts, and the establishment of specialised judicial boards to handle particular categories of cases, will, when activated, hopefully alleviate the worst of the pressures on the judicial order. In the long term, however, a more fundamental reform of the judicial system may prove necessary for the courts to be able to function effectively in the future.

One issue which will shortly need to be addressed is that of the size and composition of the Court. The Nice Treaty formalises the one-state–one-judge convention, and the revised Article 221 EC Treaty removes any upper ceiling on the number of judges at the Court. There is thus the prospect of more judges arriving at Court with the accession of new member states. While this is to be welcomed in terms of the Court's capacity to handle the cases coming before it, it should be recognised that the ECJ itself has voiced concerns that a significant increase in its membership may cause 'the invisible boundary between a collegiate court and a deliberative assembly' to be crossed (ECJ and CFI 1999). The prospect of plenary hearings involving nearly thirty judges is concerning to say the least, not only in terms of increased time and administrative costs, but also to the extent that it may compromise the construction of legally coherent judgments. The member states will undoubtedly oppose any amendment to their Treaty-based 'right' to have a judge at the Court. Instead, a workable though no doubt politically controversial solution would be to limit the membership of plenary hearings to a number of the more senior judges at the Court.

Another, more fundamental proposal for change involves a restructuring of the relationship between the Community courts and the national courts, involving the introduction of a new tier of decentralised Community courts, located in each of the member states, and given jurisdiction to hear Article 234 references coming from within their legal order (see Jacqué and Weiler 1990; Rasmussen 2000). This sharing of responsibility would undoubtedly take pressure off the ECJ and the CFI, but there is concern that it could lead to a lack of uniformity in Community law. Similar concerns have been voiced about less radical proposals designed to limit the number of Article 234 references, such as the introduction of a form of 'docket control' according to which the ECJ selects only those cases which it considers important to respond to. It has also been suggested that certain national courts, those at the lower end of the national hierarchies, should have their power to refer cases removed. The adoption of such measures would, however, place clear constraints on the cooperation and dialogue which has existed between the Community courts and national courts throughout the Community's history, a dialogue which, as we have seen, has fundamentally transformed the nature of the Community legal order.

Summary

- The EU has two judicial bodies: the European Court of Justice, and the Court of First Instance. Both consist of one judge from each of the member states, with the ECJ also comprising eight advocates general, who assist the Court in reaching its decisions.
- The courts are charged with the task of ensuring that the rule of law is observed. The different types of actions which may be brought before the Courts include: (1) actions in judicial review, in which challenges are brought against the validity of the acts of the institutions. If the claim is well founded, the Court may annul the legal act in question; (2) enforcement actions against the member states for failure to abide by their Community law obligations. If these cases are well founded, the ECJ may ultimately impose a fine against the defaulting state; (3) requests to the ECJ for preliminary rulings on the interpretation and validity of EC law, which are made by national courts. There are detailed rules governing which Court has the authority to hear the different types of cases. In general, the CFI deals with cases of lesser political salience.
- The ECJ is accredited with having 'constitutionalised' the EC Treaty, through its purposive interpretation of the law. Motivated by a desire to ensure the effectiveness of Community law, it has developed principles which have transformed a Treaty-based legal order into one resembling that of a federal state. These key principles are the supremacy of EC law, the direct effect of EC law, and the principle of state liability.
- The ECJ in particular plays an important oversight role in the policy process.

In the process of adjudging whether the Community institutions have abided by the Treaty rules, the ECJ has itself contributed to the meaning of these rules. The Court also contributes to the development of substantive policy through its interpretation of the law.

- The Nice Treaty has gone some way towards addressing the pressing need for reform of the Community judicial structure. The system is still overloaded, however, and the envisaged enlargement of the EU will exacerbate the problem. Depending on the success of the envisaged measures, further reform may be necessary. Suggestions include introducing decentralised 'courts of justice' in each member state, and imposing restrictions on the situations in which Article 234 references can be made. Both are highly disputed, as they may jeopardise the ability of the courts to maintain a uniform interpretation of the law.

Test questions

1   Explain how the European Court of Justice radically altered the nature of the Community legal order through its decisions. What significance did these decisions have for the wider integration process?
2   In what circumstances may the ECJ annul decisions taken by the EC's legislative organs? Do you believe that the ECJ should have this power? Would it make any difference to your answer if a decision had been taken by unanimity in Council?
3   Should the member state governments have the competence to overrule decisions of the ECJ? Give reasons for your answer.
4   What do you perceive to be the main challenges facing the courts at the present time?

Contact information

The courts' website contains a wealth of information about the structure and functions of the Community judicature, as well as a searchable database of recent case law. The courts' own contributions to the debate on the reform of the Community judicature can also be accessed on this site. The address is: http://www.curia.eu.int. Questions about the operation of the courts are handled by the Press and Information Division; its email address is info@curia.eu.int. The Press and Information Division also organises educational visits to the Court; further information is available on the website.

The postal address for both courts is Palais de la Cour de Justice, Boulevard Konrad Adenauer, Kirchberg, L02925 Luxembourg. The English-language contact unit telephone number is (+352) 4303 3355; the fax number is (+352) 4303 2731.

Notes

1 The Treaty of Nice will, if ratified, formalise this practice.
2 In 1999, some 543 new cases were brought before the ECJ. The 1999 figures show a continuing rise in the in the number of cases being brought each year, which has resulted in an increase in the average length of time taken to deal with each case (ECJ 2000).
3 Council Decision 88/591, OJ 1988 L 319/1.
4 The Nice Treaty will, if ratified, change this situation (see below).
5 While it is always the decision of the national court, and not the plaintiffs before it, to make a request, there is clear evidence of private parties launching strategic litigation at national level in an attempt to come before the ECJ and achieve political outcomes unattainable through other routes. See further Rawlings 1993; Barnard 1995.
6 These non-privileged applicants must clear a very high set of hurdles before they get to the CFI. They are required to demonstrate a direct and individual concern in the act complained of – a test which few succeed in passing (see the restrictive formula established in Case 25/62 *Plaumann and Co v. Commission* [1963] European Court Reports 95). The 'individual' leg of the test makes it all but impossible for groups acting in the general public interest to mount a successful action (see e.g. Case T-585/93 *Stichting Greenpeace Council v. Commission* [1995] European Court Reports II-2205, and on appeal from the CFI to the EC, Case C-321/95 P [1998] European Court Reports I-1651].

Selected further reading

Arnull, A. (1999). *The European Union and Its Court of Justice*, Oxford: Oxford University Press.
   A detailed legal account of the contribution the Court has made to the integration process and to specific policy fields.

Dehousse, R. (1998) *The European Court of Justice: The Politics of Judicial Integration*, Basingstoke: Macmillan.
   An important work which places the Court and its actions within the framework of political actors and pressures.

Mancini, G.F. (2000) *Democracy and Constitutionalism in the European Union*, Oxford: Hart.
   A collection of thought-provoking and enlightening essays written from an insider's perspective, Mancini being both a former Advocate General and Judge of the Court of Justice.

Rasmussen, H. (2000) 'Remedying the Crumbling EC Judicial System', *Common Market Law Review*, 37, 5: 1071–112.
   A review of the proposals for reform of the Court system from one of the most long-standing and influential critical commentators on the ECJ.

References

Alter, K. (1996) 'The European Court's Political Power', *West European Politics*, 19, 3: 458–87.
Alter, K. (1998) 'Explaining National Court Acceptance of European Court Jurisprudence: A Critical Evaluation of Theories of Legal Integration', in A-M. Slaughter, A. Stone Sweet and J.H.H. Weiler (eds) *The European Courts and National Courts: Doctrine and Jurisprudence*, Oxford: Hart.

Alter, K. and Meunier-Aitsahalia, S. (1994) 'Judicial Politics in the European Community: European Integration and the Pathbreaking *Cassis de Dijon* Decision', *Comparative Political Studies*, 26,4: 535–61.

Arnull, A. (1999) *The European Union and Its Court of Justice*, Oxford: Oxford University Press.

Barnard, C. (1995) 'A European Litigation Strategy: The Case of the Equal Opportunities Commission', in J. Shaw and G. More (eds) *New Legal Dynamics of European Union*, Oxford: Oxford University Press.

Burca, G. de (1998) 'The Principle of Subsidiarity and the Court of Justice as an Institutional Actor', *Journal of Common Market Studies*, 36,2: 217–35.

Burley, A.M. and Mattli, W. (1993) 'Europe Before the Court: A Political Theory of Legal Integration', *International Organization*, 47,1: 41–76.

Chalmers, D. (2000) 'The Postitioning of EU Judicial Politics within the UK', *Western European Politics*, 23,4: 169–210.

Cullen, H. and Charlesworth, A. (1999) 'Diplomacy by Other Means: The Use of Legal Basis Litigation as a Political Strategy by the European Parliament and Member States', *Common Market Law Review*, 36, 6: 1243–70.

Curtin, D. (1993) 'The Constitutional Structure of the Union: A Europe of Bits and Pieces', *Common Market Law Review*, 30, 1: 17–69.

de Witte, B. (1999): 'Direct Effect, Supremacy and the Nature of the Legal Order', in P. Craig and G. de Burca (eds) *The Evolution of EU Law*, Oxford: Oxford University Press.

Dehousse, R. (1998) *The European Court of Justice: The Politics of Judicial Integration*, Basingstoke: Macmillan.

European Court of Justice (ECJ) (2000) *Annual Report 1999*, Luxembourg: Office for Official Publications.

European Court of Justice (ECJ) and Court of First Instance (CFI) (1999) 'The Future of the Judicial System of the European Union (Proposals and Reflections)'. Available on Court's website: www.curia.eu.int

Fries, S. and Shaw, J. (1998) 'Citizenship of the Union: First Steps in the European Court of Justice', *European Public Law*, 4, 4: 533–59.

Garrett, G. (1995) 'The Politics of Legal Integration in the European Union', *International Organization*, 49, 1: 171–81.

Jacqué, J.P. and Weiler, J.H.H. (1990) 'On the Road to European Union – A New Judicial Architecture: An Agenda for the Intergovernmental Conference', *Common Market Law Review*, 27: 185–207.

Mancini, G.F. (2000) *Democracy and Constitutionalism in the European Union*, Oxford: Hart.

Mancini, G.F. and Keeling, D.T. (1994) 'Democracy and the European Court of Justice', *Modern Law Review*, 57: 175–190, reprinted in G.F. Mancini (2000) *Democracy and Constitutionalism in the European Union*, Oxford: Hart.

Mancini, G.F. and Keeling, D.T. (1995) 'From CILFIT to ERT: The Constitutional Challenge Facing the European Court', *Yearbook of European Law*, 11: 1–13, reprinted in G.F. Mancini (2000) *Democracy and Constitutionalism in the European Union*, Oxford: Hart.

Rasmussen, H. (2000) 'Remedying the Crumbling EC Judicial System', *Common Market Law Review*, 37, 5: 1071–112.

Rawlings, R. (1993): 'The Eurolaw Game: Some Deductions from a Saga', *Journal of Law and Society*, 20, 3: 309–40.

Shapiro, M. (1999) 'The European Court of Justice', in P. Craig and G. de Burca (eds): *The Evolution of EU Law*, Oxford: Oxford University Press.

Shaw, J. (2000) *Law of the European Union*, Basingstoke: Palgrave.

Stein, E. (1981) 'Lawyers, Judges and the Making of a Transnational Constitution', *American Journal of International Law*, 75, 1: 1–27.

Stone Sweet, A. (1998) 'Constitutional Dialogues in the European Community', in A-M.

Slaughter, A. Stone Sweet and J.H.H. Weiler (eds) *The European Courts and National Courts: Doctrine and Jurisprudence*, Oxford: Hart.

Tallberg, J. (2000) 'Supranational Influence in EU Enforcement: The ECJ and the Principle of State Liability', *Journal of European Public Policy*, 7, 1: 104–21.

Weiler, J.H.H. (1993) 'Journey to an Unknown Destination: A Retrospective and Prospective of the European Court of Justice in the Arena of Political Integration', *Journal of Common Market Studies*, 31, 4: 417–46.

Weiler, J.H.H. (1994) 'A Quiet Revolution – The European Court of Justice and its Interlocutors', *Comparative Political Studies*, 26, 4: 510–34.

Wincott, D. (1996) 'The Court of Justice and the European Policy Process', in J. Richardson (ed.) *European Union Power and Policy Making*, London: Routledge.

The Court of Auditors

Brigid Laffan

Key facts

Established in 1977, the Court of Auditors is a collegiate body of fifteen members, with a President elected for a three-year, renewable period. Its members are appointed by the member states, by qualified majority voting after the ratification of the Nice Treaty. Its headquarters are in Luxembourg. The Court's role is to act as an external auditing body for the EU, a function which has become increasingly important over time and which led the Court to play a role in the resignation of the Commission in 1999. Organised into twelve audit groups, the Court issues several important publications regarding the financial probity of the EU every year: an Annual Report, Special Reports, and Opinions on Financial Regulations.

The Court of Auditors: composition, powers and functions

The work of the Court of Auditors enters the political and public domain through its Annual Report and the Special Reports it produces each year. The reports make multiple references to the weaknesses of financial management in the EU within the institutions and in the member states. The weaknesses identified in the reports seem to recur year in year out and have a certain serial quality. The resignation of the Santer Commission in March 1999, when confronted with accusations of weak management, lent support to the view that the problems of budgetary management are systemic and that little has been done to address them. It could lead to the conclusion that the Court of Auditors had not fulfilled its role as 'financial conscience' of the Union. Such a conclusion would, however, fail to acknowledge the real difficulties facing the Union as it tries to administer a budget throughout the EU and in third countries. A more measured assessment leads us to conclude that the Court of Auditors had to find its place in the Union's institutional landscape and that, together with the other EU institutions, it had to enhance the norms and processes of financial control in the Union. This was done while the EU budget expanded significantly following the first Delors package in 1988. The development of the Court of Auditors highlights a number of key themes about institutionalisation and institution building in the Union. The aim of this chapter is to analyse the evolution of the European Court of Auditors from an idea into a 'living institution' in the EU. The resignation of the Commission in March 1999 must be seen in the context of a slow and faltering process of strengthening financial management in the EU. The Court of Auditors was a vital part of this process.

Provision for a European Court of Auditors was made in the 1975 Budget Treaty, a treaty that endowed the European Parliament with enhanced budgetary powers. The Court formally came into existence two years later in October 1977 when it replaced a pre-existing Audit Board and the Auditor of the European Coal and Steel Community (ECSC). The perceived need for the Court arose directly from the establishment of an autonomous EC budget based on 'own resources' in the 1970 Budget Treaty. Furthermore, the granting of limited budgetary powers to the European Parliament enhanced the powers of the European Parliament's Budget Committee and led it to seek to increase its role in the budgetary domain. Both these changes in the EU budget – 'own resources' and parliamentary power – altered the stakes in the budgetary domain and provided a 'window of opportunity' for institution building in the Union. The Chair of the Parliament's Budget Committee, Dr Heinrich Aigner, published an influential report in 1973: *The Case for a European Audit Office*. The key argument was that with the changes in the composition and size of the budget, external auditing should be taken more seriously. Publicity about a number of frauds in the agricultural sector lent urgency to the quest for a strengthening of the mechanisms of financial control and auditing in the Union. From the outset, the role of the Court of Auditors was linked to the power of discharge over the budget granted in the 1975 Treaty to the Parliament. The United Kingdom, then a new member state, was quick to support the creation of a fully fledged audit office in the Union. There was no outright opposition from other member states, since external auditing of public agencies and their use of public monies was considered part and parcel of the norms of good government and accountability. This did not, however, mean that the member states wanted a very intrusive auditing body that would hold them, and not just the Commission, accountable. From a member state perspective, the Court was created to oversee the Commission's management of the budget. Gradually, however, the member states themselves have been drawn into the web of the Court as EU expenditure is deployed at national level and the member states have considerable management discretion.

Hans Kutscher, President of the European Court of Justice, established the leitmotiv of the Court when he defined it as the 'financial conscience' of the Community at the swearing-in ceremony for the members of the first Court in 1977. The Court of Auditors adopted the mantle of 'financial conscience' of the Community, as its official description of itself and its work, from the outset (Court of Auditors 1995a: 7). There was considerable debate at the outset about the nature of the Court and the number of auditors that should be appointed. The appointment of one auditor per member state continued the practice of national representation in all EU institutions. It meant that the Court would have to be a collegiate body rather than a small, tightly knit professional body of auditors. In line with all other EU institutions its size has expanded, reflecting the continuing process of enlargement.

Like all EU institutions, the Court relies on treaty provisions to establish the broad parameters of its role in the Union's system of financial management. The role of the Court is to assist the European Parliament and the Council in exercising their powers of control over the implementation of the budget. It exercises the delegated task of financial control for the political institutions of the Union by providing them with the material to make political judgements about financial management. The work and role of the Court cannot be judged in isolation from its relationships with the other EU institutions. The precise functions of the Court as prescribed by treaty are as follows:

- examination of the legality and regularity of EU revenue and expenditure;
- analysis of whether financial management has been sound (Article 188c, TEU).

In order to do this, the Court is mandated to examine the accounts of all EU revenue and expenditure by carrying out audits. These audits are based on records of financial transactions, and if necessary include on-the-spot checks in other EC institutions and in the member states. Prior to the TEU, the rhythm of the Court's work was essentially established by the legal requirement that it produce an Annual Report following the close of each financial year, published in November. This imposed a precise time frame on the work of the Court. From the outset, the Annual Report (usually over 400 pages long, and published in the Official Journal) was the centre-piece of the Court's work. This was augmented by special reports on particular areas of EU expenditure and by the responsibility of the Court to give its opinions to the Council on laws with a financial content.

The Court is a collegiate body that has developed its own internal rules of procedure. The Council used to appoint the auditors by unanimity after consulting with the EP. The Treaty of Nice specified that the Council will in future act by qualified majority voting when appointing the auditors. The Parliament's Budgetary Control Committee has also developed a practice of holding formal hearings attended by each aspiring auditor. The Court's members elect their President for a renewable period of three years. The role of the President is that of *primus inter pares* both internally in the organisation and externally *vis-à-vis* the other EU institutions, but the role of the President has certainly increased since the Court's inception.

The work of the Court is divided into twelve audit groups representing the major EU spending programmes or audit sectors, two horizontal groups dealing with the statement of assurance and the development of audits. The audit groups are the responsibility of a senior member of the Court known as a Doyen. Each audit group works out its programme and reviews the outcome of the sectoral or programme audits before they go to a meeting of the full Court. A small *cabinet* assists the members of the Court, and the professional auditors who make up the operating core of the Court conduct day-to-day work. In 1998, the Court had 550 employees, including ninety translation staff (Desmond 1999: 115).

History and evolution of the Court

Key events

1983:   Court asked for its assessment of financial management in the Union by the European Council

1992:   Elevated to the status of a full institution by the Treaty on European Union

1992:   Role expanded to include a Statement of Assurance

1997:   Enhanced role in the Treaty of Amsterdam

1999:   Resignation of the Santer Commission

2000:   Treaty changes re appointment to the Court in the Nice Treaty

A combination of factors enhanced the salience of financial management in the Union and thus moved the Court of Auditors from the margins of the Union's institutional landscape to a position befitting its role as external auditor of EU revenue and expenditure. It is not, and never will be, a policy-making institution. Rather, it provides the external auditing component of the Union's accountability structure. In this way it works closely with those responsible for political accountability in this domain: the Budget Committee and the Budgetary Control Committee of the European Parliament. It must also work closely with those responsible for financial management in the other EU institutions and the national audit authorities. It is but one link in a chain of financial accountability in the Union. The Court of Auditors has no role in investigating fraud against the financial interests of the Union and it cannot follow up its reports to recover EU monies from the member states. These roles are exercised by OLAF (the EU's anti-fraud agency), and the Commission itself.

Notwithstanding the lack of interest of the European Council in 1983, the Court of Auditors continued to carry out its auditing work and to publish its findings. Since 1978, the Court of Auditors has published an Annual Report each year in addition to myriad reports on particular EU programmes or areas of expenditure. Successive reports highlighted weaknesses in the financial management of the Union budget. The examples of problems in financial management in a succession of Court Reports are often very similar to those noted in previous reports. Among the routine criticisms are:

- Failure by member states to collect all of the 'own resources' because of weak application of legislation and difficulties arising from the abolition of tax frontiers for VAT.
- Extensive weaknesses in the organisation and management of expenditure arising from the Agricultural Guidance and Guarantee Fund (EAGGF) including failure to recover amounts owed to the Community, failure to monitor the eligibility of declared costs, and failure to ensure that there were adequate control procedures in relation to special payments.
- inconsistent treatment of eligibility in relation to certain categories of Structural Fund expenditure. Concern about the legality and regularity of some Structural Fund operations.
- Problems of subcontracting programmes in some internal EU and some external programmes, notably Phare and Tacis.

The Court of Auditors, together with the Budget Control Committee of the EP, found themselves in a wilderness for many years as they sought to build up the commitment in the Union to improved financial management. Gradually their advocacy found a receptive political and institutional audience for a variety of reasons. The Delors I package in 1988 greatly increased the size of the EU budget from some 28 billion ECUS in 1986 to over 87 billion by 1999. The pronounced increase in the EU budget led to a growing number of 'net contributors' who in turn felt it necessary to ensure that what they considered their taxpayers' money was spent well and wisely. The 'net contributors club' in the Council was transformed into a good housekeeping club on budgetary matters. Furthermore, the ratification crisis that surrounded the Treaty on European Union in 1992 enhanced the demand for more effective accountability throughout the EU system of governance. Transparency, openness and accountability became part of the normative framework of the Union.

The growing evidence of fraud against the financial interests of the Union added to the salience of improved financial management. The British House of Lords, the Budget Control Committee of the EP, the work of the Court itself and media coverage all served to highlight problems of fraud and mismanagement of the budget. The House of Lords was particularly tenacious concerning the management of EU finances, concluding in 1989 that:

> Even with its limited existing resources the Court of Auditors has drawn attention on numerous occasions to weaknesses in administration, failure to exercise adequate control and other grave irregularities – on which neither the Community institutions nor the Member States have acted. This is the most glaring example of the lack of political will.
>
> (House of Lords 1989, par 198)

The level of fraud against the financial interests of the Union is impossible to measure but it is likely to be high (Ruimschotel 1993; Mendrinou 1994). The Union's financial instruments are vulnerable to fraud because of the highly complex and ambiguous legislation which governs many expenditure programmes, and the multi-level delivery system which involves EU-level institutions, as well as public and private authorities in the member states. The Annual Reports of the Commission's anti-fraud unit provide a catalogue of mispaid agricultural subsidies, abuses of the Structural Funds and fraud in the tourism sector masterminded in the Commission itself. An editorial in the *Financial Times*, a paper not known for its hyperbole, spoke of 'fraudsters frolicking through Europe's complex rules for disbursing funds, particularly those for agriculture and infrastructure' (*Financial Times*, 17 November 1994, p.21). This was underlined by the European Parliament's first Committee of Inquiry – an examination of the EU's transit system. The Committee highlighted major problems in the transit system and concluded: '[g]oods cross borders, criminals cross borders, profits from illegal activities cross borders, public authority stops at the borders' (EP Committee of Inquiry 1996–7, Vol.1: 13).

A recurrent theme in the Court's pronouncements about financial management was the need for changes in the management culture of EU institutions. For example, in its 1994 report the Court concluded that there was a need for a 'substantial change in what might be termed "the financial management culture" which administers and controls the collection and utilisation of budgetary resources, at Commission and Member State levels' (Court of Auditors 1994: 6). It went on to say that the evidence of problems in the culture of financial management could be detected in weak management of available funds, insufficient attention to cost-effectiveness and a failure to act quickly to recover funds that were wrongly paid (Court of Auditors 1994: 6). The Court's judgement on financial management received an unexpected endorsement in 1995 when the outgoing Budget Commissioner in the last Delors Commission, Peter Schmidhuber, left a testimonial which baldly concluded that '[t]he principle of sound financial management stated in Article 2 of the Financial Regulation and stressed repeatedly by the Court of Auditors is not acknowledged as a general maxim in the Commission' (European Commission 1995). Schmidhuber then went on to outline the main weaknesses of the Commission's internal management, which bore out what the Court of Auditors had been repeatedly saying in its Annual Reports.

Constitutional change in the 1990s provided a timely 'window of opportunity' to strengthen treaty provisions on the Court. Because the Union's treaty framework is subject to change, the role of the Court is also subject to redefinition when the member states as 'masters of the treaties' choose to enhance its powers and the scope of its jurisdiction. This they did in the Treaty on European Union (TEU), when the Court was made a full institution of the Union, together with the older institutions, the Council, the Commission, the European Parliament and the Court of Justice. This was clear recognition of the need to enhance the authority of the Court and to elevate it to a status equivalent to those institutions over which it had an auditing power. In addition, the TEU significantly added to the tasks of the Court by making provision for what is known as the 'statement of assurance' (SOA), a statement provided by the Court of Auditors to the EP and the Council on the 'reliability of the accounts and the legality and regularity of the underlying transaction' (Art. 188c, TEU). The SOA altered the work of the Court in an important manner, as it required far more extensive auditing by the Court of the Union's financial transactions.

The Court's new institutional status was accompanied by other significant changes in the financial framework of the Union, notably a direct reference to budgetary discipline (Art. 201a, TEU) and the need to implement the budget in accordance with the principle of sound financial management (Art. 205, TEU). Moreover, the TEU strengthened the responsibility of the member states in this field by specifying that they should take measures to combat fraud affecting the Community's financial interests and that they must take 'the same measures to counter fraud affecting the financial interests of the Community as they take to counter fraud affecting their own financial interests' (Art. 209a, TEU).

The Treaty of Amsterdam provided another opportunity for the Court to improve its legal framework. In its submission to the Reflection Group established prior to the 1996 Intergovernmental Conference, the Court sought to build on its gains in the TEU. The Court wanted to be mentioned in Article E of the TEU to establish its jurisdiction in pillars 2 and 3. It sought access to the European Court of Justice so that its rights and prerogatives could be upheld, if necessary through judicial review. In addition, it wanted a clear statement in the Treaty that gave it access to all organisations in receipt of EU finance so that it could follow the transaction trail down to the ultimate beneficiary (Court of Auditors 1995a).

The outcome of the negotiations was that the Court was successful in getting most of the changes that it sought. The amended Article E enables the Court to examine expenditure in the Common Foreign and Security Policy (CFSP) and in judicial cooperation. In was given the right to seek review in the ECJ to protect its prerogatives, a power already granted to the European Parliament and the European Central Bank. A series of changes to Article 188c enable the Court to publish its Statement of Assurance in the Official Journal, and under Article 206(1) the other institutions are required to take the SOA into account when granting the Commission a discharge of the budget. A further amendment to Article 188c specifically mandates the Court to 'report in particular on any cases of irregularity' (Art. 188c), a clear attempt to heighten the Court's role in exposing irregularities. The jurisdiction of the Court's auditing powers was extended to EU agencies and consultants, and its right to examine EIB transactions in respect of projects with budgetary subvention was upheld. Finally, the relationship between the Court of Auditors and national audit bodies was defined in the following terms: '[t]he Court of Auditors and the national audit bodies of the Member States shall co-operate in a spirit of trust while maintaining their independence' (Art. 188c, Treaty of Amsterdam). A proposal that would end the right of national audit offices to refuse to cooperate with the Court was not accepted by the IGC (Duff 1997: 170). A declaration on relations between the Court and the national audit offices was added to the Treaty of Nice. The declaration asks the Court of Auditors and the national auditing institutions to improve the 'framework and conditions for co-operation between them' and allowed for a contact committee consisting of the President of the Court of Auditors and the chairmen of the national audit institutions (Declaration, Treaty of Nice 2000: 61). The objective is to enhance the overall auditing capacity and reach of the Court of Auditors by creating linkages with the relevant national institutions. There remains, however, no compulsion on the national bodies to cooperate with the Court of Auditors, although there are growing institutional pressures to make them do so.

The Court in the EU system

The Court of Auditors and institutional reform

The Court's place and importance in the making of public policy at EU level has increased over time, in keeping with several changes in the wider integration process: an increase both in the size of the EU budget and member state concerns about 'value for money'; the greater attention paid by all actors, including the public, to fraud; and demands for increased transparency across the board in EU decision making. Nonetheless, the Court has been obliged to work hard to establish itself as a force to be reckoned with and also to establish its own working practices. As a financial watchdog, the Court's relations with the other EU institutions have often been strained. However, its role in prompting reform of those institutions – particularly the Commission – has enabled it to come of age.

Since its inception in 1977, we can trace the co-evolution of the Court and its institutional centre. There has been constant interaction between the internal dynamics of the Court and its external environment. The key features of the Court's external environment were the growing size of the budget, the emergence of a 'net contributors' club, the politicisation of the issue of fraud, and the public demand that all EU institutions and processes become more transparent and democratic (House of Lords 1987, 1989; Kok 1989; Alabau I Oliveres 1990; Levy 1990, 1996; Strasser 1992; March and Olsen 1995; Desmond 1996, 1999; Laffan 1997a, 1999).

The Court faced a major organisational challenge in translating Treaty provisions concerning its role into a real presence in the Union's institutional landscape. Considerable energy in the early years went into the internal development of the Court as it strove to establish an identity for itself. The challenge was both organisational and inter-institutional; it was also a problem of salience. The Court began its work having inherited thirty staff from the old Audit Board, and then had to rapidly increase its staffing resources so that it could carry out the tasks entrusted to it. By 1980, staffing levels had increased to 200. The Court had to decide how to distribute the auditing work among the auditors. At first, all of the members of the Court were involved in auditing and in the internal management of the Court itself. In other words, each member had a vertical responsibility for a sector and horizontal responsibility for an administrative task. This was described as 'inefficient: the coupling of disparate vertical and horizontal duties tended to dissipate members' attention and energy with the result that in some cases neither function was discharged adequately' (Wilmott 1984: 211).

In the early days of the Court, there were numerous conflicts about the allocation of staff to different audit areas and little coherence in the work of the Court. In evidence to the House of Lords, it was claimed that the system led to overlapping responsibilities, friction between members of the Court, and endless debates about rather trivial administrative problems (House of Lords 1987: 64). In an attempt to overcome the fragmentation of its audit work, the Court adopted a multiannual work programme which provided the basis for each year's audit cycle to ensure that all major areas of EU finance were audited every four or five years. In 1980, in an attempt to break down the 'fiefdoms' of individual auditors, audit groups, as noted above, were established. Each audit group consists of between three and five members of the Court. In addition to a designated area of responsibility, each member acts as a *contre-rapporteur* on the work of colleagues. A special unit in the Court, known as the ADAR Unit, is responsible for coordination of the Annual Report, staff training and the development of audit practices.

Given the diversity of auditing traditions in the member states and the diverse backgrounds of its staff, the first College of Auditors had to establish its approach to auditing, in terms of norms and procedures. The first Court opted for a North European approach in that it wished to embrace sound financial management, in addition to the legality and regularity of EU revenue and expenditure (Art. 188c, Treaty on European Union). In other words, the Court established a broad rather than narrow definition of external auditing. This increased the likelihood of tensions between the Court and those being audited. Like any new institution, the Court had to build an *esprit* among its members and staff. Establishing an *esprit de corps* was extremely difficult because the members of the Court were drawn from diverse backgrounds such as politics, national audit institutions and the legal profession. The professional staff in the Court tended to be lawyers and economists, with fewer qualified accountants than might be expected. Considerable work went into the production of an audit manual because the staff of the Court were drawn from such diverse auditing backgrounds. The Court has had to try to mould this diversity into a coherent approach to audit objectives and procedures (Levy 1996).

By 1981 the Court felt ready to adopt an audit approach which was suited to the context of the Community. It had to work out how best to carry out the Treaty provision that it examine 'all revenue and all expenditure'. The Court opted for a systems-based approach because it could not hope to analyse the 400,000 transactions that are involved in EU revenue and expenditure each year. A systems-based approach rests on the premise that financial management and control is dependent on the quality of internal control systems in any organisation. Thus the Court begins the audit trail by examining systems, procedures and records. Further, in-depth tests are then carried out to test a number of transactions based on a sampling technique. Both levels of analysis inform the Court's judgment on the legality and regularity of the transactions. Furthermore, the Court examines decision-making systems to assess whether or not the programmes represent 'value for money' (Desmond 1996: 21).

During its settling-in period, the Court had to grapple with establishing internal rules and procedures, deciding on its approach to auditing and attempting to mould its diverse staff and members into a cohesive external auditing body. Considerable organisational energy went into creating the new institution. Notwithstanding the clear evidence of experiential learning in the Court of Auditors in its early years, it remained on the margins of the Union's institutional landscape. It had great difficulty in making its presence felt in the wider EU framework. Officials in the other institutions considered that it was engaged in obscure, albeit worthy work. It had particular problems getting its voice heard within the Council. In 1983, the Stuttgart European Council asked the Court for a report on the management of EU finances. This was an important opportunity for the Court to raise its profile with the senior political level in the Union. The report echoed the Court's previous Annual Reports in that it covered all the main areas of expenditure and highlighted the key problems that recurred in relation to the management of the EU Budget. The Court offered specific suggestions for improving the effectiveness of EU expenditure, particularly in relation to the CAP and Structural Funds. The Court pointed out to the Council that most of what its special report contained had already been included in various other reports. The Court regretted that the Council had not established procedures to follow up its reports (Court of Auditors 1983). The Court's findings were not even discussed by the European Council and no follow-up was taken (Kok 1989: 358). This suggests that financial management had not yet become a salient issue on the EU agenda, a situation which was to change by the end of the 1980s.

Relations between the Commission and the Court of Auditors were problematic for many years. Prior to the establishment of the Court of Auditors, the Commission was largely unfettered in its management of the Community Budget because of the weakness of the Audit Board. The arrival of the Court of Auditors meant that the Commission had to come to terms with the presence of an external audit body with teeth and resources. The arrival of the Court transformed the Commission's regulatory environment. What was inevitably a difficult relationship was soured by an early conflict about the right of the Commission to reply to critical observations of the Court. The conflict about how the Court should present the Commission's replies or its observations created considerable hostility between the two bodies. Serious difficulties between the two institutions were only averted because of the moderating influence of the first Court President, Michael Murphy. Gradually, the Court worked out procedures for presenting its observations together with the replies of all institutions in its reports. Relations with the Commission were made difficult by other issues. The Commissioner for the Budget, Mr Tugendhat (1979–84), was deeply suspicious of the Court and its motives. In evidence to the House of Lords, he claimed that the Court had made two major mistakes. First, the Court believed that the European Parliament was going to be a much more important institution than it had turned out to be, and, according to the Commissioner, the Court was unwise to turn to the EP as its principal interlocutor. Second, the Court was too interested in seeking publicity for its activities (House of Lords 1987: 37). Furthermore, there was a dispute in 1979 about personal expenses incurred by individual commissioners. The Court provided evidence to the Parliament's Budgetary Control Committee about Commission expenses, which showed that they were indeed extravagant. The Commission was outraged that its President had to appear at a public hearing of the Committee to assure the members that new controls were in place. Both the Parliament and the Court of Auditors were attempting to assert their authority against the well-established Commission and wanted to put down markers about appropriate behaviour and norms. Following the departure of Commissioner Tugendhat in 1984, both institutions established a more harmonious relationship, although conflict continued about value-for-money auditing. The Commission, as would be the case for most auditees, was keen to protect its policy prerogatives and independence. In evidence to the House of Lords in 1989, the Financial Controller of the Commission suggested that the Commission had come to terms with the presence of the Court and that it recognised its useful role in the system (House of Lords 1989, Pratley evidence, p. 59).

Relations between the Court and the Commission deteriorated again, however, during Jacques Delors' tenure in Brussels. Jacques Delors and the then President of the Court André Middelhoek never met. The President of the Commission objected to the tone of a Court of Auditors' Report to the Council of Ministers in 1992 on EU spending. In its negotiations on the Delors II budget proposal (which sought to increase the overall EU Budget and especially the amount allocated to cohesion policy), the Council asked for the opinion of the Court. The Court, while accepting there had been improvements in the management of EU monies, stressed that there remained serious difficulties with the administrative and financial management of the budget. It was particularly critical of control of farm spending and the structural funds. Those who opposed a significant increase in structural spending used the report in the negotiations on the financial perspective. Delors felt that the Court was interfering in his attempt to increase the size of the budget. The following year, the presentation of the Court's report, a tome of some 450 pages, was accompanied by an information note for the press which highlighted key problems of financial management. The report received considerable exposure in the press, particularly in the UK. Euro-sceptic MP Bill Cash argued that British taxpayers were being asked to contribute to a 'bottomless, fraudulent pit' (*Financial Times*, 16 November 1994). The publication of the report coincided with the debate in the House of Commons on the increase in the EU's 'own resources' arising from the Edinburgh Agreement on the budget (Delors II). The Commission argued that the Court's resumé was inaccurate and was not a fair representation of financial management in the Union. Moreover, it protested that the Court had taken insufficient account of the improvements it had made in financial management. The Commission also stressed that it was up to the member states in the first instance to prevent irregularities in the use of EU monies (European Commission 1994). Commission officials argued that the Court felt sufficiently strong to criticise the Commission but was unwilling to take on the member states, the real culprits in their mind. President Middelhoek was criticised by the Commission as someone who 'was good at banging the drum about fraud and waste, but he's not so good at establishing the relationships to start putting things right' (quote from a Commission official, *Financial Times*, 19 November 1994). It should be noted that André Middelhoek was to return to the centre stage of EU financial management in 1999 when he was appointed by the EP as chair of the Committee of Independent Experts to investigate financial management in the Commission. In undertaking this task he was surely influenced by the older battles with the Commission.

The challenge of financial reform in the EU began increasingly to preoccupy the Commission in the latter half of the 1990s. When he assumed office in 1995, the new Commission President (Jacques Santer) placed considerable emphasis on internal Commission reform. With support from President Santer, the Budget Commissioner (Erkki Liikanen) embarked on a reform project – Sound and Efficient Management (SEM 2000) – in the Commission, designed to improve financial management (Laffan 1997b). Improving relations with the Court of Auditors was a central theme in the reform effort. However, the SEM programme, which was accompanied by other programmes of reform, was still being implemented when the question of financial management exploded on to the EU agenda in 1999.

There had been considerable tension inside the Commission about the SEM programme, largely due to a lack of internal consultation. During 1998, relations between the Commission and the European Parliament's Budgetary Control Committee deteriorated. The rapporteur of the Committee, James Ellis, recommended that the Parliament should not grant a discharge to the Commission for the 1996 budget, given a highly critical report from the Court of Auditors. By December, the discharge issue led to a major crisis between the two institutions, as the main party groups put down a motion of censure against the Commission for the January 1999 session. The Commission survived the vote in January, but only on the basis that a Committee of Independent Experts chaired by the former President of the Court of Auditors would report to the EP on financial management in the Commission. When the Committee's report was published in March 1999, the entire Santer Commission was forced to resign. The heads of state and government quickly moved to stem the crisis by nominating Romano Prodi as the next President of the Commission. Prodi took office in September 1999 with a mandate from the European Council to pursue reform within the Commission. The Commission President appointed Neil Kinnock as Vice-President for Administrative Reform in the Commission, with a key element of the reform programme being financial management.

Although the Court of Auditors did not play a major role in the resignation of the Commission, it provided the Parliament's Budgetary Control Committee with the material with which to pursue the issue of sound financial management at a political level. To a large extent, the subsequent resignation of the Commission and the ensuing reform programme elaborated by its successor have marked the Court of Auditors' coming of age in the EU system.

The Future of the Court of Auditors

The future of the Court will be determined by its role as external auditor in the Union and by the trajectory of EU finances. Given that the EU is about to expand to include a large number of new and poorer candidate countries, the EU budget will continue to form a very important instrument of public policy in the Union. EU finances are already deployed in the candidate countries, but the level of EU funding will increase dramatically following accession. We can thus anticipate a growing role for the Court in the new member states. The Court's relations with the Commission will be determined in some measure by the reform process in the Commission, and the degree to which the latter can enhance its management capacity. The Court will also need to improve its relations with the national audit offices in the future to ensure that there is extensive auditing of EU finances.

The future composition of the Court was agreed at Nice. With the prospect of twenty-seven or twenty-eight member states, the norm of one member per state was questioned during the Nice Intergovernmental Conference (IGC). However, the IGC concluded with a provision that the Court of Auditors will consist of 'one national from each Member State', thereby ensuring that the Court will grow as the EU expands (Treaty of Nice, Art. 247). The main argument in support of retaining existing practice (one member of the court for each member state) rested on the variety of auditing traditions in the member states: it was argued that the Court should have members with knowledge of each member state. The main argument for change rested on the difficulty of running an auditing body with twenty-seven or twenty-eight members. The decision at Nice will thus exacerbate the top-heavy character of the Court, and is also likely to pose managerial and efficiency problems in the future.

Summary

- Since 1977 the Court of Auditors has worked to establish itself in the Union's institutional landscape and has acted as an advocate for better management of the Union's budget. Like all EU institutions, it has to work in myriad languages, and with many auditing traditions and institutions. It has had to fashion an institutional identity for itself and also to fight for its place in the Union's institutional landscape.
- The EU's budget is deployed throughout the member states and in many third countries. The audit trail extends in many cases from the Commission to national public institutions, intermediate bodies and local agencies down to specific localities. Financial control and auditing in this environment is complex, patchy and unlikely to assure 'value for money' in all cases. There remain serious problems in relation to EU auditing and financial management.
- The Court's energies in the early years went into establishing standard operating procedures, refining its internal organisation and developing an approach to auditing that would suit the diversity of organisations that deploy the Union's budgetary resources.

- The Court has played a vital role in acting as an advocate of better financial management in the Union. It has drawn attention to all the major issues and was vindicated in the Schmidhuber testimonial of 1995. The growing size of the EU budget in addition to the expansion of the number of budgetary programmes has increased the salience of financial management. Gradually, the EU has strengthened the regulatory framework surrounding the budget, and increased the obligations on EU institutions and the member states to protect the financial interests of the Union. The constant references in the Court's reports to the need for better financial management bore fruit as the issue climbed the political agenda.
- The European Parliament used the work of the Court in its political battle with the Commission on the management of EU finances. The resignation of the Commission in March 1999 stemmed in part from the criticisms contained in successive Court reports.
- Constitutionally, legally and politically, the Court of Auditors has come in from the cold in the EU system. Its auditing function forms part of the unglamorous work necessary to ensure accountability and sound financial management in any democratic polity.

Test questions

1   What is the function of the Court of Auditors?
2   Explain the tensions in the relationships between the Court of Auditors and the main legislative institutions of the EU (Council, Commission and Parliament).
3   Why was the Court of Auditors elevated to the status of full EU institution?

Contact information

The Court of Auditors has a dedicated website: http://www.eca.eu.int.
Other means of making contact are the traditional methods.
Mail address: External Relations Department, European Court of Auditors, 12 Rue Alcide de Gasperi, L-1615 Luxembourg.
Tel: (+352) 4398 45410; *Fax*: (+352) 4398 46430.

Selected further reading

Kok, C. (1989) 'The Court of Auditors of the European Communities: The Other Court in Luxembourg', *Common Market Law Review*, 26: 345–67).
    Provides an inside view of the early development of the Court.

Laffan, B. (2001) 'Finance and Budgetary Processes in the European Union', in S. Bromley (ed.) *Governing the European Union*, London: Sage.
    Provides an overview of the EU budget and the financial context within which the Court of Auditors operates.

Levy, R. (2000) *Implementing European Union Public Policy*, Cheltenham: Edward Elgar.
This book analyses and evaluates the implementation of EU programes using the Court of Auditors' reports as the main source of data.

Ruimschotel, D. (1994) 'The EC Budget: Ten per cent Fraud? A Policy Analysis Approach', *Journal of Common Market Studies*, 32, 3: 319–42.
Provides a useful overview of the politics of fraud in the EU.

References

Alabau I. Oliveres, M.M. (1990) *Le Contrôle Externe Des Cours Des Comptes De L'Europe Communautaire*, Barcelona: University Institute for European Studies, Paper No. 1, February.

Court of Auditors (1983) *Report in Response to the Conclusions of the European Council of 18 June 1983*, Official Journal C 287, 26, 24 October 1983, pp.1–17.

Court of Auditors (1994) *Annual Report 1993*, Official Journal c327, 24 November.

Court of Auditors (1995) *Auditing the Finances of the European Union*, Luxembourg: Court of Auditors booklet.

Desmond, B. (1996) *Managing the Finances of the European Union: The Role of the European Court of Auditors*, Dublin: Institute of European Affairs.

Desmond, B. (1999) 'The European Court of Auditors', in J. Dooge and R. Barrington (eds) *A Vital National Interest: Ireland in Europe 1973–1998*, Dublin: IPA, pp. 113–25.

Duff, A. (1997) *The Treaty of Amsterdam – Text and Commentary*, London: Federal Trust/Sweet and Maxwell.

European Commission (1994) Press Release No. 39/94, 21 November.

European Commission (1995) Schmidhuber Memo on Financial Management, sect.95.26.

European Parliament (1996–7) Final Report and Recommendations, *Committee of Inquiry into the Community Transit System*, 19 February, A4–0053/97; www.europarl.eu.int/hearings/kelletta/default-en.htm

House of Lords (1987) *Report on the Court of Auditors*, Select Committee on the European Communities, Session 1986–87, 6th report (HL 102).

House of Lords (1989) *Fraud Against the Community*, Session 1988–89 (HL 27).

Kok, C. (1989) 'The Court of Auditors of the European Communities: The Other European Court in Luxembourg', *Common Market Law Review*, 26: 345–67.

Laffan, B. (1997a) *The Finances of the Union*, London: Macmillan.

Laffan, B. (1997b) 'From Policy Entrepreneur to Policy Manager: The Challenge Facing the European Commission', *European Journal of Public Policy*, 4, 3: 422–38.

Laffan, B. (1999) 'Becoming a Living Institution: The Evolution of the European Court of Auditors', *Journal of Common Market Studies*, 37: 251–68.

Levy, R. (1990) 'That Obscure Object of Desire: Budgetary Control in the European Community', *Public Administration*, 68: 191–206.

Levy, R. (1996) 'Managing Value-for-Money Audit in the European Union: The Challenge of Diversity', *Journal of Common Market Studies*, 34, 4: 509–29.

March, J.G. and Olsen, J.P. (1995) *Democratic Governance*, New York: The Free Press.

Mendrinou, M. (1994) 'European Community Fraud and the Politics of Institutional Development', *European Journal of Political Research*, 26, 1: 81–101.

Ruimschotel, D. (1993) 'The EC Budget: Ten Per Cent Fraud? A Policy Analysis', *EUI Florence, Working Papers EPU no.93/8*.

Strasser, D. (1992) *The Finances of Europe (7th edn)*, Luxembourg: EC Official Publications.

Wilmott, P. (1984) 'The European Court of Auditors: The First Five Years', *Public Administration*, 62: 211–18.

Chapter 8

The European Union Ombudsman

Philip Giddings, Roy Gregory and
Anthea Harris

Key facts

Created in 1994, following provision made in the Treaty of Maastricht (1992), the European Union Ombudsman is an office intended to promote 'good administration' within the institutions of the EU. The holder of the office is an independent official elected and financed by the European Parliament, whose principal role is to investigate complaints from European citizens of 'maladministration' by EU institutions. The Ombudsman, located in Strasburg, can also investigate possible maladministration by setting up 'own initiative inquiries'. However, he does not have powers of enforcement and so he must concentrate upon achieving a 'friendly settlement' for the complainant. In some cases the Ombudsman issues draft recommendations designed to improve administration and in others he directs a 'critical remark' towards the institution found guilty of maladministration. Even though the work of the Ombudsman has increased year on year, it is important to note that of the *circa* 1800 complaints received a year (only) about 200 result in investigations because the rest are almost all outside the Ombudsman's remit. However, in future the workload of the Ombudsman seems set to increase even more: the Charter of Fundamental Rights agreed upon at the Nice 2000 Summit includes the 'right to good administration' and the right to refer cases of maladministration to the Ombudsman.

The Ombudsman: powers and functions

Openness, accountability and citizenship are issues that in recent years have come to occupy an increasingly important place in debates about the EU and the working of its institutions. This is hardly surprising since, after almost half a century of expansion, both territorially and in terms of activities, the EU has developed a powerful administrative apparatus responsible for a vast volume of laws, rules and regulations, a growing number of which directly affect the citizen.

As one might expect, the more points of contact there have been between EU authorities and the citizen, the more opportunities have been generated for friction and the more grievances have arisen. In response, EU decision makers have sought to put in place various ways of dealing with complaints from EU citizens. These complaint-handling channels may be divided into three categories:

1   The Courts – either the Court of Justice or the Court of First Instance;
2   The Parliament – representations through MEPs or to the Petitions Committee;
3   The European Union Ombudsman (EUO) – currently Jacob Söderman.

The Courts and the Parliament are described in earlier chapters. Here we focus on the third channel – the office of the Ombudsman – which has emerged during the past five years as a key part of the EU's complaint-handling procedures and a force for change within the institutions of the EU.

Most Ombudsmen around the world operate within a nation state, at central, regional or local level (Gregory and Giddings, 2000). The EUO, although concerned like other Ombudsmen with investigating the complaints of members of the public against governmental authorities, functions at the *supranational* level. In this way the EUO is unique. There are a few other Ombudsman or Ombudsman-like agencies which function at an international level (e.g. the World Bank and the World Health Organization), but these offices are largely confined to internal staff complaints, and so cannot be compared with the office of the EUO.

Article 138e (par. 1) of the Treaty of European Union (1992) sets out the formal powers of the Ombudsman.[1] It provides that the European Parliament (EP) shall appoint an Ombudsman

> empowered to receive complaints from any citizen of the Union or any natural or legal person residing or having his registered office in a Member State concerning instances of maladministration in the activities of the Community institutions or bodies, with the exception of the Court of Justice and the Court of First Instance acting in their judicial role.

If there is one essential feature for an Ombudsman, it is that he must be entirely independent and impartial. In the case of the EUO both the Treaty provisions and the Ombudsman statute make clear that the Ombudsman shall be completely independent in the performance of his duties.[2] The Ombudsman Statute also requires that 'he must neither seek nor take instructions from any government or other body' (Statute, Article 9(1)). The Ombudsman may not, during his term of office, engage in any other occupation, whether gainful or not. His independence is underpinned by the fact that he is appointed by the EP and his office staffed and funded through it. It follows from this that the location of the office is that of the EP.

The Ombudsman may be dismissed only on the initiative of the Parliament if he 'no longer fulfils the conditions of his duties or is guilty of serious misconduct'. However, the actual decision to remove him from office is taken by the Court of Justice of the European Communities (Statute, Article 8), which in its judicial role is not open to investigation by the Ombudsman (Statute, Article 2(1)). As an impartial, independent, and yet highly informed participant in the day-to-day operations of the EU, therefore, the Ombudsman is well qualified to promote democracy and citizenship within its institutions in so far as good administrative practice is concerned. Thus, the EUO deals with faulty administration by the EU's administrative authorities. He may become involved as a result of a complaint. Any EU citizen, or any non-citizen living in a member state, can make a complaint to the Ombudsman. So can businesses, associations or other bodies which have a registered office within the Union. Complaints can be made to the Ombudsman directly or through an MEP. Most of the Ombudsman's cases arise as a result of complaints, but the Ombudsman is also empowered to begin investigations on his own initiative in an area which he believes is of concern.

The EUO is not authorised to investigate organs of government within member states of the Union; his mandate relates only to the governmental authorities of the Union itself. These are of three kinds:

- *Community Institutions*, i.e. the European Commission, the Council of Ministers, the EP, the Court of Justice, the Court of First Instance and the Court of Auditors;

- *Community bodies*, i.e. the Economic and Social Committee, the Committee of the Regions, the European Central Bank, the European Investment Bank, the European Coal and Steel Community Consultative Committee and the Euratom Supply Agency;
- *'Decentralised Agencies'*, which are located not in Brussels but in various cities across the Union, i.e. the European Foundation for the Improvement of Living and Working Conditions (Dublin); the European Centre for the Development of Vocational Training (Berlin/Thessalonica); the European Environment Agency (Copenhagen); the European Agency for the Evaluation of Medicinal Products (London); the European Monitoring Centre for Drugs and Drug Addiction (Lisbon); the European Training Foundation (Turin); the Office for Harmonisation in the Internal Market (Alicante); the Agency for Health and Safety at Work (Bilbao); the Office for Plant Varieties (Angers); the Translation Centre for Bodies of the European Union (Luxembourg); and Europol (The Hague).

As mentioned above, the EUO is a unique office as it is wholly concerned with the operations of supranational authorities. The supranationality of his office has not, however, prevented the Ombudsman from developing liaison arrangements with national Ombudsman offices. Indeed, in his first Annual Report (EUO, 1996: 31) the Ombudsman pointed out that a permanent relationship between the EU and national Ombudsmen is necessary because citizens do not always make a clear distinction between acts of national and of European Union administrations. Upon receipt of a complaint, the Ombudsman has to decide whether it falls within his mandate. At this point four questions have to be answered about the complaint:

1   Is the person complaining entitled to make a complaint?
2   Is the complaint against a Community institution, body or agency?
3   Is the complaint against the Court of Justice or the Court of First Instance acting in their judicial role?
4   Does the complaint concern a possible instance of maladministration?

If the Ombudsman decides that the complaint passed those four tests and so falls within his mandate, he then has to apply five further tests of admissibility laid down by the Ombudsman statute:

5   the author and the object of the complaint must be identified (Article 2.3);
6   the Ombudsman may not intervene in cases before the courts or question the soundness of a Court's ruling (Article 1.3);
7   the complaint must be made within two years of the date on which the facts on which it is based came to the attention of the complainant (Article 2.4);
8   the complaint must have been preceded by an approach to the administrative authorities concerned so that they have had a chance to deal with it (Article 2.4);
9   in complaints concerning personnel matters, the internal administrative and complaints process must have been exhausted before the complaint is brought to the Ombudsman (Article 2.8).

If the Ombudsman concludes that the complaint passes all these tests, he then instigates an inquiry by referring the complaint to the administrative agency concerned, which has a period of three months within which to inform him of its views. The Ombudsman encourages the administrative agency in question to seek a settlement directly with the complainant, but if this appears not to be possible, he then suggests a 'friendly settlement' arrived at through a form of mediation. On the rare occasions where neither of these approaches secure a satisfactory outcome, only then does the Ombudsman use one of the other tools at his disposal in order to make decisions about reforming decision-making procedures.

It is important to remember when looking at the EUO's decisions that nowhere do Ombudsmen exercise executive power to compel fresh decisions to be taken, or financial or other remedies to be provided. Their only weapon is the persuasive power of logic, reason and publicity. An Ombudsman's ultimate power lies in the right to report directly to the legislature, and therefore to go public. As Mr Söderman has put it:

> The European Union Ombudsman, like national Ombudsmen, is not empowered to order an administrative authority to change a decision or to give redress, even if a complaint is found to be justified. If a friendly settlement cannot be reached, the Ombudsman is limited to making reports and recommendations.
> (EUO, 1996: 12)

However, this does not mean an Ombudsman has no leverage. Results can sometimes be achieved in the face of opposition because of the power to embarrass. Failure or refusal to respond positively to an Ombudsman's findings and recommendations is to invite trouble, both in the legislature and in the media. In countries where public opinion matters, in the eyes of most administrative agencies trouble in those quarters is something to be avoided. Hence it is a major part of the EUO's work to expose instances of persistent maladministration. His role is to investigate complaints and establish in what ways the agency concerned has made a mistake or is to blame, and then if the matter is still not put right, to refer the matter to Parliament.

After an investigation the Ombudsman may of course find that the complaint was not justified. Alternatively he may find that there had been a mistake, misunderstanding or incorrect assessment on the part of the complainant. In this event, he will simply file the matter after informing the complainant. In other cases he may establish that a problem exists, and go on to secure a rapid and full settlement through conciliation or mediation. In the most serious cases, or where the administration refuses to recognise the wrongdoing he has found, the Ombudsman will draw up a formal report on the cases and refer the matter to the EP, with his own conclusions and recommendations. Parliament then has the chance to take action at the political level, particularly by taking the matter up with the Commission, which under the treaties is accountable to Parliament. The EP has various ways of bringing pressure to bear on the Commission (see Burns, Chapter 4, this volume). In this way Parliament's political power acts as the citizen's ultimate guarantee: the EP is, so to speak, 'the Ombudsman's right arm in the service of the citizens of the Union' (Giraud, 1995: 13).

A feature of some Ombudsman schemes, which can enhance their effectiveness, is a link with a committee of the legislature. A committee of this kind, monitoring official responses to Ombudsman reports, can do a great deal to help secure appropriate remedial action in cases where the agency concerned is disposed to resist their recommendations. In the EP the Committee on Petitions has taken on the role of acting as the link between the Ombudsman and the Parliament. It considers and assesses the political implications of the Ombudsman's Annual Report as well as examining reports on individual cases and submitting proposals for resolving them. Parliament, the Committee has declared, has a special relationship with the Ombudsman and a strong interest in supporting him in every respect.[3] For example, if the Ombudsman is refused information, Parliament should take steps to ensure that all the papers and documents he requests are actually forwarded to him. It is therefore the Petitions Committee's practice to invite the Ombudsman to attend its meetings in order to discuss matters of common interest – whether general or specific. In this way, the Committee and the Ombudsman have begun to work together to overcome the potential difficulties arising from the EP's earlier hostility to the Ombudsman concept.[4]

The general principle which guides Ombudsmen in deciding on remedies when they find public authorities have made mistakes is that so far as possible the complainant should be restored to the position he or she would have occupied had matters not gone wrong. According to the Ombudsman Statute, where the EUO identifies an instance of maladministration, as far as possible he 'shall seek a solution' designed to 'eliminate' it and 'to satisfy the complainant' (Statute, Article 3(5)). His first task, therefore, is to seek to work out and reach an amicable settlement which gives satisfaction to the person lodging the complaint. This action may itself lead to a satisfactory resolution. In this way the Ombudsman's role is to act as mediator, as indicated by the French translation of the word 'Ombudsman' – *Médiateur*. By seeking amicable solutions the Ombudsman helps to relieve the burden of litigation by promoting acceptable settlements and making recommendations that avoid the need for proceedings in courts. If this is achieved, he closes the case in question with a reasoned decision. He informs the citizen and the institution concerned of the decision he has reached.

If an amicable outcome is not achieved and the Ombudsman decides that maladministration has occurred, the Ombudsman has three choices: he can either close the case with a reasoned decision that may include a 'critical remark'; he can make a report which contains draft recommendations; or he can issue a 'special report' to the EP. An aggrieved person may derive some satisfaction from having his or her complaint upheld, even if no other action is taken by way of remedy. Such a situation relates to the use of the 'critical remark' by the Ombudsman. As the rules governing the internal operation of the office indicate, the Ombudsman is likely to choose the first option – to close the case with a critical remark – if he considers that it is no longer possible for the institution or body concerned to eliminate the instance of maladministration *and* that the instance of maladministration has no general implications. In such cases the Ombudsman will inform the citizen and the institution concerned of his decision.

The Ombudsman is likely to choose the second option – to make a report with draft recommendations to the institution or body concerned – if he considers *either* that it is possible for the institution or body concerned to eliminate the instance of maladministration, *or* that the instance of maladministration has general implications. In these cases the Ombudsman sends a copy of his report and draft recommendations to the institution concerned and to the citizen. Within three months the institution concerned should send the Ombudsman a detailed opinion which should consist of acceptance of the Ombudsman's decision and a description of the measures taken to implement the recommendations.

If the Ombudsman does not consider that the detailed opinion is satisfactory, he draws up a special report to the EP containing his findings and recommendations. The Ombudsman sends a copy of his report to the institution concerned and to the citizen. In practice, special reports to the EP are rarely needed. This is because in most cases the institutions, especially the Commission, respond positively to the Ombudsman's findings. As we shall see when we consider the Ombudsman's record, friendly settlements have often been reached directly with the complainant by the institution after receiving the complaint from the Ombudsman.

Some critics have suggested that the EUO is in a weaker position than most national Ombudsmen are in this respect. Mr Söderman, by contrast, points out that his powers are substantially the same as those of the Danish Ombudsman, upon which the EUO office is based: that is, 'the right to argue, to recommend and to report'. Mr Söderman's view is that this should be sufficient in a democratic society with a commitment to an open and accountable public administration. Even in those countries where the office has stronger powers (like Sweden and Finland), those powers are seldom used and the Ombudsman has 'slowly become more a conciliator than a repressive figure' (Söderman, 1997: 12). In Mr Söderman's view, this should be true at the EU level. The fact that he has had some success in seeking to achieve this can be seen in the case studies in Section 3 below.

History and evolution of the EU Ombudsman

Date	Event
1994	'Statute of the European Ombudsman' adopted by European Parliament, and thus EU Ombudsman office set up in order to deal with maladministration in the institutions of the EU.
1995	First Ombudsman, Jacob Söderman, elected by the European Parliament.
1996	First own-initiative inquiry launched, dealing with public access to documents held by Community bodies.
	First Special Report to the President of the European Parliament presented (dealing with outcome of own-initiative inquiry).
1997	The Treaty of Amsterdam extends the EUO's remit to include the Central European Bank, the Community Plant Variety Office, the European Agency for Health and Safety at Work and Europol.

> 1998   The Ombudsman begins own-initiative inquiry into the existence and public accessibility of a code of good administrative behaviour for EU officials.
>
> 2000   Jacob Söderman re-elected for a further term of five years.
>
> Nice Summit agrees to adopt the Charter of Fundamental Rights and Freedoms, which includes the 'right to good administration'.

By the late 1980s, following the expansion of the EU, there were moves to create a complaint-handling body that would overcome many of the problems associated with the traditional procedures of courts and Parliament. The new complaint-handling body needed to be less expensive to use than the courts, and more equitable in terms of opportunity of access than making a representation via one's MEP. Even in instances where citizens can afford litigation, taking a case through the courts can often be a complicated, costly and slow process. In addition, individuals have no standing at the ECJ – they must have their case brought for them by the Commission or the national courts. Moreover, even if an MEP were willing to use the political process in order to voice constituents' individual complaints, these representations may not be effective. Denied access to the internal files of public offices, they are not always in a position to see through the veil of official secrecy that may sometimes conceal governmental wrongdoing. Furthermore, the partisan structure and orientation of the EP was not seen as helping its effectiveness as a mechanism through which MEPs might secure administrative justice for their aggrieved constituents (Owen, 1993).

Although the idea of appointing a 'European Ombudsman' was mooted at least three times in the 1970s, it was not discussed in any depth either by the Commission or by the Parliament until 1985. At this juncture, it resurfaced in response to the Report of the Adonnino Committee on 'A People's Europe', but opinion in the EP proved to be firmly against it, partly because of a lack of familiarity with the Ombudsman concept among the original member states. This state of affairs had not changed two years later when, in June 1987, the Parliament passed resolutions stating its preference for a petitions committee, feeling that it would be impossible to transpose the Ombudsman institution into the different legal systems operating in the Community (Marias, 1994).

Moves to adopt the Ombudsman institution were finally given substance in February 1992 when provision for an Ombudsman was made in Articles 8d and 138e of the Maastricht Treaty.[5] This provision was one of the outcomes of the debates about democratising the EU and how notions of 'European citizenship' could be promoted. The idea was that an Ombudsman would help to establish a relationship of confidence between the institutions and the citizen, based on transparency in the Community's administration. Within two years, the provisions of Maastricht had been followed up by 'The Statute of the European Ombudsman' which was adopted by the EP on 9 March 1994. Following a false start in the autumn of 1994, when procedural difficulties made it impossible to make an appointment, the first European Union Ombudsman, Jacob Söderman (formerly Parliamentary Ombudsman of Finland), was elected by the EP on 12 July 1995 and began work in September 1995.

We shall look in more detail at the Ombudsman's record since 1995 in another section. It is important to note, however, that the workload of the office has already increased rapidly, as citizens become more willing to direct their complaints towards the Ombudsman. At the same time, Mr Söderman has developed other aspects of the EUO's role within the EU, first meeting with members of the Petitions Committee as early as January 1996, issuing an Annual Report in April of that year and opening the first own-initiative inquiry two months later.

Although the present Ombudsman has always maintained the importance of individual complaints as a focus of the EUO's work, he has also sought to develop a more far-reaching approach to decision-making procedure reform. One of the most significant steps to developing such an approach was the adoption of the Charter of Fundamental Rights and Freedoms – which includes the 'right to good adminis-tration' – by government representatives at the Nice Summit in November 2000. This step had been championed by the EUO, specifically by seeking to improve transparency. This has been done in two ways: first, by ensuring citizens have more access to documents; and second, by promoting the codification of principles of good administrative behaviour across the bodies of the EU. In October 2000 Mr Söderman was re-elected for a further term of office (five years). Therefore, we can expect to see this agenda being implemented in the near future.

The Ombudsman and EU administration: promoting good practice?

The contribution of the EUO to reforming EU administration

The EUO has two principal tools for promoting good administration in the EU: examining individual complaints, mostly from private citizens, and setting up own-initiative inquiries into areas where maladministration is suspected to be more endemic. Most of the EUO's work concerns individual complaints, but in recent years the Ombudsman has broadened the scope of his work, adopting a more proactive approach to improving citizens' experience of dealing with the EU. The 1998 to 2000 own-initiative inquiry into the development of a Code of Good Administrative Behaviour, intended to cover all areas of the EU institutions' work, can be seen in this context. So too can the push to include the 'right to good administration' in the Charter of Fundamental Rights and Freedoms which national governments finally agreed to adopt as part of the TEU at the end of 2000. Nevertheless, the Ombudsman remains limited by the fact that he has no executive powers and can only *persuade* the relevant bodies to take action.

The EUO makes an impact on the EU's administration in two ways: through the handling of complaints and through own-initiative inquiries. We first consider complaint-handling as a whole, which is the bulk of the office's work. We then consider two types of case study: (1) two environmental cases arising from complaints; and then (2) examples of the EUO's use of his own-initiative power.

The first thing to notice is that, in common with most Ombudsman offices, a large proportion of the complaints the EUO receives are either outside his mandate or otherwise inadmissible [see Figure 8.1].[6] So, of the 7000 complaints received between opening office in 1995 and the end of December 2000, only 1000 cases actually resulted in an inquiry by the Ombudsman. Overwhelmingly (see Figure 8.2), complaints come from individual citizens, with associations and companies accounting for about one in twelve. Fewer than 1 per cent were referred on by MEPs.

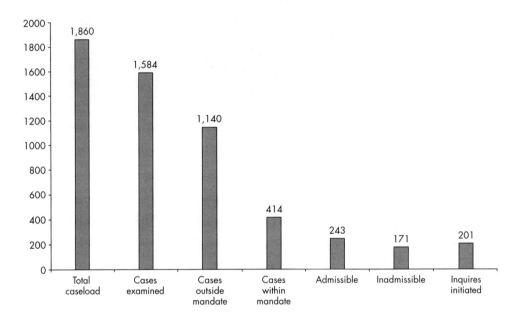

Figure 8.1 EU Ombudsman's caseload 1999

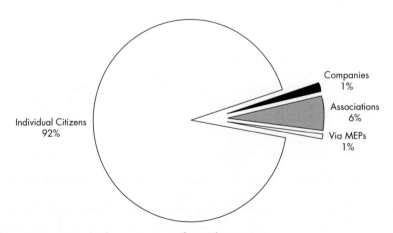

Figure 8.2 EU Ombudsman: source of complaints 1999

As one might expect given the relative size and nature of their responsibilities, of the various EU bodies it is the Commission which is the target of most of the complaints made to the EUO (see Figure 8.3). The main types of maladministration alleged (see Figure 8.4) have been lack of transparency, discrimination, unsatisfactory procedures, unfairness, avoidable delay and failure by the Commission to carry out its role as 'Guardian of the Treaties'.

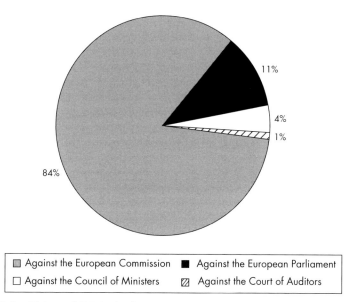

Figure 8.3 Objects of EU Ombudsman's inquiries 1995–2000 (main institutions)

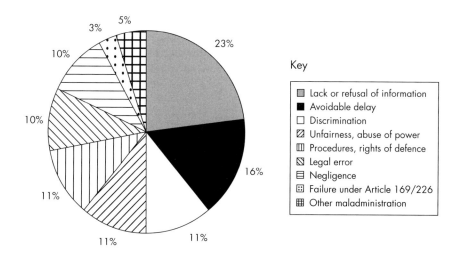

Figure 8.4 EU Ombudsman types of maladministration alleged 1999

What has the EUO achieved for the complainants? In over half of the cases no maladministration was found, and in a further quarter the institution concerned settled the case as soon as the Ombudsman began his inquiry (see Figure 8.5). One hundred and forty inquiries were closed with a critical remark to the institution concerned, and only twenty-six resulted in draft recommendations to the institutions and bodies concerned. In fifteen of these cases his recommendations were accepted. In four other cases, all of them cases taken up on his own initiative, the Ombudsman presented a special report to the EP.

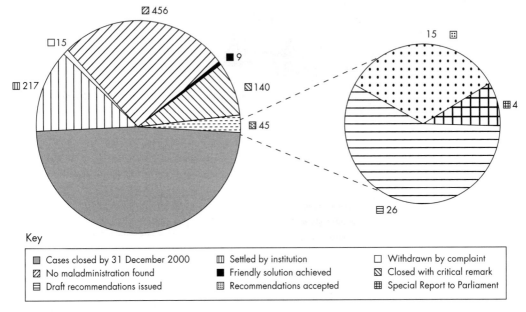

Figure 8.5 Outcomes of EU Ombudsman's inquiries (numbers of cases 1995–2000)

To what extent the outcomes achieved can be considered 'satisfactory' is a moot point. From Figure 8.5 one could perhaps deduce that about a quarter of the closed cases were settled satisfactorily, i.e. those settled by the institution after the EUO had opened an inquiry plus those in which a 'friendly solution' was achieved. It is also worth noting that in some of the many cases which he ruled were inadmissible, the Ombudsman was able to advise complainants about alternative courses of action they might take. Thus he has advised complainants to:

- complain to a national or regional Ombudsman or to petition a national Parliament (1411 cases);
- petition the EP (550 cases);
- apply to the European Commission (580 cases), the Court of Justice (five cases), the Court of Auditors (two cases) or other bodies (445 cases).

In relation to the total population of the member states of the European Union these figures are of course minuscule, and, given that most citizens of the EU have little direct contact with its institutions, that is only to be expected. From the point of view of citizens as a whole, it is the general character and culture of European administration which matters. It is thus helpful to examine a selection of important cases brought to the attention of the EUO in order to make a more solid assessment of his impact to date.

We are going to examine two cases in the field of environmental protection, the handling of which raised issues that could affect the lives of EU citizens as a whole. One case concerned the building of the Newbury Bypass in England and the other concerned the holding of French nuclear tests in Polynesia. These were initiated by citizens' complaints about the failure of the Commission to take action against a member state which appeared not to be fulfilling its Treaty obligations.

Case study 1: The Newbury Bypass

The issue

In the Newbury Bypass case the complainants argued that the British government had breached Community law by failing to carry out an environmental impact assessment of the planned bypass (EUO, 1997: 58–66).[7] They alleged maladministration by the Commission in deciding not to open infringement proceedings against the United Kingdom under Article 169 of the Treaty on European Union.[8] The issue at stake was whether and how to apply a particular Council Directive. The draft orders for the bypass were published and the public inquiry had begun before the Directive came into effect.

The Commission's response

When the complainants had put their case to the Commission in 1994, the Commission had responded with a press release. This said that, in the light of an ECJ decision in another case,[9] it had decided that the Directive did not apply to the Newbury Bypass. This was because, in the Commission's view, the Directive required only environmental impact assessments for projects where the procedure for consent started after the Directive had come into effect.

This response did not convince the complainants so they decided to take their case to the Ombudsman. They argued that the Commission had misinterpreted the ECJ's ruling on when Directives applied, and that its response to their complaint showed that its decisions on the Newbury Bypass had been arbitrary and disingenuous. The complainants also said that by announcing its decision to the media in October, but not informing the complainants until December, the Commission had failed in its obligation to keep the complainants informed of the progress of their case.

The Ombudsman's findings

In his findings the Ombudsman supported the Commission's decision that an environmental impact assessment was not required. However, he did criticise the way in which the Commission had responded to the complainants, especially in providing only a very brief, and possibly incomplete, outline of the legal backing for its conclusion. The Ombudsman also criticised the Commission for not telling the complainants of its decision before announcing it in a press release – that was not what the Ombudsman considered 'good administrative behaviour'.

As a result of this and several other complaints (including one on the M40 motorway),[10] the Ombudsman decided he should carry out a more general examination – an 'own-initiative inquiry' – into the procedural position of individual complainants under Article 169 which makes the Commission the 'Guardian of the Treaties'. His reasoning here is significant. In his view, this would help to show the EU's commitment to open, democratic and accountable forms of administration and respond to the dissatisfaction among some European citizens, who regarded the Commission's style as arrogant and high-handed. So, although the Newbury Bypass case did not result in the Ombudsman persuading the Commission to change its decision, it did help to bring about a wider review of the way in which Commission decisions are made. We will be looking at what that review led to below.

Case study 2: The French nuclear tests

The issue

In late 1995 and early 1996 the Ombudsman received complaints that the Commission had failed to respond properly to the French government's announced intention to carry out nuclear tests in the Pacific Ocean (EUO, 1997: 21–3). Although most of the complaints did not actually specify which legal provisions had been breached, the Commission took it that they referred to the provisions of Article 34 of the Euratom Treaty requiring a member state to take additional health and safety measures when carrying out a particularly dangerous experiment.

The Commission's response

The Commission argued in reply to these complaints that it had in fact sought to ensure that the Treaty provisions had been fully respected. In particular, it had gathered and assessed information, including a specialist report on the release of radioactivity in the water. It had also sent a verification mission in September 1995 to check the efficiency of the monitoring facilities. The Commission had concluded in October 1995 that as the tests did not involve a perceptible risk of significant exposure of workers or of the population to radiation, the provisions of Article 34 did not apply.

The Ombudsman's findings

The Ombudsman noted that the Commission had annexed to its comments a list of the twenty-five main documents upon which it had based its conclusions. These had been sent to the complainants but most had chosen not to comment on them. Having examined the Commission's response, the Ombudsman concluded that the Commission had not exercised its powers wrongly or incompletely and therefore that there was no instance of maladministration.

We turn now to our second pair of case studies. The own-initiative inquiries conducted by the EUO address issues that lie at the heart of the current debate on the functions and future of the EU, and particularly the character of its administration. Administrative culture is not set in stone, but can be changed by the actions of participants in the administrative process. One of the Ombudsman's designated tasks is to help shape the culture of the European institutions in such a way that good administration becomes natural to them. The principal tool he has for doing this is the 'own-initiative report', a comprehensive and systemic inquiry which potentially has the ability to affect large numbers of people throughout the EU. Of course, it is difficult to estimate how many citizens' rights to good administration have been protected in this way since the setting up of the Ombudsman's office, because the effect of these inquiries is largely 'preventative'.

Case study 3: Transparency

In the late 1990s, in the midst of a debate about the alleged lack of 'transparency' in the European Union institutions, the Ombudsman called for the EU to promote 'transparency' in its administrative dealings (Söderman, 1998). By 'transparency', he meant that the processes through which public authorities make decisions about citizens' complaints should be understandable and open; that the decisions themselves should be reasoned; and that, as far as possible, the information on which the decisions are based should be available to the public.

An increasing number of complaints which – either directly or indirectly – alleged lack of transparency had prompted the Ombudsman to undertake an own-initiative inquiry into the matter in 1996 (EUO, 1997: 81).[11] The aim of the inquiry was to ensure that rules for making information accessible to the public existed, and that the public was made aware of them. Accordingly, by August 1997, all but one of the fifteen EU bodies consulted had drawn up rules concerning public access to information. The exception was the ECJ, which argued that it was too difficult to distinguish documents relating to its judicial role from those that did not. Later, in April 1999, the inquiry was extended to those bodies which had become operational since 1997 – the European Central Bank, the Community Plant Variety Office, the European Agency for Health and Safety at Work, and Europol. They (again with one exception) responded by adopting rules concerning access to their administrative documents, and making these available to the public. Europol, which had initially resisted the recommendations of the Ombudsman, eventually adopted them to the satisfaction of his office in July 2000.

For the present, however, there is no Treaty Article or general Community legislation about public access to documents. Therefore, to persuade the EU institutions to make information more readily available to those citizens who asked for it, the Ombudsman had to employ the Declaration on the right of access to information which comprised part of the Treaty of Amsterdam's modifications of the TEU (Article A, par. 2).

Case study 4: A Code of Good Administrative Behaviour

In November 1998, the Ombudsman opened another own-initiative inquiry. This was aimed at developing a Code of Good Administrative Behaviour, which further illustrated his concerns with the everyday operations of the EU (EUO, 2000b: 19–20).[12] His intention was that such a Code would incorporate two aspects of administrative justice: substantive principles – such as lawfulness, equality of treatment, proportionality, avoidance of abuse of power, abstention in cases of personal interest, legal certainty, fairness and consistency – and procedural principles. These latter related to keeping people properly and fully informed of decisions made by the institutions, allowing them the opportunity to make their case, and making sure that they are aware of the mechanisms for appealing against decisions.

This call for a codification of good administrative behaviour received a mixed response. The Commission drafted a Code of Conduct dealing with most of the principles the Ombudsman had suggested be incorporated, but it was decided not to adopt this Code until further consultations with other institutions had taken place. This, together with the installation of a new Commission after the 'Santer crisis', resulted in the Commission making no further moves to develop a Code of Conduct during 1999.

Responses from the other institutions were even less constructive. In the face of these unsatisfactory responses from the other institutions, the Ombudsman concluded that there was no evidence of any code of good administrative behaviour being developed at an institutional level. He subsequently issued his own draft recommendations in September 1999 and spoke out about what he saw as a rejection of his efforts: 'The refusal to adopt . . . a Code . . . will show that nothing has really changed since the collapse of the last Commission. It demonstrates the gap between the fine words pronounced by the Commission President . . . and the reality of the actions put into place' (EUO, 1999b).

In April 2000, by which time still only six of the eighteen institutions addressed had adopted a Code, the Ombudsman went further. He exercised his powers under Article 3 (7) of the Statute of the European Ombudsman to present a Special Report to the EP. In this report he recommended the enactment of a European administrative law to ensure that officials of all the Community institutions observed the same principles of good administrative behaviour in their relations with the public (EUO, 2000b). Eventually the institutions started to respond, beginning with the Commission. The Commissioner with responsibility for administrative reform, Neil Kinnock, issued a Code of Good Behaviour that came into force on 1 November 2000. This is a legally binding document (both on individual members of staff and on the Commission as a whole) which sets out the obligations incumbent on officials and guidelines for good administrative practice. It also draws attention to the existence and role of the Ombudsman. At the time of writing, the Code has not yet received its first monitoring report (due end of 2001), but these are expected to become regular features of the Code's working life.

Codes, of course, still fall short of the Ombudsman's ultimate objective of an administrative law. Thus, we can see from this case study that the reform of decision making within the structures of the EU is often a complex and time-consuming matter, with a tendency for rhetoric and action to become separated. The case study illustrates, too, the fact that the Ombudsman cannot force the institutions to take one particular action or another. His methods are those of persuasion, not enforcement. Consequently, in this case, he drew on his tool of negative publicity: he published the institutions' initial responses to his proposals and drew attention to the Parliament's own resolution, stressing the urgent need to draw up a publicly accessible code as soon as possible. He then contrasted this with the slow responses he had subsequently received, making sure that his actions received wide media coverage in the appropriate quarters.

Although slow, and as yet limited in scope, these developments demonstrate the effectiveness of the Ombudsman as an agent for transforming the organisational culture and practices of EU institutions. This aspect of the Ombudsman's role should not be underestimated – cultural change is always incremental and often slow – because it has the potential to affect the many European citizens who would not otherwise come into contact with the Ombudsman.

After the Nice Treaty: Prospects for the EU Ombudsman

Prediction in government and politics is always a risky business. Predicting the future of an institution such as the EUO, the fortunes of which are so much determined by the decisions and perceptions of others, is particularly hazardous. The attitudes of citizens, Community officials, European parliamentarians and national governments are all likely to play a part in shaping the development of this unique, supranational oversight body.

The Ombudsman's jurisdiction at present covers only administrative action taken by the 'institutions and bodies' of the European Community. The most radical change in his role would be to transform the office into a body supervising the rights of European citizens under Community law at all levels in the European Union, even at the national, regional and municipal levels. This was the function originally envisaged for it by some of the architects of the scheme.

A move of that kind would have at least two advantages. First, in terms of fairness: the application of EU law would be monitored by a single oversight agency bringing to bear consistent standards of good administration, rather than by a variety of national and subnational Ombudsmen as at present. Second, with a wider mandate the EUO would not have to reject such a large percentage of the complaints referred to him. As we have seen, many complaints have to be rejected at present because they are against national administrations and consequently outside his jurisdiction. The inability to investigate cases referred to the office is always damaging to an Ombudsman's standing. On the other hand, to extend the EUO's mandate to matters currently covered by national and regional Ombudsmen would seem to run counter to the 'principle of subsidiarity'. Moreover, the task of monitoring the implementation at all levels of government in each of the member states of the large and growing body of European law would also inevitably require an EUO bureaucracy of formidable proportions. For these reasons it is not easy to see the governments of member states agreeing to such a development.

However, the EUO's caseload does seem certain to expand significantly for other reasons. It might do so if, for example, there were a further increase in Community action impinging directly on the citizen (perhaps in the areas of immigration or visa control); or an extension to the functions performed by the Commission. Likewise, the Ombudsman's caseload might expand if there was an increase in the number of 'decentralised' institutions and bodies, such as occurred as a result of the 1992 Edinburgh Summit. Such developments would result in a considerable widening of the administrative action potentially the subject of complaint to the Ombudsman.

Possibilities of that kind are highly speculative. Two other developments likely to add to the EUO's workload appear much more probable. In the first place, as EU citizens gradually become more aware of the existence of the Ombudsman and better informed about his functions, the number of complaints referred to the office will almost certainly continue to rise. Second, and more dramatically, the number of potential complainants will also rise as a result of the enlargement of the EU into Central and Eastern Europe. In most of the countries likely to be admitted in the course of the next decade or so, the Ombudsman concept is already reasonably well established. For the citizens of these new entrants, the right to complain to an Ombudsman will be neither novel nor strange.

There is one further consideration which could strengthen citizens' propensity to complain to the Ombudsman. This is the adoption at the Nice Summit in 2000 of the Charter of Fundamental Rights of the European Union. Among the rights included in the Charter is the 'right to good administration': Article 41 states that '[e]very person has the right to have his or her affairs handled impartially, fairly and within a reasonable time by the institutions and bodies of the Union'. At the same time, Article 43 declares that citizens of the Union have the right to refer to the Ombudsman 'cases of maladministration in the activities of Community institutions or bodies'. This explicit reference to the role of the Ombudsman, together with the expression of the right to good administration, could well encourage citizens to seek the Ombudsman's services – at the national as well as the European level of government – despite the Charter's limited legal force.

The fact is, however, that in terms of scale even a much larger and growing Ombudsman caseload will always remain minuscule in relation to the total population of the Union. If the Ombudsman is to make a significant impact on the quality of administrative action it is much more likely to be by means of his systemic inquiries, often undertaken on his own initiative.

If the EUO is to react to an increased workload thoroughly and expeditiously, the office will require increased resources. In the year 2000 there was a staff establishment of twenty-three and a revenue budget of 346,761 euros. Increased resources, in turn, could permit the office to operate more proactively in its efforts to promote good administration. A significant number (17 per cent) of the Ombudsman's investigations, as we have seen (Figure 8.5), are closed with a 'critical remark'. Part of the idea behind the critical remark is to *seek to avoid a repetition* in the future. However, as Mr Söderman himself has pointed out, 'the weakness of this solution consists in the fact that so far the Ombudsman has not been able, due to his heavy workload, to check systematically whether the administration takes heed of these critical remarks in future cases'. An increase in resources would allow him to tackle this problem (Söderman, 2000).

Essential to the effective performance of an Ombudsman's functions are adequate powers of investigation. Under Article 3 (2) of the Statute access to an official file can be refused on duly substantiated grounds of secrecy. Moreover, officials of Community institutions and bodies when testifying at the request of the Ombudsman are bound by their duty of professional secrecy and must speak in accordance with instructions from their administrations. These limitations, Mr Söderman argued in 1998, are unnecessary, inappropriate and unacceptable. It would be better, he maintained, for the Treaty to make clear that the Ombudsman has full access, for the purposes of his inquiries, to the files and documents held by Community institutions and bodies, and that officials must give full and truthful testimony to the Ombudsman (EUO, 1998: 12). Accordingly, in 1999 Mr Söderman did indeed present an initiative to the EP to amend those parts of the EUO Statute that had produced disputes between his office and the Commission concerning his right to inspect documents (EUO, 1999a: 12). Although not yet resolved, the outcome of this initiative will surely show the extent to which the EP is willing to support the EUO's attempts to enhance the effectiveness of his office.

Finally, speculation about the future of the office of EUO would be incomplete without reference to an additional, and crucially important, power exercised by the EP – electing the Ombudsman. To a greater extent than most other public bodies, the office of Ombudsman reflects the qualities, priorities and personality of its incumbent. At the time of writing, the post of EUO has been filled, following keenly contested elections in 1995 and 1999, by a single occupant, Jacob Söderman. Mr Söderman is a former Parliamentary Ombudsman of Finland and very much in the Nordic and Northern European tradition. He is concerned to publicise the office rather than himself, and committed both to putting individual wrongs right and to promoting high standards of public administration. In future elections for the post of EUO an increasingly important part will be played by MEPs from Eastern and Central European countries, where human rights issues occupy a more central position in the Ombudsman's mandate, which in that respect differs from the older offices in Western Europe. With national, regional and political considerations very much at work in elections conducted by the EP, future holders of the EUO office may well need to adopt a different, more campaigning, style from Mr Söderman's, one more concerned with advocacy on behalf of causes deemed worthy of support. Whether such a style would prove more or less effective in promoting democratic values and helping to underpin the legitimacy of the European Union would be a subject for much debate.

Summary

- The EUO is an independent official elected by the EP to investigate and report on individual citizens' complaints about administrative action. The Ombudsman's success and legitimacy depend upon his perceived independence and impartiality.
- The Ombudsman is entitled to investigate complaints of maladministration against EU institutions only. He cannot investigate the administrative procedures of member states and their governments, and for this reason many of the complaints addressed to the Ombudsman have to be declared 'inadmissible'. However, the Ombudsman has developed liaison arrangements with national and regional Ombudsman offices in member states.
- Reflecting his preference for a mediatorial rather than adversarial style, the Ombudsman, with the support of the EP, always aims for a 'friendly settlement' in cases where maladministration is found to have occurred. Sometimes he also chooses to make a 'critical remark' against the institution found guilty of maladministration. Other tools available to him include 'draft recommendations' and 'special reports' to the EP. The Ombudsman does not have the power to enforce his recommendations; the office is principally a persuasive and recommendatory body.
- Since the creation of the office in 1994 and the appointment of its first holder in 1995, the Ombudsman has sought to promote greater transparency in the administrative procedures of the EU, as well as participating in moves to create a stronger sense of 'citizenship' among the citizens of the Union. Most notably in recent years, he has been a strong proponent for the creation of a Code of Good Administrative Behaviour, which would harmonise and codify administrative practice.
- Although one of the youngest institutions of the EU, the Ombudsman's workload grew rapidly during the late 1990s, prompting calls for the office to be given greater resources to promote good administration. Thus, the Ombudsman looks set to become a more important and influential institution in future years.

Test questions

1. When and why was the office of the Ombudsman set up?
2. How successful has the Ombudsman been in resolving specific complaints against the institutions of the EU? How might the office's 'success' rate be increased?
3. Is the Ombudsman a useful vehicle for promoting cultural change in the administrative procedures of the EU?

Contact information

- By internet: http://www.euro-ombudsman.eu.int
- By mail: The European Ombudsman
               1 avenue du Président Robert Schuman
               BP 403
               F-67001 Strasburg Cedex
               France
- By telephone: +33 (0) 3 88 17 40 01
- By fax: +33 (0) 3 88 17 90 62
- By email: euro-ombudsman@europarl.eu.int

Notes

1   Since the signing of the Amsterdam Treaty in 1997, Article 138e has been renumbered as Article 195.
2   The Statute for the provision of the European Ombudsman can be found in full on the EUO's website, as can all other quotations from the Ombudsman's office and Jacob Söderman used in this chapter.
3   See: EP, 1994.
4   In July 1985 the EP passed a resolution saying that differences between national legal systems and the Community system made it impossible to transpose the Ombudsman institution into the Community system. A parliamentary petitions committee was thought to be preferable. See OJ C175, 15 July 1985 and EP Debates, 1987, No. 2 – 353/91 and 353/92.
5   See note 1. Article 8d has been renumbered as Article 21.
6   The statistics represented in the figures which follow, as well as the other statistics quoted in the rest of this chapter, are taken from EUO (2000c).
7   See: http://www.euro-ombudsman.eu.int/decision/en/950206.htm.
8   Since the signing of the Amsterdam Treaty in 1997, Article 169 has been renumbered as Article 226.
9   The Grosskrotzenburg Case, C431/92, *Commission v. Germany*, judgment of 11 August 1995.
10 See: EUO, 1997: 66–74.
11 See: http://www.euro-ombudsman.eu.int/recommen/en/317764.htm.
12 See: http://www.euro-ombudsman.eu.int/recommen/en/oi980001.htm.

Selected further reading

Gregory, R. and Giddings, P. (eds) (2000) *Righting Wrongs: The Ombudsman in Six Continents*, Amsterdam and Brussels: IOS Press.
    An international collaborative study of the evolution and application of the Ombudsman concept, including a definitive account of the EUO Office.

Heede, K. (2000) *European Ombudsman: Redress and Control at Union Level*, Rotterdam: Erasmus University.
    A wide-ranging study of the theory and practice of the European Union Office, set in the context of a more general examination of Ombudsmanship.

Söderman, J. (1997) 'The Role of the European Ombudsman', 6th Meeting of European National Ombudsmen, Jerusalem, 9–11 September 1997 (available on the EUO website).

A critical assessment of the evolution of the Ombudsman's Office, including the implications of the Maastricht and Amsterdam treaties.

Söderman, J. (1998) *The Citizen, the Administration and the Law: General Report Prepared for the 1998 Fide Congress*, Stockholm, Sweden (available on the EUO website).

An account by the Ombudsman of his views on citizenship and good administration, as well as the various forms of remedy available to citizens of the EU. EP (1994) *Report of the Committee on Petitions on the Role of the European Ombudsman Appointed by the European Parliament*, 25 November 1994 (Session Documents, DOC A4 – 0083/94).

References

EUO (1996) *Annual Report, 1995.*

EUO (1997) *Annual Report, 1996.*

EUO (1998) *Annual Report, 1997.*

EUO (1999a) *Annual Report, 1998.*

EUO (1999b) *Press Release No. 14/99.*

EUO (2000a) *Annual Report, 1999.*

EUO (2000b) *Special Report to the EP Following the Own-initiative Inquiry into the Existence and the Public Accessibility in the Different Community Institutions and Bodies, of a Code of Administrative Behaviour*, Brussels, April 2000.

EUO (2000c) 'Statistics Concerning the Work of the European Ombudsman on 31 December 2000'.

Giraud, J.G. (1995) 'The Ombudsman of the European Union', Fourth Meeting of the National Ombudsman of the EU organised by the Ombudsman of the French Republic, Paris, 15–16 March.

Gregory, R. and Giddings, P. (2000) 'The Ombudsman Institution: Growth and Development', in *Righting Wrongs: The Ombudsman in Six Continents*, Amsterdam and Brussels: IOS Press, pp. 1–20.

Marias, E. A. (1994) 'The Right to Petition the EP after Maastricht', *European Law Review*, 19: 169–83.

Owen, S. (1993) 'The Ombudsman: Essential Elements and Common Challenge', in L. C. Reif, M. A. Marshall and C. Ferris (eds) *The Ombudsman: Diversity and Development*, Edmonton: International Ombudsman Institute, University of Alberta.

Söderman, J. (1997) 'The Role of the European Ombudsman', 6th Meeting of European National Ombudsmen, Jerusalem, 9–11 September 1997 (available on the EUO website).

Söderman, J. (1998) *The Citizen, the Administration and the Law: General Report Prepared for the 1998 Fide Congress*, Stockholm, Sweden (available on the EUO website).

Söderman, J. (2000) 'The Effectiveness of the Ombudsman in the Oversight of the Administrative Conduct of Government'. Paper presented to the 7th International Ombudsman Institute Conference, Durban, 30 October to 3 November 2000 (available on the EUO website).

Part IV

THE ADVISORY BODIES

Chapter 9

The Economic and Social Committee

Alex Warleigh

Key facts

Created in 1957 by the Treaty of Rome, the Economic and Social Committee (ESC) is the means by which organised interests have formal access to EU decision making. The Committee is divided into three groups: employers, workers and 'various interests'. The ESC thus exists to bring the diverse interest groups to a common view on proposed legislation, and to provide the Commission with a source of expert advice. The ESC is a consultative body, regularly asked for comment on legislative proposals by the Commission, but without legislative power. The Committee can also issue opinions on its own initiative if it deems this appropriate. Since the Amsterdam Treaty (1997), the European Parliament has also had the right to consult the ESC. The Committee has 222 members, appointed by the member governments and formally approved by the EU Council, selected on a quota basis roughly according to the population size of each member state. It generates opinions by building consensus between its component groups, expressed by a simple majority vote in plenary sessions. ESC members are unpaid for their work on the Committee (although they do receive expenses), and are primarily based not in Brussels but in their member state of origin.

The Economic and Social Committee: composition, powers and functions

The Economic and Social Committee (ESC; the Committee) was set up by the Treaty of Rome, and is thus one of the EU's original bodies. Its purpose is to allow economic and social interest groups formal access to the decision-making system of the EU. This access was deemed necessary for three main reasons. First, such interests were considered useful links to society in general, and thus a suitable instrument to use in making the process of European integration more accessible to the public. Second, such interest groups were held to be sources of helpful policy advice, given the expertise which their members accumulate through direct involvement with policy making and its impacts on everyday life. Third, by providing the various groups with a venue for compromise between their diverse standpoints, it was hoped that the ESC would allow its members to agree on a single set of advice upon which the Commission would be more readily able to act. The Committee thus reflected the corporatist style of governance prevalent in the 1950s in several of the original member states (Lodge and Herman 1980). Since 1994, the Committee has also been responsible for the Single Market Observatory, a body which monitors the impact and problems of the internal market. The ESC also plays a minor role in the EU's external relations, establishing joint consultative committees with its equivalent bodies in some of the Central and Eastern European countries waiting to join the EU. Moreover, the ESC has contributed to EU development policy, organising meetings with its equivalents in the countries of the African, Caribbean and Pacific (ACP) regions (within the framework of the ACP–EU Joint Assembly).

The ESC has 222 members, all of whom are appointed by their respective member governments and then formally approved by the EU Council on the basis of qualified majority voting. Each member state has a set number of ESC members, decided according to a sliding scale roughly in keeping with the size of the country's population – for example, Germany (twenty-four) has more members of the Committee than Luxembourg (six). The Committee is divided into three groups: Group I is for employers' organisations, Group II for trade unions and Group III for 'various interests', which range from farmers to consumers. The groups are formally equal in influence and status, although historically Group III has fared less well than the others thanks to its internal diversity and the view of many in Group II that the 'various interests' are subject to relatively easy 'capture' by the employers (McLaughlin 1976). ESC members are unpaid, and come to Brussels only for ESC work unless they happen to live there already; ESC membership is considered very much a part-time occupation since members are there to provide their expertise, itself gained through their primary employment. Members are appointed for a four-year period, which is renewable.

The Committee is run by a Bureau of twenty-four members, of which each of the three groups delegate eight. The Bureau is elected by the members every two years. The formal head of the institution is the President, also elected for two years by the ESC members, on the principle that each Group should hold the Presidency in turn. Thus, a troika system by which each group plays a role in the Committee Presidency is in operation in order to ensure continuity and consistency. The President runs the Bureau, and is also responsible for the external representation of the Committee. The Bureau has overall responsibility for the organisation of the Committee's work. As well as the three groups, the ESC is divided into six sections, which have responsibility for specific policy areas and are composed of members from each group. The sections are: Economic and Monetary Union/Economic and Social Cohesion; the Single Market, Production and Consumption; Transport, Energy, Infrastructure and the Information Society; Employment, Social Affairs and Citizenship; Agriculture, Rural Development and the Environment; and External Relations. When proposals address the remit of more than one section, the Committee can establish a temporary subcommittee to deal with that particular issue. Finally, there is a Budget Group, appointed by the Bureau and composed of Bureau members. The Budget Group is appointed for two years, and has two members each from the employers, workers and various interests groups. Its task is to advise the President, Bureau and Committee about the correct exercising of the ESC's budgetary and financial powers, within the parameters set by the Council and Parliament acting as budgetary authorities for the EU as a whole.

The ESC works primarily by issuing opinions written by individual members from the dedicated section on legislative proposals from the Commission, although the Council and, since the Amsterdam Treaty, the European Parliament (EP), also have the right to consult it. Opinions are voted on in plenary sessions and require a simple majority to be carried. The Committee seeks to build inter-group consensus before the plenary session is held in order to allow such meetings to proceed smoothly. This means that the member responsible for the drafting of each opinion – the Rapporteur – must attempt to ensure the support of as broad a base as possible within his or her section and group, as well as in the Committee as a whole. Having issued its opinion as requested, the ESC has no means of obliging the other institutions to take its findings into account. However, the Committee receives reports on the impact of its opinions from both the Commission (quarterly) and from the Council (annually), which indicate that at least some of its suggestions find their way into eventual legislation (see below). Two other kinds of opinion are issued by the Committee. First, the own-initiative variety. This allows the ESC members to deliver an opinion on a matter which the committee considers important in the absence of formal consultation by either the Commission or EP. Second, and more interesting, is the 'Exploratory Opinion'. This is a mechanism which allows both the Commission and Parliament to request the Committee to consider a particular issue and make recommendations for EU action in that field, which could in turn result in a legislative proposal being issued. This procedure thus in principle allows other institutions to make use of the ESC in order to justify the production of new legislation, and allows the Committee a source of influence which should not be overlooked. However, the Committee is asked to produce very few exploratory opinions, and there is no doubt that its general impact on legislation is minor. The quarterly reports from the Commission indicate that the ESC's opinions are usually disregarded when they request action which departs significantly from the Commission's intent, and the Council's reports indicate even less receptiveness (Van der Voort 1998).[1]

Policy areas on which the ESC must formally be consulted are: *the internal market* (especially the 'four freedoms' of movement of people, goods, services and capital, but also policies with implications for the single market such as agriculture); *social policy* (equal treatment between the sexes; the Report on Social Policy; directives under the co-decision procedure and measures adopted unanimously by the Council; measures to combat social exclusion; Social Policy under Protocol 14 of the Treaty on European Union); *employment* (guidelines and measures; 4th and 5th Articles of the Title on Employment; training (vocational training and education measures); *economic and social cohesion* (coordination of the structural funds; the Report on Economic and Social Cohesion; cohesion funds; regional funds); *environment, public health and consumer protection policies*; *research* (research and development policy; Framework Programmes for Research and Development); *industrial policy*; *transport* (rail, road and inland waterway travel; trans-European networks); *the Report on EU Citizenship*; and *tax*.

History and evolution of the Economic and Social Committee

Date	Event
1957	Economic and Social Committee (ESC) established by the Treaty of Rome as an advisory committee comprising representatives of social and economic interest groups.
1972	Paris Summit gives ESC the right to issue reports on its own initiative.
1986	Single European Act extends the range of policy issues on which the ESC must be consulted by the Commission and Council.

1992   Maastricht Treaty further extends the range of issues on which ESC must be consulted.

1994   ESC tasked with running the Single Market Observatory by the Council, Commission and Parliament.

1997   Amsterdam Treaty further extends the ESC's range of mandatory consultation issues and also gives the European Parliament the right to consult the ESC.

2000   Nice Treaty sets the maximum number of ESC members at 350 and reinforces the civil society element of the Committee. It also stipulates that in future ESC members will be appointed by qualified majority rather than unanimous vote.

The formal history of the Committee is one of growth, albeit unspectacular. Created by the Rome Treaty, the Committee has seen the range of issues on which it must formally be consulted expand by successive revisions of the Treaty, a significant factor since ESC opinions are likely to have greater weight if they result from an official consultation. The 1972 Paris Summit of the member states' heads of state/government allowed the Committee to produce reports on its own initiative, thereby granting it an opportunity to raise its profile and prompt the other institutions into action.[2] The Single European Act and Maastricht Treaty (TEU) added to the number of policy areas in which the ESC must be consulted, although they did not increase the Committee's powers as such. In 1994, the Committee was requested to set up the Single Market Observatory by the Council, Commission and Parliament, granting it a useful function in monitoring the EU's major achievement to date, and reinforcing the Committee by increasing its involvement with a policy area at the top of the EU agenda. In 1997, the Amsterdam Treaty allowed the EP formally to consult the Committee. This initiative was noteworthy, since the EP's own growth in legislative influence (see Burns, Chapter 4, this volume) had clearly distanced it from the early days of the EU when the Committee was often considered more influential than the then-unelected EP (Zellentin 1962). With the new consultation linkage, the co-decision powers of the EP potentially offer the Committee a means of affecting legislation indirectly: it is thereby liberated from total dependence upon either the Commission or the Council to enact its wishes. However, the ESC has clearly failed to evolve into a powerful body, remaining on the periphery of EU decision making. This can only partially be explained by the fact that the EU has in general yet to reach its nebulous *finalité politique*. In this section of the chapter I argue that various factors, including the preference of interest groups to access decision makers directly, the institutional weaknesses of the Committee, and the frequent creation of rival bodies, have severely constrained the ESC's development.

Weaknesses were deliberately built into the ESC by the Rome Treaty, and they have not been removed since. The Committee was only reluctantly included in the institutional arrangements of the EU (McLaughlin 1976), and was not designed as a radical or even 'democratic' body but rather reflected an uneasy compromise between the predominantly Christian Democratic governments of the day and the trades union movement (Zellentin 1962). Most member governments did not want the Committee to be too powerful, fearing that it might become a tool for the trade unions to use in an attempt to radicalise the policy agenda (Zellentin 1962). Fearful of empowering groups which were weak domestically at the EU level, the German government did not wish to see the creation of the Committee at all (McLaughlin 1976). The role assigned to the Committee was thus less than extensive. It was also somewhat confused, the result of a compromise which truly satisfied no single party, rather than a clear design (Lodge and Herman 1980). Given the size of the national representation quotas, it has been impossible for any member state to send a suitably broad range of members to the Committee, thus rendering moot its representative capabilities (Kirchner and Schwaiger 1981; McLaughlin 1976). Moreover, the fact that member governments rather than EU-level associations of interest groups appoint the members of the Committee has reduced its capacity to reflect the goals of the very interest groups it is supposed to represent (Kirchner and Schwaiger 1981). Initially necessary given the lack of organised interests at the EU level in the early days of the European integration process, the retention of this appointment system has certainly contributed to the frequent decisions of Committee members to pursue their interests via other channels. The ESC's resultant low profile has allowed member governments to ignore it, and the public at large to be unaware of its existence.

In terms of patronage, the ESC has never been fortunate; to date it has never been championed in a sustained way by an important EU institution or national actor, which means that no powerful demand for its removal from the periphery of decision making has ever been made. As pointed out by Streeck and Schmitter (1992), the ESC has not been a beneficiary of policy changes which could have bolstered its role considerably. In the 1970s, trade unions seeking a stronger EU social policy rejected the Committee, considering it irretrievably captured by employers. Moreover, predictions that the Committee might prosper along with the expected growth of EU social policy to counterbalance the neoliberal bias of the single market (Morgan 1991) have not been borne out, since the premise on which they were made – the significant growth of EU social policy competence – has so far proved false, even if EU competence in this area has clearly increased over time.[3]

Even more seriously, the Committee has had to endure the creation of rival bodies within its field of competence on a regular basis. As well as the EP – an initial competitor, but now clearly its superior and, possibly, its occasional sponsor – the Committee has at various times been outflanked by such bodies as the now-defunct Tripartite Conference (McLaughlin 1976), the Committee of the Regions (Warleigh 1999) and the Employment Committee (Duff 1997). The first brought together the Council, Commission and 'social partners' – many of the last being nonetheless members of the ESC – in a new forum dedicated to finding solutions to the economic problems of the Union. The Committee of the Regions, though a younger body than the ESC, was initially foisted upon its administrative system, thereby draining the ESC of scarce resources. Through the membership of several heavyweight politicians and its admittedly often unfortunate press coverage, the Committee of the Regions succeeded in generating a higher profile for itself in five years than the ESC had achieved in over forty (Warleigh 1999).

The Amsterdam Treaty was highly ambivalent about the Committee. By this Treaty, the EU gained new competence in social and employment matters, but despite the fact that the Committee's consultation range was correspondingly extended, it was faced with a new competitor: the Employment Committee, created especially to help the EU enact its new powers (Duff 1997). The Nice Treaty established a new Social Protection Committee, whose remit is to promote cooperation on matters of social policy both horizontally (between the member governments) and vertically (between the national capitals and the Commission). Thus, functions which could easily be given to the ESC often continue to be awarded to entirely different bodies created specifically for the purpose.

If the European Council has thus often treated the ESC with less than complete respect, ESC members have themselves done the same. The member governments have tended to follow their own various preferences on matters of whom to appoint to the Committee, meaning that the latter has had to cope with a highly diverse membership (McLaughlin 1976; Kirchner and Schwaiger 1981).[4] As a result the Committee has been prone to internal cleavage, a problem compounded by the concerns of many members of the workers' group that the employers had gained control of the 'various interests' in Group III (McLaughlin 1976), whose inclusion in the Committee they had anyhow opposed at the outset (Lodge and Herman 1980). Moreover, when drafting reports the ESC has had to rely very heavily on outside experts rather than its own members, making its claim to represent technical competence based on real-world experience rather difficult to justify (Van der Voort 1998). Committee members from every group have accordingly preferred to develop other means of accessing EU decision makers, including direct lobbying and the formation of EU-level interest group umbrella organisations. A key example here is the decision by the agricultural lobby to focus on direct lobbying of the Commission, considering the ESC to be too divided and too weak to provide real influence (Caporaso 1974). Today, the majority of members regard the Committee as a place for information exchange rather than a useful tool for political leverage (Van der Voort 1998).

The broader systemic features of the EU have also presented difficulties for the ESC. As an institution, it is too diverse to be a coherent member of any of the policy networks which are the real source of EU policy (Van der Voort 1998). On the level of individual members, this gap is often not made good, since although ESC members may well have privileged positions in several networks this is usually due to their status as representatives of other, high-profile associations – (federations of) interest groups, major corporations, favoured non-governmental organisations. Their primary loyalty and focus are thus not centred on the ESC. Moreover, given their part-time membership of the ESC, many Committee members simply cannot spend sufficient time in Brussels to build the necessary contacts either with each other or with members of other bodies. This relative absence from the networking process perhaps also helps explain the occasional lapse in political judgement by the ESC leadership. For example, ESC requests to the 1996 Intergovernmental Conference (ESC 1995) included several likely to displease the EP (the Committee asked to be an observer at conciliation committee meetings, which would have granted it access to the heart of the EP's newly won and much prized legislative powers), as well as clog up the Committee's own agenda (by requesting to be consulted on every matter affecting the interests of its members). Included alongside perfectly sensible (if also ambitious) requests to be granted full institutional status and powers to take cases to the European Court of Justice, these demands showed the Committee to be lacking a pragmatic development strategy, perhaps exasperated by years of under-development.[5] For several reasons, then, the history of the Committee has not been one of great success.

Out on the edge: the Economic and Social Committee in the EU policy-making system

The contribution of the ESC to EU policy making

The ESC is one of the many committees used in the EU system of policy making, all of which serve to foster common interests between diverse actors and help produce policy outcomes whose quality and legitimacy are thereby higher. However, as with all such committees, the influence of the ESC is hard to establish. In the system of networks on which EU governance depends, it is hard to attribute influence to any single actor, since the obtention of policy goals depends on making coalitions. However, the ESC's influence on legislation is not likely to be great, given its structural weaknesses. As a result, the Committee is seeking to define a new role for itself as the voice of civil society rather than socioeconomic interests, a strategy which may yet bear fruit as the EU seeks to reduce the 'democratic deficit'.

As pointed out by Marinus Van Schendelen (1998), advisory committees tend to play a more important role in EU governance than in that of the member states, because the 'European' political structures are far more porous than those at national level. The EU system is not as fully developed, and the relationships between the various institutions are not as clear. The fact that the EU is a transnational and still incomplete system means that it is always likely to depend fairly heavily on its component states for suitable extra staff, who then require a mechanism for making their contributions to policy. Hence it is necessary to formalise meetings of the relevant officials. This system of 'comitology' can certainly be interpreted as a device by which the member states seek to control the decision-making process while formally ceding a degree of decision-making power to the Commission and EP (Dinan 1999: 227–9). However, such committees undoubtedly serve to increase trust between the various national actors, foster deliberation between them, and increase the levels of (admittedly elite) representation and participation (Van Schendelen 1998). Advisory committees can thus contribute to the legitimacy of the EU in that its policy output thereby benefits from wider stakeholding and, hopefully, better formulation.[6] The ESC is certainly able to replicate some of these processes and benefits (Smismans 2000), even if it is qualitatively different from the issue-specific entities created under comitology thanks to its broad membership base and competence.

Moreover, and despite the real problems encountered by ESC members in the process of participation in EU policy networks discussed above, informal politics *may* lend itself to successful exploitation by the ESC. Empirical research indicates that the

Committee can certainly be part of winning policy coalitions when it shares the desires of the Commission and EP for a high level of EU regulation in a given policy area (Eichener 1997). Exploiting symmetrical concerns with other institutions and bodies can thus allow the Committee to reach its objectives more often than its formal weakness would suggest. However, the crucial factor here is the pre-existence of such shared concerns – it is highly unlikely that the Committee could persuade any of the other EU institutions to take a course of action against which they were clearly ill disposed. Moreover, as set out above, the structural weaknesses of the ESC make it unable to achieve as much from informal politics as other institutions. Consequently, the Committee is seeking another way of promoting itself within the policy-making process, namely reinvention as a potential and partial means of helping to rectify the 'democratic deficit' through its links to civil society.

Many scholars seeking ways to eradicate the problems of democracy in the EU have pointed to the use of sectoral representation as a complement to elected representation in the liberal democratic sense, building on the functionalist tradition in international relations theory, which advocates the use of special parliament-like assemblies for each policy area (Mitrany 1971). Antje Wiener (1998) has pointed to the role which non-governmental organisations might play both in representing citizens' concerns about specific issues such as ecology and encouraging them to develop a more active engagement with EU policy making. Stijn Smismans (2000) argues that the ESC is not merely a source of expert advice for EU decision makers, but also an arena in which diverse socioeconomic groups deliberate and reach agreed joint policy positions they would otherwise lack. This helps ensure that a broad range of stakeholders gains a voice in EU policy making, and also contributes to the formation of a culture of consensus among at least certain elite actors.[7] In her radical proposal for democratising the EU, Heidrun Abromeit (1998) argues that the ESC should be able to veto legislation which displeases the majority of its members, in order to make more visible the influence enjoyed by interest groups and to capitalise on the genuinely transnational nature of many such organisations.

There are, however, certain practical problems to be overcome in order to make even a less radical transformation. Although the Nice Treaty includes consumer groups specifically in the list of those to be represented on the ESC and makes clear its duty to represent 'the various economic and social components of organised civil society' (Article 257, Treaty Establishing the European Economic Community as amended by the Nice Treaty), to date the Committee has been anything but a source of access to EU power circles for the groups most likely to appeal to the citizen and which can claim broad support, such as the World Wide Fund for Nature or Greenpeace. Indeed, the Treaty requirement that all the ESC groups must be of equal number means that the 'social' groups (employers and workers) must automatically outnumber the 'societal' (various interests), whose membership is in any case highly disparate and unlikely to reach consensus easily. Moreover, it could be argued that not even the largest member states have sufficient members of the Committee to send representatives of a suitably broad range of civil interest groups to the ESC. Thus, if it is to be a platform for groups which would otherwise find it either difficult to compete with those privileged nationally or to call on large resources, the ESC must discriminate in their favour within the limits of its rules of procedure and press for further Treaty change (Van der Voort 1998).

In this respect it is interesting to note that the Committee has been at pains to emphasise its claim to be a 'bridge to civil society' – a metaphor which features in much of the Committee's publicity material – in recent years, especially perhaps under the leadership of Beatrice Rangoni Machiavelli (1998 to 2000). In 1999 it held the 'First Convention of Civil Society', and in 2000 the Committee organised hearings on environment policy, health and safety issues, education and development policy. While the influence of such activities is difficult to measure, they are a useful indicator of the Committee's attempt to move beyond its image as a rather unsatisfactory and unfashionable exercise in corporatism by seeking a new role which no other EU body is equally well placed to play (the EP represents individuals rather than sectional interests; the Committee of the Regions exists to give local and regional government a voice). The ESC has also requested that the EU undertake a 'civil dialogue' with non-governmental organisations to accompany the social dialogue it has already begun. Should this dialogue emerge, the ESC would be well placed to act as a coordinator, and could expect to profit from such a dialogue if its own internal reform allows actors thus brought into the EU decision-making process to consider the Committee a suitable vehicle for their interests.

After the Nice Treaty: looking to the future

The crucial indicator for analysing the future of the ESC is thus twofold: the Committee's own will to press for internal reform, and the readiness of the European Council to sanction or even direct those efforts by the mechanism of Treaty change. Admittedly, there is nothing new about attempts to present the ESC as a potential means of helping democratise the EU; like much else in the discourse about European integration, it is an idea that has been put forward since at least the 1970s (McLaughlin 1976). However, it is the kind of strategy which may resonate with the thinking of member governments in the coming decade, as they seek further means of 'democratising' the EU without, in all probability, fully and directly addressing the really key issues such a process raises – institutional balance, accountability and political identity (Warleigh 2002). It is thus interesting to note that the priorities of the ESC for the coming years are: improvements in internal transparency, in particular that of the Bureau; more extensive use of the media and other public relations devices in order to raise the Committee's profile; and concentration on defining key ESC concerns which should be reflected consistently in all Committee opinions (Frerichs 2000).

The Committee is also seeking to foster new relationships with the other institutions. Its priorities include the request for more exploratory opinions to be sought by the Commission, with which the Committee also wants to establish closer patterns of working focused on key directorates general. The Committee is also seeking to be used more often as a consultant or as a consultation coordinator, pursuing the latter goal by organising hearings and workshops. The Committee is also hoping to use the new right of the EP to consult it to foster closer links between its sections and the relevant committees of the EP, a process which, if successful, could allow the Committee great informal influence via the powers enjoyed in Rue Wiertz. Finally, the Committee is also seeking to improve its links with the Council, by attempting to meet more regularly with Council working parties and producing work which fits the priorities of each Presidency (ESC 2000). If successful, these efforts would certainly bring the Committee much closer to the centre of decision making even without 'civil society'-flavoured reforms in the wider context of the EU structure. However, it is difficult to predict more than partial accomplishment of these goals, given that they are not always complementary and also that the ESC has few resources. For example, adapting to Council Presidency priorities might mean reduced capacity to produce routine opinions on proposals. The Committee may thus seek to change itself into a kind of think-tank, focusing on exploratory opinions, and the use of its resources and members to organise hearings/workshops on key policy issues. This would mean reducing the Committee's role as a source of advice on legislative proposals – but given the strength of direct lobbying in the EU, such a re-evaluation might well add value to the Committee by differentiating it further from the traditional function of interest representation and enhancing its putative claim to a more broadly societal pertinence (Morgan 1991). Should such a scenario be realised, links with the EP would clearly need to be renegotiated since the legislative function of the ESC would have been altered.

A further and equally important variable which will affect the future of the ESC is the enlargement of the EU. Already, the Committee sees itself as a potential training ground for interest groups in the future member states, a means of training them in the ways of EU policy making and the socioeconomic values of Western Europe. As well as being patronising – despite the obvious factor that new members of any club usually benefit from being told by old hands how the place works – this function would contradict the 'civil society' reform of the Committee to at least some extent. This is because a 'training' function for the Committee would necessitate the inclusion of as broad a range of interests as possible, thereby delaying the restructuring of the Committee in favour of the present Group III. Thus, the future of the Committee is unclear. A rationale for reform and greater influence is already present; but the will of either the member governments or the Committee itself to act on it, while certainly not impossible either to imagine or even currently in some way to detect, cannot be taken for granted.

Summary

- The ESC is an advisory committee, part of the EU throughout its history but never removed from the periphery of decision making. It issues opinions on legislative proposals, whose impact is difficult to quantify but attested by both official documents and by academic studies.
- The Committee exists to give interest groups a formal voice in EU decision making. It is the arena in which these actors can debate their diverse views and reach a compromise, something not always attainable through direct lobbying of decision makers.
- However, the ESC has often been sidelined. It has never been championed by any powerful sponsor, and has often been viewed by interest groups as less useful than direct lobbying. Moreover, rival bodies have regularly been set up to undertake functions which could have been given to the Committee. Thus,

behind the ESC's longevity lies a question of how useful it can be either for its members or for the process of integration more generally.

- The future of the ESC is thus summarised by the concept of 'reform or perish'. The ESC may never be abolished, but without change it is likely to slide into further obscurity.
- As a potential contributor to the solution of the 'democratic deficit' problem, the Committee has several assets. It could be reconfigured as a venue for civil society interests to gain access to the EU system, and play a significant part in the creation of new legislation with a 'civil society' flavour. However, this would require significant changes in the composition and working methods of the Committee which may not be favoured by all its members.

Test questions

1   Why was the ESC created? Account for its institutional purpose and weaknesses.
2   Why has the ESC remained on the periphery of EU decision making?
3   What contribution might the ESC make to the eradication of the 'democratic deficit'?

Contact information

The easiest way to contact the ESC is via its webpage on the Europa site: http://www.ces.eu.int.

This page has a wealth of information about the organisation, members and work of the Committee. It also has several ready-made virtual factsheets. Direct queries can be sent via email: info@esc.eu.int.

Traditional contact methods are also available using the following information:

Address: Rue Ravenstein 2, B -1000 Brussels, Belgium.
Telephone: (+32) 2 546 90 11
Fax: (+32) 2 513 48 93

Notes

1   See Van der Voort (1998) for a detailed survey of ESC legislative influence.
2   However, the own-initiative power can be difficult to use, encouraging a Committee to stretch itself too far and lose coherence – see Warleigh (1999) on the Committee of the Regions.
3   As argued by Leibfried and Pierson (2000), although the single market has eroded national competence in social policy, there has not been a corresponding relocation of competence to the EU level, resulting in something of a policy vacuum filled only partially by rulings of the European Court of Justice.
4   The shift to qualified majority voting in the Council when appointing members of the ESC, as sanctioned by the Nice Treaty, may reduce this diversity somewhat.

5   It is worth noting that the ESC's requests to the 2000 IGC were much more sensible, and included a canny request to be consulted before a proposal has been formally issued, that part of the law-making process at which legislation is usually the most open to change.

6   Of course, legitimacy is about far more than this. See Banchoff and Smith (1999) for an excellent set of essays on this subject.

7   However, Smismans also rightly notes that the fact that ESC plenaries offer little chance for real debate restricts the ability of the Committee to be truly deliberative, as does the still narrow range of interests formally represented in its ranks.

Selected further reading

The relative unimportance of the ESC in EU decision making is reflected in the small number of academic studies of which it has been the focus. However, the following are three of the most useful sources.

McLaughlin, D. (1976) 'The Work and Aims of the Economic and Social Committee of the EEC and Euratom', *Journal of Common Market Studies*, 15, 1: 9–28.
    Written by an ESC official, this nonetheless balanced view offers an insightful understanding of the Committee in the 1970s, by which time it had already encountered many of the problems with which it has been beset.

Van der Voort, W. (1998) 'The Economic and Social Committee', in M.P.C.M. Van Schendelen (ed.) *EU Committees as Influential Policymakers*, Aldershot: Ashgate.
    Drawing on a wealth of empirical study (published elsewhere in Dutch), this chapter presents an in-depth and convincing account of the Committee as it seeks to find a role for itself in the developing European Union.

Zellentin, G. (1962) 'The Economic and Social Committee', *Journal of Common Market Studies*, 1, 1: 22–8.
    An intriguing reflection on the Committee from the early days of the EU. In parts prophetic, in parts rendered obsolete by the subsequent evolution of the integration process, this article shows the reader how the ESC was viewed initially, and succinctly introduces many of what have proved to be its main dilemmas.

References

Abromeit, H. (1998) 'How To Democratise a Multi-level, Multi-Dimensional Polity', in A. Weale and M. Nentwich (eds) *Political Theory and the European Union*, London: Routledge.

Banchoff, T. and Smith, M. (eds) (1999) *Legitimacy and The European Union*, London: Routledge.

Caporaso, J. (1974) *The Structure and Function of European Integration*, Pacific Palisades, CA: Goodyear.

Dinan, D. (1999) *Ever Closer Union* (2nd edn), London: Macmillan.

Duff, A. (1997) *The Treaty of Amsterdam – Text and Commentary*, London: Federal Trust/Sweet & Maxwell.

Economic and Social Committee of the European Community (ESC) (1995) *Intergovernmental Conference 1996 and the Role of the Economic and Social Committee*, Brussels: Economic and Social Committee, ref. ESC-95-019bis-EN.

ESC (2000) *The ESC: Frequently Asked Questions* (http://www.ces.eu.int/en/faq/fr_faq.htm).

Eichener, V. (1997) 'Effective European Problem-solving: Lessons from the Regulation of Occupational Safety and Environmental Protection', *Journal of European Public Policy*, 4, 4: 591–608.

Frerichs, G. (2000) 'Address to the Plenary Session of the ESC', 29 November. (http://www.ces.eu.int/en/docs/misc/speeches/Frerichs_plen_291100_e.htm)

Kirchner, E. and Schwaiger, K. (1981) *The Role of Interest Groups in the European Community*, Aldershot: Gower.

Leibfried, S. and Pierson, P. (2000) 'Social Policy: Left to Courts and Markets?', in H. Wallace and W. Wallace (eds) *Policy-Making in the European Union* (4th edn), Oxford: Oxford University Press.

Lodge, J. and Herman, V. (1980) 'The Economic and Social Committee in EEC Decision Making', *International Organization*, 34, 2: 265–84.

McLaughlin, D. (1976) 'The Work and Aims of the Economic and Social Committee of the EEC and Euratom', *Journal of Common Market Studies*, 15, 1: 9–28.

Mitrany, D. (1971) 'The Functional Approach in Historical Perspective', *International Affairs*, 47, 3: 532–43.

Morgan, R. (1991) *The Consultative Function of the Economic and Social Committee of the European Community* (EUI Working Paper 91/11), Badia Fiesolana: European University Institute.

Smismans, S. (2000) 'The European Economic and Social Committee: Towards Deliberative Democracy via a Functional Assembly', *European Integration On-line Papers*, 4, 12 (http://eiop.or.at/eiop/texte/2000-012a.htm).

Streeck, W. and Schmitter, P. (1992) 'From National Corporatism to Transnational Pluralism: Organized Interests in the Single European Market', in W. Streeck, *Social Institutions and Economic Performance – Studies of Industrial Relations in Advanced Capitalist Societies*, London: Sage.

Van der Voort, W. (1998) 'The Economic and Social Committee', in M.P.C.M. Van Schendelen (ed.) *EU Committees as Influential Policymakers*, Aldershot: Ashgate.

Van Schendelen, M.P.C.M. (1998) 'Prolegomena to EU Committees as Influential Policymakers', in M.P.C.M. Van Schendelen (ed.) *EU Committees as Influential Policymakers*, Aldershot: Ashgate.

Warleigh, A. (1999) *The Committee of the Regions: Institutionalising Multi-level Governance?*, London: Kogan Page.

Warleigh, A. (2002) 'Towards Network Democracy? The Potential of Flexible Integration', in M. Farrell, S. Fella and M. Newman (eds) *European Unity in Diversity: Challenges for the Twenty-First Century*, London: Sage.

Wiener, A. (1998) *'European' Citizenship Practice: Building Institutions of a Non-State*, Oxford: Westview Press.

Zellentin, G. (1962) 'The Economic and Social Committee', *Journal of Common Market Studies*, 1,1: 22–8.

Chapter 10

The Committee of the Regions

Alex Warleigh

Key facts

Established by the Treaty on European Union, the Committee of the Regions is an advisory body which exists to allow actors from subnational authorities formal access to the EU policy-making process. It was created as part of the process of eradicating the 'democratic deficit', but its ability to meet this goal is not yet clear. Like the Economic and Social Committee, it offers Opinions on proposals for legislation from the Commission, but has no legislative power. It is consulted obligatorily on a range of issues relevant to local and regional government, and can issue Opinions on its own initiative if it so chooses. Since the Amsterdam Treaty, the Committee can also be consulted by the European Parliament. Research indicates that the Committee is able to influence the content of EU policy, but that this influence can often be small and is not automatic. The 222 members of the Committee are appointed by member governments rather than directly elected, on a quota basis roughly corresponding to the population size of each member state. The Committee passes its Opinions by majority vote in plenary, but real influence is held by its Executive Bureau. Members are not paid for their activities on the Committee, although they do receive financial allowances. They are based primarily in their member state of origin.

The Committee of the Regions: composition, powers and functions

The Committee of the Regions (CoR; the Committee) is one of the European Union's most interesting bodies despite the fact that it is by no means its most powerful. This is due to a paradox in the essential nature of the Committee: it is an advisory body composed not of supposedly neutral experts but elected politicians. This tension not only gives CoR its novelty; it also helps explain many of its strengths and weaknesses, as I make clear below. CoR marks the first channel of representation for actors from subnational authorities (SNAs) to the EU institutions recognised by the Treaty. It constitutes a mechanism by which SNA actors can give policy advice on EU proposals, thereby in theory improving both their quality and their democratic legitimacy. As such, CoR represents a qualitative leap from the patterns of lobbying which such actors had used before its creation in the Treaty on European Union (TEU) (Loughlin 1996a). Moreover, it brings to an end the principle that all territorial representation within the EU must be a matter for national (i.e. central) governments (Loughlin 1996b).

The Treaty establishes CoR as an advisory body to the Commission and Council, very much on the model of the Economic and Social Committee (ESC) (see Chapter 9). However, the Amsterdam Treaty (ToA) also gave the European Parliament (EP) the right to consult the Committee. CoR has 222 full members, together with the same number of deputies or 'alternates'. Members are appointed by the EU Council for a (renewable) mandate of four years, on the basis of lists of candidates supplied by each member government. As for the ESC and EP, the number of members of the

Committee per member state varies roughly according to the size of the national population. The Treaty of Nice (ToN) made it imperative that CoR members either hold elected office at the local/regional level, or are at least accountable to an elected local/regional authority. Even before the ToN, the vast majority of its members met this criterion. As a result, CoR members are not normally based in Brussels, but rather travel there for Committee business. CoR members are unpaid, but do receive travel allowances. Although it can be consulted on any matter of the other institutions' choosing and can also offer Opinions on its own initiative, CoR must be consulted on the following issues: education; vocational training and youth; public health; trans-European networks and certain other transport issues; economic and social cohesion; certain aspects of the Structural Funds; cross-border cooperation; employment; social policy and environmental policy. The Committee is able to convene itself, appoint its own executive and, since the ToA, also has the power to devise its own rules of procedure. Against these strengths, however, must be weighed the following formal weaknesses: the Committee is obviously advisory rather than legislative; it has no power to insist on feedback regarding its Opinions or ensure they are taken into account; and it has no control over its budget, which is decided by the Council and EP. Nonetheless, CoR is able to make an impact on EU legislation, as attested by both public and private feedback supplied by the Commission and academic research (Loughlin 1996b; Farrows and McCarthy 1997; Warleigh 1997; Warleigh 1999).

Organisationally, CoR is divided into seven standard 'commissions' responsible for particular portfolios, plus a special commission on institutional affairs, giving a total of eight.[1] The Committee is managed by a large and powerful Bureau, composed of a President, first Vice-President, a further Vice-President for each member state, the leaders of the political groups and other members appointed to bring each member state up to its allocated quota (a total of three members each for Germany, Spain, France, Italy and the UK; two members each for the other member states). The Bureau sets out the Committee's programme of work and ensures that the latter is implemented. It coordinates and organises the work both of the commissions and of the plenary sessions. Also responsible for the overall financial and administrative management of the Committee, the Bureau prepares a draft statement of accounts for the Committee, authorises the occasional CoR meetings outside Brussels and manages the payment of members' allowances. The Bureau's powers are political as well as administrative; it is the Bureau which approves requests by CoR members to write own-initiative Opinions, and which allocates Opinions to the commissions. CoR is thus a distinctly elitist body (Warleigh 1999); plenary debates are rarely significant, and members are influential through either membership of the Bureau or securing rapporteurships (the authorisation to prepare a CoR Opinion on a given subject). Consequently, the Presidency of the Committee has been a sought-after position, and one which has so far alternated between the major political groups (Christian Democrats and Socialists), each of which has provided two presidents.[2]

CoR members are drawn from across the variety of types of local and regional authority in the EU, which range from the powerful regions and Länder of federal member states such as Belgium, Germany and Austria to the weak local authorities of Greece and the UK. As such they are appointed to represent subnational *authorities*, rather than citizens from a specified area. Indeed, given the size of the Committee, it is impossible for even a majority of SNAs to be represented on it directly, which makes the link between the average citizen and the members of CoR tenuous at best. As discussed below, this has significant implications for CoR's role in the rectification of the 'democratic deficit'; it is important here to note that most CoR members consider themselves to primarily represent the SNAs of their member state, with party political loyalties helping bridge the differences between national delegations and different tiers of government (Warleigh 1999). Representatives from the regions of federal member states have a more clearly and narrowly defined territorial loyalty, but even in these cases coordination of policy between the national delegates is common (Morass 1997).

History and evolution of the CoR

Date	Event
1988	Commission creates CoR's predecessor body, the Consultative Council of Regional and Local Authorities. It has no Treaty status, but serves to cement links between the Commission and the various European associations of SNA actors.
1991	Commission makes two proposals for CoR. The first, rejected by the Council, would have linked the Committee exclusively to the Commission. The second is for CoR to be an independent advisory committee composed of democratically elected SNA politicians.
1992	Maastricht Treaty creates CoR. It is independent, but less powerful than sought by the Commission, and also joined administratively to the ESC. There is no obligation that its members be elected SNA actors.
1997	Amsterdam Treaty extends the range of issues on which CoR must be consulted, separates it administratively from the ESC, and gives the EP the right to consult the Committee.
2000	Nice Treaty makes it obligatory for CoR members to be elected to a local/regional authority, or at least politically accountable to an SNA. The maximum membership of CoR is set at 350, and it is agreed that in future members are to be appointed by the Council using qualified majority voting rather than unanimity.

To understand the advent of CoR it is necessary briefly to delve into the context of the recent, albeit partial, shift towards a 'Europe of the Regions'. This term, current in much commentary on European integration during the early 1990s, remains controversial. At its strongest, it denotes a federal EU in which national governments have all but disappeared; in its weaker sense, it means a Union in which SNA actors have been given a direct and expanded role in 'European' decision making (Loughlin 1996a). The first variant remains a distant possibility. However, the 'weak' definition is reflected in the fact that the EU has been moving towards a system of multi-level governance, in which actors from below the national level of government are given a formal and direct role in Union decision making – at least in structural and cohesion policies – since the late 1980s (Marks *et al.* 1996). This process of change was provoked by the Single European Act and subsequent reforms to EU structural and cohesion policies, which set up the 'partnership principle' as a key feature. According to this principle, SNAs play an important role in policy formulation and implementation, alongside the Commission, national governments and a range of public and private sector actors at the local/regional level (Hooghe 1996). The TEU took the process further, enabling component regions of a federal member state to represent that state in meetings of the EU Council (although in such meetings their brief is to promote the national, rather than regional, interest). Although this has clearly not resulted in the disempowerment of national governments, it has given a new salience to SNAs in the EU process, and results from activism by various sets of actors. Tömmel (1998) emphasises the role of the Commission, which had sought to bring SNAs closer to the heart of Union policy making as an exercise in legitimation, the construction of political and economic links across national borders, and, it hoped, alliance building. Jeffery (1997, 2000) stresses the role of the powerful SNA players, particularly the German Länder, which sought to ensure that European integration did not allow central governments to deprive them of competences over which they had domestic control. Relatedly, Christiansen (1997) argues that pressure from such SNA actors obliged the federal and heavily regionalised member states (then Germany, Belgium, Spain) to agree to changes in the EU's policy-making style and institutions. Taken together, these pressures impacted upon the EU agenda; the related debate on subsidiarity during the early 1990s clearly reflected the understanding in most member states (with the usual exception of the UK) that actors from below the national tier of government had a useful role to play in the formulation and implementation of EU policy.

Against this background, it was not surprising that the CoR was established by the Maastricht Treaty. A predecessor body, the Consultative Council of the Regions and Local Authorities, had been in existence since 1988 as a semi-formal source of policy advice for the Commission. This served to raise the profile of SNAs and as a mechanism by which actors from that tier were able to learn how to play the EU system. However, there was no agreement at Maastricht that CoR should be a powerful legislative body, a potential second chamber of the EP, as many advocates of regionalisation had wanted. During early negotiations, Luxembourg and Denmark proposed that instead of a new committee, SNA actors should be included in the membership of the ESC. However, CoR emerged as an independent consultative body, with its structural weaknesses due largely to the recalcitrance of the UK (Warleigh 1999).

Still a young body – thanks to the delays in ratifying the TEU, the Committee first met only in 1994 – the CoR has so far evolved quite impressively. It has survived a shotgun administrative marriage with the ESC, an arrangement which pleased neither body. It has established itself clearly, and been able to absorb two separate sets of members and alternates (as well as changes to the Treaty and its own remit) in that short period of time. It has not fallen victim to a grand split along the regional/local cleavage, as many feared (Christiansen 1995; Warleigh 1999), thus retaining cohesion despite often marked differences of opinion between its members, who often divide along three main axes: nationality, political party, and type of SNA. The system of alternates has worked well, and has not on the whole been a means by which powerful SNA actors absent themselves from the Committee while remaining nominal members. The CoR has also established political party groups, whose strength and coherence is debated, but which do at least mean that the Committee is not organised entirely according to nationality. The CoR has also been able to establish a fairly clear agenda and voice, seeking to promote the sub-sidiarity principle in the interests of SNAs while promoting the value of diversity of SNA structures across the member states (Warleigh 1999). However, by the same token it has not been a vehicle for the most powerful regions to force radical change from the member states, partly thanks to its legislative weakness and partly as a consequence of the differences between its members in terms of their domestic influence and powers. In addition, powerful regional governments are in a minority on the Committee, meaning that they cannot dictate the Committee's line. As discussed below, this is an important variable to examine when considering the Committee's future.

The Amsterdam Treaty brought CoR several important gains, but did not transform it radically. Many of the Committee's structural weaknesses were removed, such as its uneasy cohabitation with the ESC, its dependence on the Council to agree its rules of procedure, and its lack of a formal link with the EP. The ToA also increased the range of issues on which CoR must be consulted, thereby in principle giving the Committee's Opinions on those matters greater weight. However, it is clear that during the intergovernmental conference (IGC) which led up to the ToA, no member state championed the cause of the Committee. Spain and Belgium would have supported greater changes, but were not prepared to risk their partners' decisions on their eligibility for economic and monetary union, which were to be made shortly after the IGC, by pushing actively for more powers to be given to CoR (Christiansen 1997). Austria supported the promotion of CoR to full institution, but was not prepared to make it a veto matter (Morass 1997). Crucially, the Länder of Germany reversed their position. At Maastricht, they had considered both European integration and its regionalisation to be important goals. At Amsterdam, they were far more introverted and cautious about the potential for integration to eradicate their domestic powers. Thus, they prevented German support both for deepening integration (Devuyst 1998) and the powers of CoR (Jeffery 2000). In this context, the continued and undoubted support of the Commission (both President Santer and Commissioner Wulf-Matthies) was insufficient, although it has certainly aided the evolution of CoR on a day-to-day basis (Warleigh 1997, 1999).

The Nice Treaty continued CoR's progress along this slow but certain develop-ment trajectory. The decision to appoint members by qualified majority rather than unanimity in the Council is potentially significant, since by removing the veto of reluctant member states it may allow actors with domestic leverage over their national governments to push for a greater number of powerful SNA politicians to be appointed to CoR. Of course, whether this proves to be the case remains to be seen. More definite gains are already clear, however. By making it compulsory for CoR members to be elected SNA politicians, or at least politically accountable to an elected SNA, the member states added significantly to the Committee's legitimacy, and took an action they were not prepared to agree at Amsterdam. This was reinforced by the new obligation placed on members to resign from CoR if they lose their local/regional mandate during their time on the Committee. Any CoR member thus affected is to be replaced by the Council, again on the basis of qualified majority voting. Given the fact that SNA elections are not synchronised either across the EU or with CoR mandates, this is a significant provision which further buoys up the Committee's credibility and removes the threat that it could be filled with members who not only had little public recognition but had actually been rejected at the ballot-box. The capping of members after enlargement to the applicant countries from Eastern and Central Europe (plus Malta and Cyprus) at 350 matches the treatment given to the ESC, and should ensure the Committee does not become unwieldy. However, these gains should not be overstated. The Committee has yet to be promoted to full institutional status (see Laffan, Chapter 7, this volume, on the Court of Auditors' progress in this regard), and is thereby deprived of certain highly significant rights – notably the right to take cases to, and protect its interests at, the European Court of Justice. Similarly, two of the Committee's other key targets – to achieve Treaty recognition of the principle of local self-government, and to have a role in the policing of subsidiarity – have not been met. Nonetheless, in the three intergovernmental conferences since 1990, the Committee has been created and reinforced, thereby constituting a solid if unspectacular achievement for advocates of SNA involvement with the integration process.

The CoR in the EU policy-making system: smoke without fire?

The contribution of the CoR to EU policy making

Like the ESC, the Committee of the Regions has an advisory function, issuing Opinions on proposals for legislation. This is a lesser role than had been hoped for by many of those who sought the Committee's creation. However, unlike the ESC, the CoR is composed of elected politicians, many of whom appear concerned that the Committee should make an impact on EU legislation. Consequently, CoR has to date revealed itself as a fairly ambitious body, seeking to advance its interests and ensuring that its output is generally of good quality in order to ensure a good reputation. It is clear that the Committee is able to influence EU legislation, but as with the ESC this influence can be difficult to quantify. The Committee's efforts to carve itself a niche in the institutional system have been successful after a difficult start, but its primary relationship has so far been with the Commission. Moreover, CoR faces a dilemma between its role as provider of expert advice and its members' desire to exert political influence, since the former is arguably both its most legitimate function and that which is most useful to its sponsors in the Commission.

As pointed out by Christiansen (1995), many initial expectations of CoR were excessive, which has inevitably meant that some of its advocates have been disappointed by the solid but unspectacular progress made by the Committee. Similarly, assessments of its role in the EU policy-making system depend on the lens through which the Committee is observed; those seeking a powerful legislative chamber which could act as a catalyst for a federalisation of the EU will probably be less than satisfied by the impact CoR has made, concluding that the Committee is a case of smoke without fire. However, the Committee has certainly been able to shape EU legislation, and has also impacted upon the inter-institutional relations of the Union. A critical test is whether its Opinions are taken into account either by the Commission or by the Council. Here, the evidence is clear. As with the ESC, it is difficult to quantify exactly how much influence CoR Opinions have, since they are often broadly supportive of the proposal in question and constitute but one of the many sources of advice available to Union policy makers. However, much academic research indicates that the CoR is able to shape agendas, provide ideas for policy change/innovation, and influence the final shape of legislation (Loughlin 1996b; Farrows and McCarthy 1997; Warleigh 1999). This influence may even extend to Committee Opinions issued on its own initiative (Schwaiger 1997). That said, CoR influence is by no means either automatic or extensive. It depends largely on two factors: the perceived quality of its advice – the ability to fill an information gap, or supply a workable new idea – and the ability to network successfully with the other institutions, in order to find champions for its ideas. CoR also needs to be seen to work by consensus, i.e. to produce Opinions which result from genuine agreements between its disparate membership rather than the agenda of one particular type of SNA. With this in mind, the Committee is under the obligation to cultivate strong working relations between its various internal groups and also with the Commission, EP and Council. In the case of the latter three institutions, CoR's efforts have so far been markedly more successful with the Commission and EP.[3]

This is particularly interesting given the context sketched out at the beginning of this chapter, namely the partial and limited shift towards a 'Europe of the Regions'. The Committee has undoubtedly provided actors from weak systems of local and regional government the ability to escape their limited domestic roles to some extent, an opportunity which at least certain of its members have seized. However, as made clear by Hooghe and Marks (1995), the CoR is just one of the means available to SNA actors seeking to influence EU policy alongside direct lobbying both at EU and at national levels, the partnership principle, and, in some cases, the opportunity to sit in Council: it is by no means clear that SNA actors will regularly select the CoR as their preferred channel of influence. The Committee is thus obliged to make a name for itself by acquiring a reputation for solid advice, and also by the exploitation of opportunities for advancement. During its early period it was by no means clear that the CoR would be able to achieve these tasks. In addition to the normal problems of establishing a new institution, the CoR managed to attract adverse attention as a result of the policies of its first President, Jacques Blanc, whose staffing policies and approach to the other institutions were publicly criticised by many Committee members as well as the EP and privately bemoaned by the Commission (or at least its Directorate General for Regional Policy). Administrative scandals continued to trouble the CoR for several years, but under its second and later presidents inter-institutional networking greatly improved, facilitating the generation of influence on policy making.

However, there continues to be an important debate concerning the path to optimal influence for the Committee. The CoR faces a dilemma in that its members are (almost entirely) elected SNA politicians who can be expected to seek influence by exploiting the system of networks in Brussels and Strasburg to their own advantage. To reinforce its links with the EP, it needs to develop its political groups and thus provide organisational links other than those based either on nationality or on type of SNA. However, this contradicts to some degree the CoR's other claim to legitimacy and influence: the provision of non-partisan expertise based on its members' experience in government below the national level (Barker 1995). Given the structural weaknesses of the Committee, it is possible that influence will come from a reputation for excellent advice rather than through entering the maelstrom of networks in which the Committee might be expected to fare less well than its more powerful fellow institutions. A further handicap is the infrequency of the Committee's meetings; most CoR members are present in Brussels only a handful of times a year in that capacity, meaning that their potential access to EU networks is reduced. Developing the role of expert adviser might enable the CoR to maximise its visibility, differentiate it from other institutions, capitalise on its symbolic potential and help reify the idea of a 'Europe of the Regions' (Christiansen 1997). It would thereby also enable the Committee to serve the interests of its patrons in the Commission, who above all seek policy legitimacy and the diffusion of the idea that SNAs are part of the integration process (Tömmel 1998; Warleigh 1999). Although the two options are not entirely impossible to reconcile, since expertise is a prerequisite for successful networking, it is clear that CoR cannot both be a think tank 'above' the political fray and regularly thrust itself into the heart of the Union's morass of networks. For the moment, it appears that the Committee prefers life as a political animal (Warleigh 1999), but this does not rule out a reversal of tactics in the future.

Beyond the Nice Treaty: future perspectives for the CoR

Much of the CoR's potential lies in its ability to prevent the growth of unbridgeable internal cleavages. It is thus noteworthy that political groups are increasingly used as a means of organisation in the Committee, and that its first enlargement – with the accession to the EU of Austria, Finland and Sweden in 1995 – did not result in demands for the creation of further 'commissions' in order to provide each national delegation with a commission chair.[4] Similarly, it also appears that the Committee has safely ridden out the threats of a split along regional/local lines. Thus, CoR is well placed to capitalise on whatever strategy for advancement it decides to adopt. However, there is also no doubt that without a bigger budget, CoR will be severely limited in its capacity to act as the regional face of the EU. The elitist internal structure of the Committee may also prove a significant impediment should it frustrate demands for greater influence by the rank and file of its members.

The most decisive factor shaping the development of the CoR in the coming years, however, is likely to be found in the domestic politics of the member states. SNAs are likely to be a key contributor to the resolution of the democratic deficit if they are empowered domestically as well as in the EU context, since even symbolically they rely for this purpose on being considered important by the citizen (Christiansen 1997). Yet such empowerment is not without risk for the Committee. Jeffery (1997, 2000) warns that much of the SNA support for the regionalisation of

EU governance may be attributed to the activism of the German Länder, whose goal was to ensure that the German federal government did not use European integration as an excuse for the removal of their policy prerogatives and powers. However, regionalising the EU has become a second-string strategy for the Länder; their main goal was to secure constitutional reform in Germany, and, having achieved this, their interest in pursuing EU regionalisation further appears to have waned considerably. As always, however, the picture is unclear. The new President of the CoR (2000 to 2002) is a powerful regional politician: Jos Chabert, Vice-President of Brussels Capital region, with a history both of activism in the AER and of involvement with the Committee itself. In his capacity as Vice-President for Brussels Capital, Chabert helped negotiate both the TEU and the ToA, including the provisions for the Committee and participation in Council meetings by SNA politicians (*European Voice*, 3 August to 6 September 2000). It is thus to be expected that Chabert will use his contacts and experience to advance the Committee's cause whenever possible. Beyond 2002, the Committee will have to entrust itself to a similar figure if it is to harness the support of key SNA players and thereby secure further advances.

Such evolution may be possible since, as demonstrated by its approach to the Nice Treaty, the CoR is developing a sound set of relationships with the other EU bodies, particularly the EP. This may lend it the ability to live up to one of its principal purposes, the eradication of the 'democratic deficit', through improving its ability to shape legislation and raising its profile. Lest too strong a parallel with the ESC be drawn, it should be noted that any role in this process played by the CoR would be qualitatively different from that of its fellow consultative committee – it would result from giving a voice to elected SNA politicians rather than civil society representatives. Given the need to broaden the range of voices heard in the EU policy-making process, the CoR might even be less suited to such a role than the ESC, since it is more clearly linked to traditional political structures and concerns than to 'the people' and their various interests. Moreover, its structural weaknesses (the fact that members are appointed rather than elected directly; the CoR's status as a consultative rather than legislative body) mean that the Committee's potential to help improve the perceived democracy of the Union is likely to be limited in the absence of significant reform. However, there are reasons to be more sanguine. First, some reform may be forthcoming, as member states continue to seek means of appearing to address the 'democratic deficit' while omitting to deal with the central institutional and identity issues (Warleigh 2002). Second, even without reform, the Committee could play a vital part in developing the symbols and rituals of legitimacy which are currently lacking in EU politics (Christiansen 1997). Symbols rely primarily on perception rather than reality; the Committee might through its mere existence entrench the myth that there is a European level of regional government (instead of a highly diverse assortment of SNA actors), and thereby alter popular appreciation of the Union's institutional balance. The CoR certainly creates an arena in which (SNA) politicians are seen to be active, which again may help reduce perceptions of the transparency gap in EU decision making (Christiansen 1997). Nonetheless, despite the clear importance of symbols in improving the perceived levels of democracy in the EU, it remains to be seen whether the CoR will make an appreciable impact in this regard.

As with all the EU institutions, the forthcoming enlargement of the Union to the countries of Central and Eastern Europe will cause difficulties for the CoR. Traditions of local democracy are weak in many applicant countries, and while the Committee might help them to flourish, it could equally suffer from lack of familiarity with the idea and practice of local democracy in many of the likely new member states. Enlargement is already causing problems with the Structural Funds: the fifteen current member states are battling to retain as much EU financial aid as possible in the face of enlargement to a set of countries which all have better claims to it than even the poorest existing member state. It is thus possible that the CoR will become an arena for parochial dispute between regional politicians. In order to prevent this, the CoR is already forging links with SNA actors in the applicant states, aided in this both by the ToA (which gave the Committee competence as adviser on matters of cross-border cooperation) and by the European SNA associations.[5] Again, the future will determine how successful the Committee is either in preventing new cleavages occurring or in bridging the differences between its members.

Summary

- The CoR is a consultative committee, established by the Treaty on European Union to give actors from SNAs a voice in EU decision making and to help reduce the democratic deficit. It issues Opinions on legislative proposals, whose impact is clear but by no means always extensive.
- The Committee reflects the partial shift in the EU towards a 'Europe of the Regions' through both its existence and its limitations. Although this concept can be exaggerated, it helps explain the successful exertion of pressure for the creation of the CoR by the Commission, SNAs and the federal or regionalised member states.
- However, the Committee's role in EU decision making is by no means central. Its early years have seen it successfully establish its identity and prevent internal cleavages from damaging its coherence, but they have also seen the support of some of its most vital members – those from powerful SNAs – wax and wane.
- The CoR's future depends on three factors: (1) its ability to present expert advice; (2) its capacity to network successfully with the other EU institutions; and (3) the retention of positive input from key SNA players. The issue of democratic reform in the EU is a further crucial variable: the CoR could be promoted both to the public and up the institutional hierarchy as an important symbol of democratisation, but this depends in turn both on the strategy adopted by the Committee and on the pattern of intergovernmental relations within, as well as between, the member states.

Test questions

1 Why did the member states establish a Committee of the Regions in the Treaty on European Union and not at the outset of European integration?

2   How is the CoR able to influence EU policy outcomes?

3   What are the key variables affecting the future of the CoR?

Contact information

The most direct way to contact the CoR is via the internet. Its homepage has the following address: http://www.cor.eu.int. This page includes various virtual factsheets, as well as information on such matters as the CoR's opinions, rules of procedure, plenary agendas and internal organisation. If you are looking to contact officials with specific responsibilities or have particular queries (for example, about traineeships, the political groups, the various commissions, press relations, etc.), their respective email addresses are indicated on the following webpage: http://www.cor.eu.int/contact/contact.html.

Traditional contact methods are also available. You can write to the Committee at Rue Montoyer 92–102, B-1000 Brussels, Belgium. The switchboard telephone number is (+32) 2 282 22 11. Faxes can be sent on (+32) 2 282 23 35.

Notes

1   The list of commissions is as follows: Commission 1 – regional policy, structural funds, economic and social cohesion, cross-border/inter-regional cooperation; Commission 2 – agriculture, rural development and fisheries; Commission 3 – trans-European networks, transport, information society; Commission 4 – spatial planning, urban issues, energy, the environment; Commission 5 – social policy, public health, consumer protection, research, tourism; Commission 6 – employment, economic policy, single market, industry, small and medium sized enterprises; Commission 7 – education, vocational training, culture, youth, sport, citizens' rights.

2   The Presidency changes half-way between each four-year mandate, as President and First Vice-President exchange roles. Presidents to date are: Jacques Blanc (Christian Democrat); Pasquall Maragall (Socialist); Manfred Dammeyer (Socialist); Jos Chabert (Christian Democrat).

3   The Commission has so far displayed an almost paternalistic approach to the CoR, and the EP appears to be overcoming initial wariness about a possible rival. The Council appears to have an attitude of beneficent neglect during day-to-day matters; in terms of Treaty change, no member state has yet insisted on radical transformation of the Committee.

4   However, the influence of nationality as a factor in determining access to important positions within the Committee remains important. I am grateful to Thomas Christiansen for the suggestion that its importance may even currently be somewhat masked: had Norway joined the EU in 1995 as expected, the CoR would have been able to offer a Presidency or Vice-Presidency of one of its eight 'commissions' to nationals of each member state, a fact which may well have influenced the decision to choose this as the number of CoR commissions.

5   AER (Association of European Regions); CEMR (Conference of European Municipalities and Regions).

Selected further reading

Christiansen, T. (1997) 'The Committee of the Regions at the 1996 IGC: Institutional Reform', *Regional and Federal Studies*, 7, 1: 50–69.

A thought-provoking article which sets out and analyses the evolution of the CoR up to and including the Amsterdam Treaty.

Dehousse, R. and Christiansen, T. (eds) (1995) *What Model for the Committee of the Regions? Past Experiences and Future Perspectives* (EUI Working Paper 95/2), Florence: European University Institute.

A perceptive collection of essays tracing the early development of the Committee and placing it in the context of advisory committees in the EU, the UK and the USA.

Jeffery, C. (ed.) (1997) *The Regional Dimension of the European Union: Towards a Third Level in Europe?*, London: Frank Cass.

An excellent volume which sets the CoR in the context of the changing relations between central and subcentral government in the member states.

Warleigh, A. (1999) *The Committee of the Regions: Institutionalising Multi-level Governance?*, London: Kogan Page.

A rare single-authored volume which gives a rounded and in-depth introduction to the CoR during its first mandate (1994 to 1998).

References

Barker, A. (1995) 'Political Authority and "Knowledge Authority": A Distinctive Role for the Committee of the Regions?', in R. Dehousse and T. Christiansen (eds) *What Model for the Committee of the Regions? Past Experiences and Future Perspectives* (EUI Working Paper 95/2), Florence: European University Institute.

Christiansen, T. (1995) 'Second Thoughts: The Committee of the Regions After its First Year', in R. Dehousse and T. Christiansen (eds) *What Model for the Committee of the Regions? Past Experiences and Future Perspectives* (EUI Working Paper 95/2), Florence: European University Institute.

Christiansen, T. (1997) 'The Committee of the Regions at the 1996 IGC: Institutional Reform', *Regional and Federal Studies*, 7, 1: 50–69.

Devuyst, Y. (1998) 'Treaty Reform in the European Union: The Amsterdam Process', *Journal of European Public Policy*, 5, 4: 615–31.

Farrows, M. and McCarthy, R. (1997) 'Opinion Formulation and Impact in the Committee of the Regions', *Regional and Federal Studies*, 7, 1: 23–49.

Hooghe, L. (ed.) (1996) *Cohesion Policy and European Integration*, Oxford: Clarendon Press.

Hooghe, L. and Marks, G. (1995) 'Channels of Subnational Representation in the European Union', in R. Dehousse and T. Christiansen (eds) *What Model for the Committee of the Regions? Past Experiences and Future Perspectives* (EUI Working Paper 95/2), Florence: European University Institute.

Jeffery, C. (1997) 'Farewell to the Third Level? The German Länder and the European Policy Process', in C. Jeffery (ed.) *The Regional Dimension of the European Union: Towards a Third Level in Europe?*, London: Frank Cass.

Jeffery, C. (2000) 'Subnational Mobilization and European Integration: Does it Make a Difference?', *Journal of Common Market Studies*, 38,1: 1–23.

Loughlin, J. (1996a) '"Europe of the Regions" and the Federalization of Europe', *Publius*, 26, 4: 141–62.

Loughlin, J. (1996b) 'Representing Regions in Europe: The Committee of the Regions', *Regional and Federal Studies*, 6, 2: 147–65.

Marks, G., Hooghe, L. and Blank, K. (1996) 'European Integration from the 1980s: State-centric versus Multi-level Governance', *Journal of Common Market Studies*, 34, 3: 341–78.

Morass, M. (1997) 'Austria – The Case of a Federal Newcomer in European Union Politics', in C. Jeffery (ed.) *The Regional Dimension of the European Union: Towards a Third Level in Europe?*, London: Frank Cass.

Schwaiger, P. (1997) 'The European Union's Committee of the Regions: A Progress Report', *Regional and Federal Studies*, 7, 1: 11–22.

Tömmel, I. (1998) 'Transformation of Governance: The European Commission's Strategy for Creating a "Europe of the Regions"', *Regional and Federal Studies*, 8, 2: 52–80.

Warleigh, A. (1997) 'A Committee of No Importance? Assessing the Relevance of the Committee of the Regions', *Politics*, 17, 2: 101–7.

Warleigh, A. (1999) *The Committee of the Regions: Institutionalising Multi-Level Governance?*, London: Kogan Page.

Warleigh, A. (2002) 'Towards Network Democracy? The Potential of Flexible Integration', in M. Farrell, S. Fella and M. Newman (eds) *European Unity in Diversity: Challenges for the Twenty-First Century*, London: Sage.

Appendix

Political representation in the EU[1]

NB: This table relates the agreements on political representation made in the Treaty of Nice both for existing member states and for applicant countries. Current member states (as of March 2001) of the EU are in **bold** text.

Country	Population (millions)	Votes in council	Number of MEPs
Germany	82	29	99
UK	59.2	29	87
France	58.9	29	87
Italy	57.6	29	87
Spain	39.4	27	64
Poland	38.7	27	64
Romania	22.5	14	44
Netherlands	15.8	13	25
Greece	10.5	12	22
Belgium	10.2	12	22
Czech Republic	10.2	12	20
Hungary	10.1	12	20
Portugal	9.9	12	22
Sweden	8.8	10	18
Bulgaria	8.2	10	17
Austria	8.1	10	17
Slovakia	5.4	7	13
Denmark	5.3	7	13
Finland	5.2	7	13
Ireland	3.8	7	12
Lithuania	3.7	7	12
Latvia	2.4	4	8
Slovenia	1.9	4	7
Estonia	1.4	4	6
Cyprus	0.8	4	6
Luxembourg	0.4	4	6
Malta	0.4	3	5

Source: Adapted from Euopean Parliament: *Draft Treaty of Nice (Initial Analysis)*, PE 294.737.

Note: 1 The Draft Nice Treaty allows for qualified voting in the European Council in order to appoint the Commission President and the rest of the Commission College (Article 214).

Index